Britannica®

From its launch in 1768 in Edinburgh, Scotland, 15 editions and constant revisions of the printed encyclopædia have contained contributions from the greatest names in science, mathematics, literature, history, religion, philosophy, and the arts. Since the 1990s it has been the most respected continuously updated, worldwide encyclopædia online. More than 4,000 expert contributors, backed by a staff of professional fact-checkers and editors, ensure that Britannica's text and visual resources are clear, current and correct.

Introducer

Anthony Grayling is Professor of Philosophy at Birkbeck College, University of London. He also often writes for the *Observer*, *Economist*, *Times Literary Supplement*, *Independent on Sunday*, and *New Statesman*, and is a frequent broadcaster on BBC Radios 4, 3, and the World Service. He has written a number of highly acclaimed works of philosophy and history including *Towards the Light: The Story of the Struggles for Liberty and Rights that made the Modern West*, a biography of Rene Descartes and *The Heart of Things: Philosophy in the 21st century*.

Also available from Robinson and Britannica

The Britannica Guide to Modern China

THE Britannica® GUIDE TO

THE IDEAS THAT MADE THE MODERN WORLD

The people, philosophy, and
history of the Enlightenment

Constable & Robinson Ltd
3 The Lanchesters
162 Fulham Palace Road
London W6 9ER
www.constablerobinson.com

Encyclopædia Britannica, Inc.
www.britannica.com

First published in the UK by Robinson,
an imprint of Constable & Robinson Ltd, 2008

A copy of the British Library Cataloguing in
Publication Data is available from the British Library.

ISBN 978-1-84529-804-3

Printed and bound in the EU

1 3 5 7 9 10 8 6 4 2

CONTENTS

LIST OF ILLUSTRATIONS

Denis Diderot, oil painting by Louis-Michel van Loo, 1767; in the Louvre, Paris. *Giraudon/Art Resource, New York*

John Wilkes, engraving from a manifesto commemorating his fight against general warrants and for the liberty of the press, 1768. *Courtesy of the trustees of the British Museum; photograph, J.R. Freeman & Co. Ltd*

Declaration of Independence in Congress, at the Independence Hall, Philadelphia, July 4 1776, oil on canvas by John Trumbull, 1819; in the United States Capitol Art Collection, Washington, DC. *The Granger Collection, New York*

Thomas Paine, detail of a portrait by John Wesley Jarvis; in the Thomas Paine Memorial House, New Rochelle, NY. *Courtesy of the Thomas Paine National Historical Association*

Edmund Burke, detail of an oil painting from the studio of Sir Joshua Reynolds, 1771; in the National Portrait Gallery, London. *Courtesy of the National Portrait Gallery, London*

Mary Wollstonecraft, detail of an oil painting on canvas by John Opie, *c.* 1797; in the National Portrait Gallery, London. *Courtesy of the National Portrait Gallery, London*

Adam Smith, paste medallion by James Tassie, 1787; in the Scottish National Portrait Gallery, Edinburgh. *Courtesy of the Scottish National Portrait Gallery, Edinburgh*

Immanuel Kant, engraving. *The Granger Collection, New York*

INTRODUCTION

The Enlightenment

A. C. Grayling

Enlightenment Values

When one thinks of the "the Enlightenment" one immediately considers an historical phenomenon whose main centre of gravity was eighteenth-century France, but which spilt across geographical and temporal borders, in particular westward towards England, Scotland, and North America (in which latter place it received its fullest contemporary realisation), and backward into the scientific, political, and philosophical revolutions of the seventeenth century.

Reference to "Enlightenment values" is an even more capacious matter, because this term not only denotes the ideas and ideals of the historical phenomenon of "the Enlightenment", but the ideas and ideals which we speak of nowadays as derived from them, and which are still very much alive in defining a rational, secular, liberal, scientifically-minded, and democratic outlook.

Because the historical circumstances are of course different as between the eighteenth century and now (one major motor of that change having been the Enlightenment itself), "Enlightenment values" in today's sense have to be understood as evolved descendents of the values that the historical Enlightenment articulated.

There is, of course, mostly overlap, but the changing conditions over 300 years have their effect. For a salient example: anti-clericalism in eighteenth-century France was a form of secularism, but secularism in its neutral meaning of separation of church and state does not have quite the same overtones of hostility. In the historical Enlightenment one major target of freeing the mind of man was the oppression of religion, and the form that the struggle took was anti-clericalism.

Today the nature of that endeavour is somewhat different. Arguments about the intrinsic merits or otherwise of religious claims about the origins of the universe, and whether or not it contains supernatural entities of some kind, are separable from the question of the place of religion and religious institutions in the public domain, and both are separable again from the question of the basis of ethics.

The three forms of debate are linked, but can be and often are now conducted separately; and almost everywhere in the Western world there has ceased to be anything like the degree of intrusive and oppressive priestcraft as was suffered by the French before 1789.

Another example is Deism. Functionally, deism is less than a whisker away from atheism, and eighteenth-century deists were by no means religious. But there were two principal reasons why they retained use of the name. One was that until the geological and biological discoveries of the nineteenth century, there was a more or less sceptical acceptance that some sort of agency had to be invoked as historically responsible for setting the clockwork of the universe going. The other was the fact that the word "atheist" then had the same kind of profoundly negative cachet that "murderer" and "rapist" does, as a result of demonization by the church of those who refused to accept its authority. The orthodoxy then was that anyone without religion could not possibly be moral, so an atheist is effectively if not in fact the same thing as a murderer and a rapist, for what stops him from being either if he lacks the fear of certain punishment?

Scarcely anyone is a deist today, that is, a believer in there having been a god to get the world started, but who has since vanished from the picture. Instead, people can now openly report that they have no religious beliefs or commitments without being socially shunned and barred from work, still less being arrested and (as so often happened in the past) executed for the fact.

These two examples of changes which make the values of the historical Enlightenment ancestors rather than identical twins of "Enlightenment values" as understood today should not however be taken to imply that a large difference has come about in that process of descent. This can be seen by a direct comparison between how one might give a summary characterisation of the values of the historical Enlightenment and today's "Enlightenment values".

Reason, tolerance, autonomy, conceptions of the rights of

man, the application of scientific method to social and political thinking, and rejection of superstition and priestcraft as barriers to human progress, are among the distinctive features of the historical Enlightenment. It can be thought of as the period in which the tyranny of traditional absolutes was challenged, chiefly absolute monarchy and absolute truth as claimed by religion. In place of these rejected sources of authority the Enlightenment thinkers raised the standard of reason and free enquiry. Among the central assumptions of this outlook was the idea that the natural and social universes are rationally ordered and that human enquiry can grasp their nature through empirical observation and rational reflection, which are jointly the foundations of truth. The world can be made a better place by these means and by education: and the Enlightenment *philosophes* accordingly saw history as the record of mankind's progress.

Despite the many forms of counter-Enlightenment that immediately rose and have continued to flourish since, the aspirations of this new intellectual temper have remained and indeed flourished as defining characteristics of modern Western societies. Democracy, commitment to regimes of human rights and civil liberties, secularism and an associated tolerance of religious variety, the ethical autonomy of the individual, and the scientific outlook, are today's versions of the historical Enlightenment's values. Some commentators on the latter, usually its critics, make the mistake of thinking that the historical Enlightenment was perfectibilist in its hopes, that is, took itself to be directing mankind towards an ideal future state. In fact it was meliorist, that is, committed to the idea that things can be made better; and this remains true of contemporary Enlightenment thinking.

Autonomy and Responsibility

Today's proponents of Enlightenment ideals find their direct inspiration in contemplating what the leading figures of the historical Enlightenment saw as the problems of the Age and their solution in the realm of thought. There could be no better hook upon which to hang such a contemplation than the fictional dream recounted by Denis Diderot in his novel *Les Bijoux indiscrets*. In this work Diderot describes a building without foundations, whose pillars, among which deformed and crippled old men totter about, soar upwards into swirling mists. The building is the Palace of Hypotheses, and the old men are theologians and metaphysicians. Then an energetic little child appears, and as he approaches the building he grows into a giant; his name is Experiment, and when he arrives at the Palace of Hypotheses he gives it a mighty blow which smashes it into ruins.

Thus science shatters the systems of theology and metaphysics. But it is not just the victory of scientific knowledge as such, but the scientific method and mindset, which routs the old and obfuscatory orthodoxies. Indeed it is also a question of attitude that is the key here, as indicated by Immanuel Kant in his celebrated essay, *What Is Enlightenment?* "Enlightenment," he wrote, "is man's emergence from his self-imposed immaturity. Immaturity is the inability to use one's understanding without guidance from another. This immaturity is self-imposed when its cause lies not in lack of understanding, but in lack of resolve and courage to use it without guidance from another. *Sapere Aude*! 'Have courage to use your own understanding!' that is the motto of enlightenment."

In common with his leading contemporaries Kant did not believe that enlightenment had actually been attained. "If it is now asked, 'Do we presently live in an enlightened age?' the answer is, 'No, but we do live in an age of enlightenment'," he wrote, and proceeded to urge further progress towards independence of thought. In describing intellectual immaturity as the state of pupillage, of the need for guidance from another, he was also attacking the various hegemonies which keep the human mind dependent.

To mature the intellect needs liberty; but that, said Kant, was precisely what was lacking in every direction: "Nothing is required for this Enlightenment except freedom; and the freedom in question is the least harmful of all, namely, the freedom to use reason publicly in all matters. But on all sides I hear: 'Do not argue!' The officer says, 'Do not argue, drill!' The tax man says, 'Do not argue, pay!' The pastor says, 'Do not argue, believe!' "

Officers and tax men are authorities who might dislike anyone's questioning the political and social status quo, but the pastor represents authority which disliked questioning at all.

Kant was a little more discreet on this subject than the editors of the great *Encyclopédie*, Diderot and Jean Le Rond D'Alembert, who declared war on religion as a barrier to intellectual progress, and to the task of finding a sound basis for morality and justice in society. In this respect Diderot and D'Alembert were following the lead given by Voltaire who had relentlessly employed logic, satire, and ridicule to *ecrasez l'infame* to attack and destroy superstition and priestcraft.

Voltaire was circumspect enough to cloak his attacks by saying that criticism of superstition was not the same as criticism of faith, and that criticism of the Church did not mean criticism of religion. He said he was a deist, that is, one who did not believe in a revealed religion but accepted that a deity created the universe, although it has no interest in mankind's affairs and does not intervene in the world, which runs according to natural laws alone.

Diderot did not find it necessary to invoke deism, regarding it as an evasion; it represented decapitation of a dozen heads of the Hydra of religion, he said, but from any remaining ones the rest would all grow again. "In vain, o slave of superstition," he makes Nature say to Mankind in his *Supplement to Bougainville's Voyage*, "have you sought your happiness beyond the limits of the world I gave you. Have courage to free yourself from the yoke of religion. Examine the history of all peoples in all times and you will see that that we humans have always been subject to one of three codes: that of nature, that of society, and that of religion and that we have been obliged to transgress all three in succession, because they could never be in harmony." As a result, Diderot wrote, there has never been "a real man, a real citizen, a real believer."

The same outright rejection of religion's assertion of authority over thought occured in Baron d'Holbach's *Natural Politics*, where in the conclusion he wrote that religion teaches people to fear earthly despots by teaching them to fear invisible ones, and this in consequence prevents people from thinking for themselves and seeking an independent direction for their own lives.

The rejection of religion's hegemony over thought was the crucial starting point for the task that the *philosophes* urged each person to undertake: to become autonomous, relying on reason and applying scientifically-minded rationality to building better lives and societies. The Enlightenment project was accordingly a creative and a reforming one, premised on the promise and demand of freedom – most especially intellectual freedom.

This is the underlying tenet of today's conception of Enlightenment values. Both facets of individual liberty are implicit: the freedom to be self-creating and self-determining in a society that respects the right to be both. In addition, the individual's responsibility to be thus included respect for the rights of others to be the same. Reciprocal responsibility in this respect is a condition of a society, and in the form of the "harm principle" ("do not harm") is a principle of classical and contemporary liberalism.

One can say, then, that the liberal ideal is a major offspring of the historical Enlightenment, for it was the historical Enlightenment's explicit aim to break strangleholds of orthodoxy and traditional authority over thought, action, and progress.

The point about autonomy as the premise of contemporary liberalism merits expansion. By "autonomy" Kant and the *philosophes* meant self-government, independence of thought, and therefore, concomitantly, the right and responsibility to choose and pursue the goals that one sees as giving meaning to one's life. Autonomy is self-government in the light of reason and experience; its opposite, heteronymy, means control over one by someone or something else; it means subjection of one's will to the will of an external authority, traditionally a deity or a monarch.

Of course the fact that people live in society means that they are subject to many contingent constraints and limitations; no one is free of the obligations of relationship, nor would many wish to be. Rather, the autonomy at issue is that of thought and moral responsibility. When Kant and his contemporaries spoke of "Enlightenment" they meant progress in this latter but all-important respect; and it is this which has such a powerful hold on the moral and political imagination of the modern Western world, expressing itself through commitments to democracy and the impartial rule of law, and the civil liberties (freedom of belief and expression, privacy, freedom in choosing a life partner and having children, and so on) that are constitutive of what it is to be a participant in that dispensation.

Education and the Good Society

It is by no means an arbitrary matter that the *Encyclopédie* of Diderot and D'Alembert should be nominated as the flagship of the historical Enlightenment, and the endeavour that most captures its essence. Given that the aim of enlightenment was to get people thinking for themselves and choosing for themselves, it was essential that they should be able to think well and choose wisely. That required information organized into knowledge, which in turn contributed to individual insight and understanding through the operation of reason.

Acquiring the abilities requisite for knowing, thinking, reasoning requires education. On this the historical Enlightenment and present-day subscription to Enlightenment values are as one: both see education as one of the chief keys to the best individual and social possibilities, because they both see education as a tool for the illumination and thus liberation of the mind.

Thus it was that the historical Enlightenment's monument is a work whose whole *raison d'etre* is education: the *Encyclopédie, ou Dictionnaire raisonne des sciences, des arts et des metiers*. In his introduction Diderot described its aim as "collect[ing] all the knowledge scattered over the face of the earth, to present its general outlines and structure to the men with whom we live, and to transmit this to those who will come after us, so that the work of the past centuries may be useful to the following centuries, that our children, by becoming more educated, may at the same time become more virtuous and happier, and that we may not die without having deserved well of the human race."

By asserting that education in the sciences and humanities was the basis of good individual lives and good societies, Diderot was repudiating faith or any submission either to traditional pieties or present tyrannies as alternatives. With D'Alembert and the other *philosophes* who abetted the grand project, Diderot thus constituted himself as a propagandist for a rational and secular view of the world. At the same time he and his colleagues were openly and proudly popularising learning and its advances in all subjects. This is seen in particular when we take into account that the historical Enlightenment was a period of advances made in the natural and social sciences, and the *Encyclopédie* saw its role as to introduce them to wider audiences.

An ever-recurring theme of the *Encyclopédie*, but especially of course of such articles on method and enquiry as "Observation", "System", and "Hypothesis", is that the empirical method governed by rational reflection is the proper route to knowledge. For its editors, the empirical method was not only inconsistent with invocations of the authority of tradition or scripture, but in fact controverted them. In the *Encyclopédie*'s "Preliminary Discourse" D'Alembert began by extolling empiricism, and then drew the implication of commitment to it: that the fundamental concepts of justice and morality have to be derived from facts about human nature and mankind's material condition, not from any supposed basis in theology or metaphysics.

This theme is fully present in one side of today's debates about, for example, ethical questions that arise in medical research and treatments. To someone of D'Alembert's persuasion the great advantages for sufferers from Alzheimer's Disease, paralysis, muscular dystrophy, blindness and deafness, and other catastrophic diseases and disabilities, of therapies that might be derived from stem cell research, would justify such research without hesitation. For those guided by religious considerations it is wrong to use embryos as sources of stem cells. Here is exactly the contrast, and the contest of views, in which the Enlightenment *philosophes* were engaged, and which remain at the centre of today's debates.

Counter-Enlightenments

What also defines "Enlightenment values" in the contemporary world is the battery of views, beliefs, and movements that oppose the way of life and outlook of modern Western liberal democracies. From long before the moment that the historical Enlightenment became self-conscious in the eighteenth century, the values and aims that became distinctive of it were vigorously opposed. Later critics blamed the Enlightenment for the excesses of the French Revolution, for Nazism and Stalinism, and for what they lament as the increase of immorality and amorality consequent on the weakening of religious traditions. In the eighteenth century itself, charges of atheism and immorality, and fears of what would follow the overthrow of tradition and authority, inspired an immediate plethora of counter-Enlightenments, of which these later versions are successors.

One immediate reaction to the historical Enlightenment was Romanticism, in its many forms. In place of universal reason and the empirical methods of science Romanticism sought (and in its contemporary forms still seeks) to privilege other sources of authority, some of them very traditional, over our minds and lives: love, ecstasy, poetry, tradition, genius, membership of a tribe, blood ties, God, indeed a variety of other non-rational or even irrational abstractions were invoked to defy what it saw as the desiccating, cold, emotionless rule of reason.

Arguably one can see nineteenth and twentieth century nationalism as an outcome of Romanticism, along with its penumbra of notions like race, "volk" and patriotism. Reflection on such a view makes it easy to see how criticism of Enlightenment values is to be met. For example, the argument

that the historical Enlightenment spawned Nazism and Stalinism is answered by noting that these are in fact counter-
Enlightenment phenomena, because they share with the monolithic authority structures of religion and absolute monarchy
that which the historical Enlightenment emphatically repudiated: the desire to impose on everyone a single outlook to
which everyone is obliged to conform and whose rule everyone
is obliged to obey, on pain of punishment even to death.

Some critics of Enlightenment values have a more general
thesis to argue. They argue that we live in thrall to a utopian
ideal of rational society which, contrary to the hopes of the
philosophes, has enslaved rather than liberated humanity, by
subjecting it to a form of bureaucratic corporatism which,
concerned only with satisfaction of its own immediate short-
term interests, stumbles without moral purpose from one crisis
to another.

Such critics say that the endeavour to replace arbitrary
monarchical or priestly power by the rule of reason collapsed
because of reason's limitations. It succeeded only in spawning
a form of technocratic corporatism, which has transformed the
world into a fiefdom of managers. Capitalists do not control
the capital they invest; voters do not control the politicians
they elect; it is managers who control these things, because
only they know how the structural complexities of society
work. And the goals that managerial activity is directed
towards are not chosen on grounds of morality, but for out-
comes of profit or election victories.

It has been easy for critics of the historical Enlightenment to
say that the first of its "nightmare children" was the Terror in
Paris, and to continue by reciting the objections to frigid
rationalism that are a commonplace of the genre. It is evident
that the objections are based on reaction, not knowledge of
what the historical Enlightenment's proponents thought a

reasoned approach to life would be like. Consider Diderot on sex, and wonder whether the liberalization of attitudes to sex and sexuality in our recent and contemporary Western world is not both an outcome of Enlightened principles, and better than too familiar alternatives:

If there is a perverse man who could take offence at the praise that I give to [sexual love] the most noble and universal of passions, I would evoke Nature before him, I would make it speak, and Nature would say to him: why do you blush to hear the word pleasure pronounced, when you do not blush to indulge in its temptations under the cover of night? Are you ignorant of its purpose and of what you owe to it? Do you believe that your mother would have imperilled her life to give you yours if I had not attached an inexpressible charm to the embraces of her husband? Be quiet, unhappy man, and consider that pleasure pulled you out of nothingness.

The propagation of beings is the greatest object of nature. It imperiously solicits both sexes as soon as they have been granted their share of strength and beauty. A vague and brooding restlessness warns them of the moment; their condition is mixed with pain and pleasure. At that time they listen to their senses and turn their considered attention to themselves. But if an individual should be presented to another of the same species and of a different sex, then the feeling of all other needs is suspended: the heart palpitates, the limbs tremble; voluptuous images wander through the mind; a flood of spirits runs through the nerves, excites them, and proceeds to the seat of a new sense that reveals itself and torments the body. Sight is troubled, delirium is born; reason, the slave of instinct, limits itself to serving the latter, and nature is satisfied.

This is the way things took place at the beginning of the world, and the way they still take place in the back of the savage adult's cave.

This passage is more truly representative of the Enlightenment attitude than the caricatures of it as the embodiment of heartless utilitarian calculation. In this same passage Diderot writes of how the sexual impulse draws us to a partner "who experiences the same sensations, the same ecstasies, who brings her affectionate and sensitive arms towards yours, who embraces you, whose caresses will be followed with the existence of a new being who will resemble one of you, who will look for you in the first movements of life to hug you, whom you will bring up by your side and love together": hardly the stuff of Scrooge in his counting house, which the imagination of some critics seems to be limited to in their depiction of a life lived according to Enlightenment principles.

Reason and Relativism

Yet given that Enlightenment values are so consistently opposed by those who see them as responsible for the French revolution's excesses, by those who agree with Romanticism's charges against its supposed frigidities, by those who see it as the ultimate source both for Fascism and Stalinism, by those yet more recently who blame it for the liberal ideas (in the pejorative sense of "liberal" as this term is understood by some conservatives in the United States) which threaten "family values" – and by everyone who sees it as the antithesis of all that most matters to the human spirit in encounters with the ineffable, the numinous, and the divine it is worth examining the deeper causes of counter-Enlightenment, because it reveals, by contrast, what has been most central and enduring in the Enlightenment's challenge to history.

The first opponents of the historical Enlightenment fall into one of two categories: those whom we might now describe as being "right wing" in political or ideological terms – ranging from churchmen contemporary with the *philosophes* to such figures as Edmund Burke and Joseph le Maistre – and those whom we now called Romantics, who asserted the claims of nature, imagination, and the emotions, over what they regarded as Enlightenment rationalism's reductively mechanistic world-view.

Burke, and those with a similar conservative outlook, saw the Enlightenment's rejection of tradition, and especially its role as the basis of moral and political authority, as the cause of everything that was worst in the French Revolution. Indeed their hostility turned on an objection to a view that had deeper roots than the historical Enlightenment itself: the view that the source of political authority is not tradition or monarchical divine right, but the people, whose consent is required in all things, and who possess rights, some of them inalienable.

The *philosophes* of the Enlightenment adopted this view reflexively, and despite Burke and the conservative lineage that descends from him, it has been the source of Western liberal democracy and internationalism, both of which are globally ascendant in today's world. Yet it has to be remembered that for Burke and many of his contemporaries "democracy" was a term of horror, as was "the people," which denoted an anarchic and unruly entity that could not be trusted. "Democracy" simply meant "ochlocracy", mob rule. In Burke's estimation the *philosophes* were no better than the French Revolution's *sansculottes* proved to be, and he regarded their principles as despicable likewise.

What the conservative political mind saw as a threat to the

order premised on traditionalist values, Romantic thinkers saw as a threat in broader cultural terms. They took the Enlightenment's championing of science to be a claim that "scientific development" and "progress" are synonyms, implying that history can only be understood properly in mechanistic, even indeed in deterministic, terms. In their recoil from this the Romantics insisted on the primacy of emotion over reason, and accordingly celebrated the subjective, the visionary and the non-rational. This gave a privileged position to moods and passions as sources of insight and truth, and exulted in responses to sublimity and natural beauty.

In this light Enlightenment attitudes are typically taken to be descendents of the classical preference for balance, harmony, and order in art, architecture and music, not incorrectly as eighteenth century applied aesthetics shows. By deliberate contrast Romanticism prefers spontaneity and variety, trusting emotion instead of the rules and principles of reason.

Of course we would not now wish to be without either the eighteenth century's neo-classicism or the nineteenth century's Romantic poetry and music, so there is no question of taking sides between the best of both. Nor, however, do we think that these entirely recompense history for their respective worst sides. The Enlightenment can be criticised for its reductivism, but the Romantic tradition's worst aspect is the irresponsible thinking that led to such catastrophes as nationalism and racism. In addition, the capacious and deliberately unreflective side of Romanticism gave refuge to many of the evils that the Enlightenment had worked to overcome, superstition not least among them.

What is at issue here is the question of the place of reason in the good life. According to the Enlightenment, reason is the mind's chief tool; it is not only the instrument for adjudication of fact, but for resolution of conflicts of opinion. This makes reason an absolute which, when used responsibly, is the secure guide to truth even when truth is disputed.

Naturally enough, this uncompromising attitude to reason has always provoked opposition. As a matter of historical fact the main opponent has always been religion, with its claim that revelation, whether in the form of mystical experience or as scripture, conveys profound truth from outside the world of ordinary experience, which human enquiry therefore could never otherwise know.

Another opponent is relativism, which in its most robust form is the claim that different ways of thinking, even when they are mutually contradictory, are equally valid, and that there is no independent standpoint from which they can be comparatively evaluated. By contrast the Enlightenment's insistence that reason, whatever its fallibilities even when employed with scrupulous care, provides standards to which competing viewpoints have to submit. This view survives in the reliance placed on the public, repeatable and conditional methods of science at their best, and on the idea that responsibility in public affairs is essentially a matter of rationality, evidence, and reflective judgement.

And this implies that the inheritors of Enlightenment, which these practitioners of the virtues of reason are, implicitly reject the claim that there are authorities equal to or more powerful than reason, such as race or emotion. Enlightenment defence of reason does not have to be unqualified, and indeed it is better if it is not, especially in our contemporary world where answers to questions about human nature are more conditional and ironic than they have ever been.

As it happens, this was something that the *philosophes* of the eighteenth century understood very well. One proof is Voltaire's satire on the excessive rationalist optimism of Dr

Pangloss in *Candide*. In addition, the leading philosophers (not *philosophes*) of the Enlightenment – Hume and Kant – were even more careful not to misplace confidence in reason, even while using it to describe its own nature and limits.

Twentieth-Century Criticisms

A significant later critical reaction to the Enlightenment focused on what it saw as its self-destructive over-optimism. In *Dialectic of Enlightenment*, which is said to have begun in conversations in a New York kitchen between its authors Max Horkheimer and Theodor Adorno during the worst days of the Second World War, it is claimed that the Enlightenment's principles metamorphosed into their opposites. The *philosophes* sought individual freedom, but that freedom became enslavement to economic powers for those who came afterwards. Science was seen as the rational alternative to religion, but "scientism", taking the form of a salvation myth in which science promises to explain everything and solve all problems simply replaced religion and began to exercise an equally malign influence.

Horkheimer and Adorno believed they were witnessing the moment at which the promise of scientific rationality had become poisonous and destructive. For Enlightenment thinkers, scientific rationality promised progress in all spheres, simultaneously undermining the dogmas of religion and with them the hegemony of traditional forms of oppression. The *philosophes* believed it could do this because of its objectivity and its already-proven pragmatic successes.

By fulfilling these promises scientific rationality would promote freedom and tolerance. But according to Horkheimer and Adorno, scientific rationality has a dynamic which gradually turns against the very values that were responsible for its own first success. Reason is transformed from a weapon against oppression into an instrument of oppression. The dream turned into a nightmare, and the ghosts that the Enlightenment sought to exorcize rose again in new and equally terrible disguises – chief among them (so Horkheimer and Adorno held), Fascism.

This view profoundly influenced the Frankfurt School, and prompted a vigorous debate after the Second World War. Indeed, a major theme of postwar French philosophy was the historical role of reason and science as instruments of domination and oppression, whether of class, race, gender, or culture. Michel Foucault, Emmanuel Lévinas, and Julia Kristeva, among others, pursued the radical implications of this idea, influencing not only philosophy but also literary theory and psychoanalysis in the second half of the 20th century.

Reflection on Horkheimer's and Adorno's views is highly illuminating as to the nature of Enlightenment values in the contemporary world, not least because of the way they survive this pessimistic evaluation. The briefest way to see why is to grasp the implausibility of Horkheimer's and Adorno's equation of scientific mastery over nature (which for the Enlightenment thinkers had as its aim the liberation of humankind) with mastery over the masses exercised by elite or vanguards who, as a result of the material progress that the Enlightenment had made possible, had acquired control of the levers of political and economic power in the period since the eighteenth century.

In the crisis of the 1930s and 40s the oppressive power that Horkheimer and Adorno had in mind was Nazism, which they saw as the Enlightenment's self-fulfillingly paradoxical outcome: in their terminology, "instrumental rationality" had been transformed into "bureaucratic politics". In effect, Horkheimer and Adorno were claiming that the Enlightenment empowered capitalism and with it a deeply oppressive form of managerialism that served its interests to the exclusion of all others.

This analysis does not survive scrutiny. Nazism drew its principal strength from a peasantry and petit-bourgeoisie that mostly felt threatened by capitalism, so it is not the latter which was the source of oppression, but in fact the former, viewed as descendents of the various constituencies that had most to lose from Enlightenment and which therefore reacted against it. The votaries of Nazism, had they lived in the eighteenth century, would have defended the traditions of absolutism, whether in Versailles or in heaven, against the "nstrumental rationality" which expressed itself in the eighteenth century as secularizing and democratizing impulses.

As this implies, the same answer can be addressed to the other example cited by critics as an inheritor of Enlightenment principles, namely Stalinism. The general point to be made is that totalitarianism, of which Nazism and Stalinism are paradigms, is a monolithic ideology that demands the unwavering loyalty and obedience of all. Whether in the form of a religion or a political movement, it is precisely opposed by the Enlightenment values of individual liberty, freedom of thought, consent of the people, rational argument, the constraints of evidence, and the absence of controlling hegemonies.

Perhaps the most famous aspect of Horkheimer's and Adorno's *Dialectic of Enlightenment* is its attack on what the authors saw as the repressive nature of the "culture industry". They took mass culture to be another consequence of Enlightenment instrumental rationalism, and therefore rejected it; but here too they are arguably wrong. Mass culture is not incapable of producing valuable things, whether in the arts or knowledge; and the same is true of the technologies designed to serve its interests, as exemplified in the sphere of popular culture by the best work in cinema and television.

By resisting the counter-Enlightenment pessimism of Horkheimer and Adorno in this way one sees, by the intended contrast, how much of the Enlightenment remains operative in the contemporary world as the same force it was historically intended to be: a force for progress, for liberty, for rationality.

For its admirers and inheritors, and it must be obvious that these words are written by one, the historical Enlightenment is one of the signal achievements of humankind, which makes a good knowledge of it important. That is what the following pages offer, and they provide a basis for all that is positive in the application of Enlightenment ideals to the conflicts, dilemmas, and possibilities of today.

I

A HISTORY OF THE ENLIGHTENMENT

The Enlightenment (in French the *Siècle des Lumières* ("Age of the Enlightened"), in German *Aufklärung*) swept through Europe in the 17th and 18th centuries. With new ideas concerning God, reason, nature, and man, the Enlightenment offered a world view that gained wide assent and instigated revolutionary developments in art, philosophy, and politics. Central to Enlightenment thought were the use and the celebration of reason, the power by which man understands the universe and improves his own condition. The goals of rational man were considered to be knowledge, freedom, and happiness.

The Enlightenment was both a movement and a state of mind. The term represents a phase in the intellectual history of Europe, but it also serves to define the programmes of reform advocated by influential French writers, philosophers, and scientists, known as "philosophes", who were inspired by a common faith in the possibility of a better world. The special significance of the Enlightenment lies in its combination of principle and pragmatism.

There are two traditional schools of thought regarding its character and achievements. The first sees the Enlightenment as the preserve of an elite centred on Paris and as primarily a French movement, while the second perceives it as an international phenomenon with as many facets as there were countries affected. Although most modern interpreters incline to the latter view, there is still a case for the French emphasis, given the genius of a number of the philosophes and their associates. Unlike other terms applied by historians "the Enlightenment" was used and cherished by those who believed in the power of the mind to liberate and improve.

The Meaning of the Enlightenment

In 1702, Bernard de Fontenelle, the French scientist and man of letters, wrote optimistically of the new century "which will become more enlightened day by day, so that all previous centuries will be lost in darkness by comparison". Reviewing the experience in 1784, the German philosopher Immanuel Kant saw an emancipation from superstition and ignorance as having been the essential characteristic of the Enlightenment.

Before Kant's death in 1804 the spirit of the *siècle des lumières* had been spurned by Romantic idealists, its confidence in humanity's sense of what was right and good mocked by revolutionary terror and dictatorship, and its rationalism decried as being complacent or downright inhumane. Yet much of the tenor of the Enlightenment survived in the liberalism, toleration, and respect for law that have persisted in European and other Western societies. There was therefore no abrupt end or reversal of enlightened values.

Nor had there been a sudden beginning. The perceptions and propaganda of the philosophes have led historians to locate the

Enlightenment within the 18th century or, more comprehensively, between the two revolutions – the English of 1688–9 and the French of 1789 – but in conception it should be traced to the humanism of the Renaissance, which encouraged scholarly interest in classical texts and values. It was formed by the complementary methods of the Scientific Revolution: the rational and the empirical. Its adolescence belongs to the two decades before and after 1700 when writers such as Jonathan Swift were employing "the artillery of words" to impress the secular intelligentsia created by the growth in affluence, literacy, and publishing. Ideas and beliefs were tested wherever reason and research could challenge traditional authority.

Sources of Enlightenment Thought

In a cosmopolitan culture it was the pre-eminence of the French language that enabled Frenchmen of the 17th century to lay the foundations of cultural ascendancy and encouraged the philosophes to act as the tutors of 18th-century Europe. The notion of a realm of philosophy superior to sectarian or national concerns facilitated the transmission of ideas. "I flatter myself", wrote the encyclopaedist Denis Diderot to the Scottish philosopher David Hume, "that I am, like you, citizen of the great city of the world." "A philosopher", wrote Edward Gibbon, "may consider Europe as a great republic, whose various inhabitants have attained almost the same level of politeness and cultivation." This magisterial pronouncement by the author of *The History of the Decline and Fall of the Roman Empire* (1776–88) recalls the common source: the knowledge of classical literature.

The scholars of the Enlightenment recognized a joint inheritance, Christian as well as classical. In rejecting, or at least reinterpreting, the one and plundering the other, they had the confidence of those who believed they were masters of their destiny. They felt an affinity with the classical world and saluted the achievements of the Greeks – who discovered a regularity in nature and its governing principle, the reasoning mind – as well as the achievements of the Romans, who adopted Hellenic culture while contributing a new order and style; on their law was founded much of church and civil law. Enlightenment thinkers were steeped in the ideas and language of the classics but unsettled in their beliefs. Some Enlightenment thinkers found an alternative to Christian faith in science and some in a form of neopaganism, and they characteristically aspired to a morality based not on religion but on reason.

The Role of Science and Mathematics

"The new philosophy puts all in doubt," wrote the English poet John Donne. Early 17th-century poetry and drama abounded in expressions of confusion and dismay about the world, God, and humanity. As the new heliocentric astronomy of Copernicus and Galileo was accepted, the firm association between religion, morality, and the traditional scheme of nature was shaken.

In this process, mathematics occupied the central position. In the words of the French philosopher René Descartes, mathematics was "the general science which should explain all that can be known about quantity and measure, considered independently of any application to a particular subject". It enabled its practitioners to bridge gaps between speculation and reasonable certainty: the German astronomer Johannes Kepler thus proceeded from his study of conic sections to the laws of planetary motion. When, however, Fontenelle wrote of Descartes: "Sometimes one man gives the tone to a whole century," it was not merely of his mathematics that he was thinking. It was the system and philosophy that Descartes derived from the application of mathematical reasoning to the mysteries of the world – all that is meant by Cartesianism – which was so influential.

A different track had been pursued by the English philosopher Francis Bacon, whose influence eventually proved as great as that of Descartes. He called for a new science, to be based on organized and collaborative experiment with a systematic recording of results. General laws could be established only when research had produced enough data, and then by inductive reasoning, which, as described in his *Novum Organum* (1620), derives from "particulars, rising by a gradual and unbroken ascent, so that it arrives at the most general axioms last of all". These must be tried and proved by further experiments.

Bacon's method could lead to the accumulation of knowledge. It also was self-correcting. Indeed, it was in some ways modern in its practical emphasis. Significantly, whereas the devout English humanist Thomas More had placed his Utopia in a remote setting, Bacon put *The New Atlantis* (1627) in the future. "Knowledge is power," he said, perhaps unoriginally but with the conviction that went with a vision of humankind gaining mastery over nature. Thus were established the two poles of scientific endeavour, the rational and the empirical, between which enlightened human beings were to map the ground for a better world.

While Descartes maintained his hold on French opinion, across the English Channel Sir Isaac Newton, a prodigious mathematician and a resourceful and disciplined experimenter, was mounting a crucial challenge. His *Philosophiae Nat-*

uralis Principia Mathematica (1687; *Mathematical Principles of Natural Philosophy*, usually called the *Principia*) ranks with Descartes' *Discourse on Method* in authority and influence in the 17th-century quest for truth. Newton did not break completely with Descartes and remained faithful to the latter's fundamental idea of the universe as a machine. But Newton's machine operated according to a set of laws, the essence of which was that the principle of gravitation was everywhere present and efficient. The onus was on the Cartesians to show not only that their mechanics gave a truer explanation but also that their methods were sounder.

The Dutch mathematician Christiaan Huygens, a loyal disciple of Descartes, had worked out the first tenable theory of centrifugal force. He acknowledged that Newton's assumption of forces acting between members of the solar system was justified by the correct conclusions he drew from it, but he would not go on to accept that gravitational attraction was affecting every pair of particles, however minute. According to Huygens, Newton's conception of gravitation as a property inherent in corporeal matter was absurd; many others joined Huygens in believing that Newton was returning to medieval "occult" qualities.

Gradually, however, Newton's work won understanding. In 1732 Pierre-Louis de Maupertuis put the Cartesians on the defensive by supporting Newton's right to employ a principle the cause of which was yet unknown. In 1734, in his *Lettres philosophiques* or *Lettres sur les Anglais* (*Philosophical Letters*, or *Letters on England*), Voltaire introduced Newton as the "destroyer of the system of Descartes". His authority clinched the issue.

Newton's physics was also justified by its successful application in different fields. The return of Halley's Comet was accurately predicted. The torsion balance invented by the

French physicist Charles Coulomb proved that Newton's law of inverse squares was valid for electromagnetic attraction. Cartesianism reduced nature to a set of habits within a world of rules; the new attitude took note of accidents and circumstances. Observation and experiment revealed nature as untidy, unpredictable – a tangle of conflicting forces.

In classical theory, reason was presumed to be common to all human beings and its laws immutable. In Enlightenment Europe, however, there was a growing impatience with systems. The most creative of scientists found sufficient momentum for discovery on science's front line: Robert Boyle, the English natural philosopher who advocated a "mechanical philosophy" that saw the universe as a huge machine, the motion of whose parts accounted for all natural phenomena; William Harvey, the English discoverer of the true nature of the circulation of the blood; and Antonie van Leeuwenhoek, the Dutch microscopist whose powers of careful observation enabled him in 1674 to study bacteria and protozoa. The controversy was creative because both rational and empirical methods were essential to progress.

Newton was supremely important among those who contributed to the climate of the Enlightenment, because his new system offered certainties in a world of doubts. The belief spread that Newton had explained forever how the universe worked. This cautious, devout empiricist lent the imprint of genius to the great idea of the Enlightenment: that human beings, guided by the light of reason, could explain all natural phenomena and could embark on the study of their own place in a world that was no longer mysterious.

Yet one might otherwise have been aware more of disintegration than of progress or of theories demolished than of truths established. This was true even within the expanding

field of the physical sciences. To gauge the mood of the world
of intellect and fashion, of French Salons or of such institutions
as the Royal Society, it is essential to understand what constituted the crisis in the European mind of the late 17th
century.

At the heart of the crisis was the critical examination of
Christian faith, its foundations in the Bible, and the authority
embodied in the church. In 1647 the French philosopher Pierre
Gassendi had revived the atomistic philosophy outlined in
Lucretius' *On the Nature of Things*. Gassendi insisted on the
divine providence behind Epicurus' atoms and voids. Critical
examination could not fail to be unsettling, because the
Christian view was not confined to questions of personal
belief and morals or even history but comprehended the entire
nature of God's world. The impact of scientific research must
be weighed in the wider context of an intellectual revolution.
Different kinds of learning were not then as sharply distinguished, because of their appropriate disciplines and terminology, as they are in an age of specialization.

The Influence of Locke

The writings of the English philosopher John Locke reveal the
range of interests that an educated man might pursue and its
value in the outcome: discrimination, shrewdness, and originality. The journal of Locke's travels in France (1675–9) is
studded with notes on botany, zoology, medicine, weather,
instruments of all kinds, and statistics, especially those concerned with prices and taxes. It is a telling introduction to the
world of the Enlightenment, in which the possible was always
as important as the ideal and physics could be more important
than metaphysics.

Locke spent the years 1683 to 1689 in Holland, in refuge from high royalism. There he associated with other literary exiles, who were united in abhorrence of Louis XIV's religious policies, which culminated in the revocation of the Edict of Nantes (1685) and the flight of more than 200,000 Huguenots. During this time Locke wrote the *Essay on Toleration* (1689). The coincidence of the Huguenot dispersion with the English Revolution of 1688–9 engendered a cross-fertilizing debate in a society that had lost its bearings. The avant-garde accepted Locke's idea that the people had a sovereign power and that the prince was merely a delegate.

Locke's *Second Treatise of Civil Government* (1690) offered a theoretical justification for a contractual view of monarchy on the basis of a revocable agreement between ruler and ruled. It was, however, Locke's writings about education, toleration, and morality that were most influential among the philosophes, for whom his political theories could be only of academic interest. Locke was the first to treat philosophy as a purely critical inquiry, having its own problems but essentially similar to other sciences.

The avowed object of his *An Essay Concerning Human Understanding* (1689) was "to inquire into the original, certainty, and extent of human knowledge; together with the grounds and degrees of belief, opinion, and assent". For Locke, the mind derives the materials of reason and knowledge from experience. Unlike Descartes' view that man could have innate ideas, in Locke's system knowledge consists of ideas imprinted on the mind through observation of external objects and reflection on the evidence provided by the senses. Moral values, Locke held, are derived from sensations of pleasure or pain, the mind labelling good what experience shows to give pleasure. There are no innate ideas; there is no innate depravity.

Locke did, however, open a way to disciples who proceeded to conclusions that might have been far from the master's mind. One of them was the Irish bishop George Berkeley, who affirmed, in his *Treatise Concerning the Principles of Human Knowledge* (1710), that there was no proof that matter existed beyond the idea of it in the mind. Most philosophers after Descartes decided the question of the dualism of mind and matter by adopting a materialist position; whereas they eliminated mind, Berkeley eliminated matter – and he was therefore neglected.

Locke was perhaps more scientific and certainly more in tune with the intellectual and practical concerns of the age. In the debate over moral values, he provided a new argument for toleration. Beliefs, like other human differences, were largely the product of environment. Did it not therefore follow that moral improvement should be the responsibility of society? Finally, since human irrationality was the consequence of false ideas, instilled by faulty schooling, should not education be a prime concern of rulers? To pose those questions is to anticipate the agenda of the Enlightenment.

The Proto-Enlightenment

If Locke was the most influential philosopher in the swirling debates of fin-de-siècle Holland, the most prolific writer and educator was the French philosopher Pierre Bayle, whom Voltaire called "the first of the sceptical philosophers". He might also be called the first of the encyclopaedists, for he was more publicist than philosopher, eclectic in his interests, information, and ideas. The title *Nouvelles de la république des lettres* (1684–7) conveys the method and ideal of this superior form of journalism. Bayle's *Dictionnaire historique et critique*

(1697) exposed the fallacies and deceits of the past by the plausible method of biographical articles. "The grounds of doubting are themselves doubtful; we must therefore doubt whether we ought to doubt." Lacking a sound criterion of truth or a system by which evidence could be tested but hating dogma and mistrusting authority, Bayle was concerned with the present state of knowledge.

Bayle's seminal role in the cultural exchange of his time points to the importance of the Dutch Republic in the 17th century. Wealth – derived from trade, shipping, and finance – and toleration – which attracted Sephardic Jews, Protestants from Flanders and France, and other refugees, as well as simply those who sought a relatively open society – combined to create a climate singularly favourable to enterprise and creativity. It was pervaded by a scientific spirit. Pieter de Hooch's search for new ways of portraying light, Benedict de Spinoza's pursuit of a rational system that would comprehend all spiritual truth, van Leeuwenhoek's use of the microscope to reveal the hidden and minute, Hermann Boerhaave's dissection of the human body, the accuracy of Jan Blaeuw in making maps and of Huygens in creating the new pendulum clock – each represented that passion for discovery that put 17th-century Holland in a central position between the Renaissance and the Enlightenment, with some of the creative traits of both periods.

It was fitting, therefore, that much of the writing that helped form the Enlightenment emanated from the printing presses of the Huguenot emigré Louis Elsevier at Amsterdam and Leiden. There was no lack of material for them. Not only did learning flourish in the cultural common market that served the needs of those who led or followed intellectual fashions; also important, though harder to measure, was the influence of the new relativism, grounded in observable facts about an ever-widening world. Of Descartes, Huygens had written that he had substituted for old ideas "causes for which one can comprehend all that there is in nature".

Allied to that confidence in the power of reason was a prejudice against knowledge that might distort argument. The French mathematician Blaise Pascal perfectly exemplified that rationalist frame of mind prone to introspection. In France, the object of the protagonists of the prevailing classicism had been to establish rules: for language (the main role of the French Academy), for painting (as in the work of Nicolas Poussin), even for the theatre, where Jean Racine's plays of heightened feeling and pure conflict of ideal or personality gained effect by being constrained within the framework of their Greek archetypes.

The Scottish Enlightenment

In 1762 Voltaire wrote in characteristically provocative fashion that "today it is from Scotland that we get rules of taste in all the arts, from epic poetry to gardening." Contemporaries referred to Edinburgh as a "hotbed of genius": it was here that the conjunction of minds, ideas, and publications in Scotland came together during the second half of the 18th century and beyond. Benjamin Franklin caught the mood of the place in his *Autobiography* (1794): "Persons of good Sense seldom fall into [disputation], except Lawyers, University Men, and Men of all Sorts that have been bred at Edinburgh."

While France and England supplied the sources of some of the ideas that were absorbed by Edinburgh, the Enlightenment in Scotland did not draw upon aristocratic patronage as did its counterpart in France. The driving forces were, on the one hand, a remarkably well-educated population (a legacy of the

Reformation in Scotland) and, on the other, the absence of what gave form and direction to English society – a long-developed history of authority being derived from a common-law system based upon tradition and precedent. There was no such history in Scotland. As John Knox, the leader of Scottish Reformation, discovered, Scotland needed an alternative method of settling disputes, one that avoided an appeal either to the naked power of the largest warring faction or to English traditions of order and precedence. The ideas of the Enlightenment found in Edinburgh a recipe for development that differed from either Paris or London, founded on the appeal to reasons, arguments, and evidence.

The personalities were fundamental: most prominent in retrospect were philosopher David Hume and the economist Adam Smith, matched at the time by Thomas Reid and Dugald Stewart. However, the Scottish Enlightenment was neither a single school of philosophical thought nor a single intellectual movement. But movement it was: a movement of ideas and the disputation of those ideas. The men who developed and disputed those ideas as they met in the societies and ate and drank in the taverns of the Old Town in Edinburgh created momentum on many fronts.

It was a movement of taste in architecture – seen in the work of Robert Adam and his brother James, followed in due course by William Playfair – and in literature and belles lettres, where notables included Hugh Blair, the holder of the first chair of rhetoric in the University of Edinburgh, the poets James Thomson, Allan Ramsay, and the incomparable Robert Burns, as well as the playwright John Home. It was also a movement in the arts, especially in portraiture where Allan Ramsay (the son of the poet) and Henry Raeburn dominated, along with the miniature wax and paste portraitists James Tassie, his nephew William Tassie, and John Henning. Equally central were those who made lasting and formative impacts on the development of the sciences of mathematics (Colin Maclaurin), medicine (William Cullen), chemistry (Joseph Black), engineering (James Watt and Thomas Telford), and geology (James Hutton).

Underlying and stimulating the activity in all these fields were developments in philosophy, which, although they do not define a single school, set a context for the intellectual endeavours that were integral to the Scottish Enlightenment. These developments had four key characteristics. The first was a scepticism about various forms of rationalism and about the attempts by such thinkers as Descartes in France and Gottfried Wilhelm Leibniz in Germany to find a single method or set of rules of rationality from which all truths might be deduced. The second was the central place given to what was connoted by the terms sentiment and sense (as in the "moral sense" school founded by the 3rd Earl of Shaftesbury, and as in the "philosophy of common sense", which emerged in Scotland in the 18th century). The third was the drive toward empirical methods of inquiry. The fourth, which draws on all of these, was given a prominent position in the title of the first and ultimately most important of Hume's writings: *A Treatise of Human Nature* (1739–40), one of the two most significant books to come out of the period. Hume's dream, shared by others, was to replace the appeal to forms of rationalism as a means of distinguishing true from false beliefs with the development of a science of human nature.

Some state that the Scottish Enlightenment began in 1740, but this fails to take account of the date of publication of Hume's *Treatise*, the product of agonized labours in France in the 1730s. Its first two volumes preceded the other truly great work of the Scottish Enlightenment, Smith's *An Inquiry into the Nature and Causes of the Wealth of Nations*, by 37 years. Also very influential was the first major work of Francis Hutcheson,

An Inquiry into the Original of Our Ideas of Beauty and Virtue
(1725). Hutcheson, a professor at the University of Glasgow,
was a major source of inspiration for his pupil Smith as well as
for Smith's professorial successor, Thomas Reid.

The primary focus of the activity of the Scottish Enlightenment was the city of Edinburgh – but it was part of a broader
Scottish phenomenon, not least in Glasgow and Aberdeen. The
disputatious men of Edinburgh to whom Franklin referred
honed their skills in many ways – over a bottle of claret, over
the dining tables of the taverns in which they gathered, in
many printed papers and books, and in the learned societies
that waxed and waned at that time. The societies were var-
iously inquisitive and intellectually improving: they included,
for example, the Honourable Society of Improvers in the
Knowledge of Agriculture in Scotland, active in 1723, and
the Society for the Improvement of Medical Knowledge,
founded in 1731, with a parallel student society founded in
1734. The first volume of published papers from the Society
for the Improvement of Medical Knowledge appeared in 1733
as *Medical Essays and Observations*. Even more definitive of
the Scottish Enlightenment were the activities of the Edinburgh
Philosophical Society for Improving Arts and Sciences and
Particularly Natural Knowledge; its range of topics, officials,
and contributors are well illustrated in the three volumes of
Essays and Observations, Physical and Literary, published
intermittently from 1754. Henry Home, later Lord Kames,
who helped reinvigorate the society, begins the first of these
published papers ("Of the Laws of Motion") in a way that
provides a manifesto-like statement for the society's activities:
"Nothing has more perplexed philosophy than an unlucky
propensity, which makes us grasp at principles without due
regard to facts and experiments." A page later, however, he
adds a complementary thought: "Facts and experiments are

useless lumber if we are not to reason about them, nor draw
any consequences from them."

Showing its aspirations to a place in the international
firmament, the society elected Voltaire a foreign member in
the mid-1740s. In 1743, the American Philosophical Society
was founded under Franklin's impetus. Comparable societies
were also to be found in Glasgow and Aberdeen.

History and Social Thought

Order, purity, clarity: such were the classical ideals. They had
dominated traditional theology as represented by its last great
master, the French bishop Jacques-Bénigne Bossuet. His *Politique tirée des propres paroles de l'Écriture sainte* (*Statecraft
Drawn from the Very Words of the Holy Scriptures*) and
Discours sur l'histoire universelle (*Discourse on Universal
History*) offered a world view and a history based on the
Old Testament. Bossuet believed in the unity of knowledge as
so many branches of Christian truth. His compelling logic and
magisterial writing had a strong influence. When, however, the
hypotheses were tested and found wanting, the very comprehensiveness of the system ensured that its collapse was complete. Bossuet had encouraged Richard Simon when he set out
to refute Protestantism through historical study of the Bible
but was shocked when he saw where it led. Inevitably, scholarship revealed inconsistencies and raised questions about the
ways in which the Bible should be treated: if unreliable as
history, then how sound was the basis for theology? Simon's
works were banned in 1678, but Dutch printers ensured their
circulation. No censorship could prevent the development of
historical method, which was making a place for itself in the
comprehensive search for truth. With Edward Gibbon, Jean

Mabillon, and Louis Tillemont, historians were to become more skilled and scrupulous in the use of evidence. Gibbon, perhaps the most famous of the three, published the first quarto volume of his *Decline and Fall of the Roman Empire* in February 1776; the last lines were written in June 1787. The first half of the work covers a period of about 300 years to the end of the empire in the West, about AD 480. In the second half nearly 1,000 years are compressed. Yet the work is a coherent whole by virtue of its conception of the Roman Empire as a single entity throughout its long and diversified course. Gibbon imposed a further unity on his narrative by describing an undeviating decline from those ideals of political and, even more, intellectual freedom that he had found in classical literature. The material decay that had inspired him in Rome was the effect and symbol of moral decadence. The epilogue of chapters describing medieval and Renaissance Rome give some hope that the long decline is over and that humankind has some prospect of recovering intellectual freedom.

The vindication of intellectual freedom is a large part of Gibbon's purpose as a historian. When toward the end of his work he remarks, "I have described the triumph of barbarism and religion," he reveals epigrammatically his view of the causes of the decay of the Graeco-Roman world. But there is the further question of whether the changes brought about are to be regarded as ones of progress or retrogression. Writing as a mid-18th-century "philosopher", Gibbon saw the process as retrogression, and his judgement remains of perpetual interest. Both in his lifetime and after, he was attacked and personally ridiculed by those who feared that his scepticism about belief would shake the existing establishment. While he treated the supernatural with irony, his main purpose was to establish the principle that religions must be treated as phenomena of human experience.

The philosophes characteristically believed that history was becoming a science because it was subject to philosophical method. It also was subject to the prevailing materialist bias, which is why, however scholarly individual writers like Hume might be, the Enlightenment was in some respects vulnerable to fresh insights about human beings – such as those of Étienne Bonnot de Condillac, who believed that humans could be moulded for their own good – and by further research into the past – which, for Claude-Adrien Helvétius was simply the worthless veneration of ancient laws and customs.

In 1703 the French soldier and writer Baron de La Hontan introduced the idea of the "noble savage", who led a moral life in the light of natural religion (i.e., religion as given by or revealed through nature). In relative terms, the uniquely God-given character of European values was questioned; Louis XIV's persecution of the Huguenots and the Jansenists (followers of the Dutch Augustinian theologian Cornelius Jansen) offered an unappealing example. Philosophers were provided, through the device of *voyages imaginaires*, with new insights and standards of reference. As Archbishop Fénelon was to show in *Télémaque* (1699) – where the population of his imaginary republic of Salente was engaged in farming and the ruler, renouncing war, sought to increase the wealth of the kingdom – a utopian idyll could be a vehicle for criticism of contemporary institutions. A bishop and sentimental aristocrat might seem an unlikely figure to appear in the pantheon of the Enlightenment. But his readers encountered views about the obligations as well as rights of subjects that plainly anticipate its universalism, as in the *Dialogue des morts*: "Each individual owes incomparably more to the human race, the great fatherland, than to the country in which he is born."

Reason, Nature, and Providence

It is easier to identify intellectual trends than to define enlightened views, even where, as in France, there was a distinct and self-conscious movement, which had by mid-century the characteristics of a party. Clues can be found in the use commonly made of certain closely related cult words such as Reason, Nature, and Providence. From having a sharp, almost technical sense in the work of Descartes, Pascal, and Spinoza, reason came to mean something like common sense, along with strongly pejorative assumptions about things not reasonable. For Voltaire, the reasonable were those who believed in progress: he lived "in curious times and amid astonishing contrasts: reason on the one hand, the most absurd fanaticism on the other". Nature in the post-Newtonian world became a system of intelligible forces that grew as the complexity of matter was explored and the diversity of particular species discovered. It led to the pantheism of the Irish writer John Toland, for whom nature replaced God, and to the absolute doubt of the French physician Julien La Mettrie, who in *L'Homme machine* (1748) took the position that nothing about nature or its causes was known.

In England, in the writings of the 3rd Earl of Shaftesbury and the physician David Hartley, nature served the cause of sound morals and rational faith. One of the foremost theologians, Joseph Butler, author of the *Analogy of Religion* (1736), tested revelation against nature and in so doing erased the troublesome distinction in a manner wholly satisfying to those who looked for assurance that God could be active in the world without breaking the laws of its being.

Finally, to the French philosopher Jean-Jacques Rousseau, "nature" – the word that had proved so useful to advocates of an undogmatic faith, of universal principles of law and even (in the hands of the physiocrats) economic laissez-faire – acquired a new resonance. In his *Discourse on the Origin of Inequality* (1755), he wrote: "We cannot desire or fear anything, except from the idea of it, or from the simple impulse of nature." Nature had become the primal condition of innocence in which man was whole – not perfect, but imbued with virtues that reflected the absence of restraints.

Along with the new view of the universe grew belief in the idea of a benign providence, which could be trusted because it was visibly active in the world. Writers sought to express their sense of God's benevolent intention as manifest in creation. To the Abbé Pluche domestic animals were not merely docile but naturally loved humanity. Voltaire, equally implausibly, observed of mountain ranges that they were "a chain of high and continuous aqueducts which, by their apertures allow the rivers and arms of the sea the space which they need to irrigate the land". The idea of providence could degenerate into the fatuous complacency that Voltaire himself was to deride and against which Samuel Taylor Coleridge was memorably to rebel – in particular, dismissing the idea that the universe was just a vast theatre for the divine message. Faith, wrote the English poet, "could not be intellectually more evident without being morally less effective; without counteracting its own end by sacrificing the life of faith to the cold mechanism of a worthless because compulsory assent". The Enlightenment, it seemed, carried the seeds of its own disintegration.

No less unsettling were the findings of geologists. Jean-Étienne Guettard concluded that the evidence of fossils found in the volcanic hills of the Puy de Dôme in south-central France conflicted with the time scheme of the Old Testament. Whether, like the Count de Buffon, geologists attributed to matter a form of life, speculated about life as a constant, shapeless flux, or postulated a history of the world that had evolved over an immensely long time, scientists were dispensing with God as a necessary factor in their calculations. Some theologians sought compromise, while others retreated, looking to a separate world of intuitive understanding for the justification of faith. Butler pointed to conscience, the voice of God speaking to the human soul. He deplored the enthusiasm that characterized the tireless preaching of John Wesley and his message of the love of God manifested in Christ. "A true and living faith in God", Butler declared, "is inseparable from a sense of pardon from all past and freedom from all present sins." It was not the freedom understood by the philosophes, but it touched hearts and altered lives.

Meanwhile the path of reason was open for the avowed atheism of Baron d'Holbach, who declared in his *Système de la nature* (1770; *The System of Nature*) that there was no divine purpose: "The whole cannot have an object for outside itself there is nothing towards which it can tend." Another approach was taken by Hume, author of the *Treatise* and the *Dialogues Concerning Natural Religion*, published posthumously in 1779. The notion of miracles was repugnant to reason, but he was content to leave religion as a mystery, to be a sceptic about scepticism, and to deny that man could reach objective knowledge of any kind.

These may appear to have been intellectual games for the few. It could only be a privileged, relatively leisured minority, even among the educated, who actively participated in debate or could even follow the reasoning. The impact was delayed; it was also uneven. In Samuel Johnson's England the independence bestowed by the Anglican clergyman's freehold and the willingness of the established church to countenance rational theology created a shock absorber in the form of the Broad Church. In Protestant countries criticism tended to be directed

toward amending existing structures: there was a pious as well
as an impious Enlightenment.

Among Roman Catholic countries France's situation was in
some ways unique. Even there orthodox doctrines remained
entrenched in such institutions as the Sorbonne; some bishops
might be worldly but others were conscientious; monasteries
decayed but parish life was vital and curés (parish priests) well
trained. Nor was theology neglected: in 1770, French publishers brought out 70 books in defence of the faith. Of course the
philosophes, endowed with the talents and the means to mount
sustained campaigns, ensured that the question of religion
remained high on the agenda. There was also a ready market
for writers who sought to apply rational and experimental
methods to Hume's science of human nature.

Man and Society

Chief among these writers was Charles-Louis de Secondat,
Baron de la Brède et de Montesquieu. His presidency in the
parlement of Bordeaux supported the career of a litterateur,
scholarly but shrewd in judgement of men and issues. In the
Lettres persanes (1721; *Persian Letters*), he had used the
supposed correspondence of a Persian visitor to Paris to
satirize both the church (under that "magician", the pope)
and the society upon which it appeared to impose so fraudu-
lently. His masterpiece, *De l'esprit des lois* (*The Spirit of the
Laws*), appeared in 22 editions within 18 months of publication in 1748. For this historically minded lawyer, laws were
not abstract rules but were necessary relationships derived
from nature. Accepting completely Locke's sensationalist psychology, he pursued the line of the Italian philosopher Giambattista Vico, the innovative author of *Scienza Nuova* (1725;

New Science), toward the idea that human values are the evolving product of society itself. Among social factors, he listed climate, religion, laws, the principles of government, the example of the past, and social practices and manners and concluded that from these a general spirit is formed.

Montesquieu's concern with knowledge as a factor in shaping society is characteristic of the Enlightenment. Nor was he alone in his Anglophile tendency, though it did not prevent him from misinterpreting the English constitution as being based on the separation of powers. The idea that moral freedom could be realized only in a regime whose laws were enacted by an elected legislature, administered by a separate executive, and enforced by an independent judiciary was to be more influential in the New World than in the Old. His theories reflected a Newtonian view of the static equilibrium of forces and were influenced by his perception of the French government as increasingly arbitrary and centralist; they were conceived as much as a safeguard against despotism as an instrument of progress.

Montesquieu's political conservatism belonged to a world different from that of the younger generation of philosophes, for whom the main obstacle to progress was privilege; they put their trust in "the enlightened autocrat" and in his mandate for social engineering. They might fear, like Helvétius, that his theories would please the aristocracy. Helvétius – a financier, amateur philosopher, and author of the influential *De l'esprit* (1758; *On the Mind*) – advocated enlightened self-interest in a way that found an echo in physiocratic economic theory and argued that each individual, in seeking his own good, contributed to the general good. Laws, being man-made, should be changed so as to be more useful. The spirit of the Enlightenment is well conveyed by his suggestion that experimental ethics should be constructed in the same way as experimental physics. By contrast, Montesquieu, whose special concern was the sanctity of human law, saw the problem of right conduct as one of adapting to circumstances. The function of reason was to bring about accord between human law and natural law (a system of justice derived from nature rather than from society). While the objective nature of his inquiry encouraged those who trusted in the power of reason to solve human problems, it was left to those who saw the Enlightenment in more positive terms to work for change.

François-Marie Arouet, whose nom de plume Voltaire was to become almost synonymous with the Enlightenment, was a pupil of the Jesuits at their celebrated college of Louis-le-Grand; his political education included 11 months in the Bastille. The contrast between the arbitrary injustice epitomized by his imprisonment, without trial, for insulting a nobleman and the free society he subsequently enjoyed in England was to inspire a life's commitment to the principles of reason, liberty, justice, and toleration. Voltaire at times played the role of adviser to princes (notably Frederick II of Prussia) but learned that it was easier to criticize than to change institutions and laws.

Like other philosophes living under a regime that denied political opportunity, he was no politician. Nor was he truly a philosopher in the way that Locke, Hume, or even Montesquieu can be so described. His importance was primarily as an advocate at the bar of public opinion. The case for the reform of archaic laws and the war against superstition was presented with passion and authority, notably in his *Dictionnaire philosophique* (1764; *Philosophical Dictionary*). With astute judgement, he worked on the reader's sensibilities. "The most useful books", he wrote, "are those to which the readers themselves contribute half; they develop the idea of which the author has presented the seed." He could lift an episode – the executions of

Admiral Byng (1757) for failing to win a battle; of Jean Calas, seemingly, for being a Huguenot (1762); and of the Chevalier de la Barre, after torture, for alleged blasphemy (1766) – to the level at which they exemplified the injustices committed when man would not listen to the voice of reason or could not do so because of archaic laws. In *Candide* (1759), he presented the debate between the optimistic Dr Pangloss (a satirical portrait of Leibniz), who affirms that this is the "best of all possible worlds", and Martin, who believes in the reality of evil, in a way that highlights the issues and is as significant now as then.

Voltaire mounted his campaigns from a comfortable base, his large estate at Ferney. He was vain enough to relish his status as a literary lion and freedom's champion. He could be vindictive and was often impatient with differing views. In his reluctance to follow ideas through or consider their practical implications and in his patrician disregard for the material concerns of ordinary people, he epitomized faults with which the philosophes can be charged, the more because they were so censorious of others. He was generous chiefly in imaginative energy, in the indignation expressed in the celebrated war cry "Écrasez l'infâme" (literally "crush infamy", signifying for Voltaire the intolerance of the church), and in the time he devoted to the causes of wronged individuals with whose plight he could identify. He had little to put in place of the religion he abused and offered no alternative vision. He did succeed notably in making people think about important questions – indeed, his questions were usually clearer than his answers.

The *Encyclopédie*

The Marquis de Condorcet, a mathematician and one of the more radical of his group, described his fellow philosophes as "a class of men less concerned with discovering truth than with propagating it". That was the spirit which animated the *Encyclopédie*, a 35-volume compendium encompassing contemporary belief and knowledge which sought to mould public opinion. Diderot's coeditor, the mathematician Jean le Rond d'Alembert, had, in his preface, presented history as the record of progress through learning. The title page proclaimed the authors' intention to outline the present state of knowledge about the sciences, arts, and crafts. Among its contributors were craftsmen who provided the details for the technical articles. Pervading all was Diderot's moral theme: through knowledge "our children, better instructed than we, may at the same time become more virtuous and happy." Such utilitarianism, closely related to Locke's environmentalism, was one aspect of what d'Alembert called "the philosophic spirit". If it had been only that, it would have been as useful as Ephraim Chambers' *Cyclopaedia* (1727), which it set out to emulate. Instead, it became the textbook for the thoughtful – predominantly officeholders, professionals, the bourgeoisie, and particularly the young, who might appreciate Diderot's idea of the *Encyclopédie* as the means by which to change the common way of thinking.

In the cause, Diderot sustained imprisonment in the jail at Vincennes (1749) and had to endure the condemnation and burning of one of his books, *Pensées philosophiques* (1746; *Philosophic Thoughts*). There was nothing narrow about his secular mission. Most of the important thinkers of the time contributed to it. Differences were to be expected, but there was enough unanimity in principles to endow the new gospel of scientific empiricism with the authority that Scripture was losing. It was also to provide a unique source for reformers. Catherine II of Russia wrote to the German critic Friedrich Melchior Grimm for suggestions as to a system of education for young people. Meanwhile, she said she would "flip through the *Encyclopédie*; I shall certainly find in it everything I should and should not do".

Rousseau and his Followers

Diderot prefigured the unconventional style that found its archetype in Jean-Jacques Rousseau. In his novel of the 1760s, *Le neveu de Rameau* (*Rameau's Nephew*), Diderot's eccentric hero persuades his bourgeois uncle, who professes virtue, to confess to actions so cynical as to be a complete reversal of accepted values. Rousseau was close to this stance when he ridiculed those who derived right action from right thinking. He understood the interests of the people, which the philosophes tended to neglect and which the American revolutionary Thomas Paine considered in the *Rights of Man* (1791). If virtue were dependent on culture and culture the prerogative of a privileged minority, what was the prospect for the rest? "We have physicians, geometricians, chemists, astronomers, poets, musicians and painters in plenty; but no longer a citizen among us."

Rousseau is thus of the Enlightenment yet against it, at least as represented by the mechanistic determinism of Condillac or the elitism of Diderot, who boasted that he wrote only for those to whom he could talk – i.e., for philosophers. Rousseau challenged the privileged republic of letters, its premises, and its principles. His *Confessions* depicted a well-intentioned man forced to become a rogue and outcast by the artificiality of society. His first essay, *Discours sur les sciences et les arts* (1750; *Discourse on the Arts and Sciences*), suggested the contradiction between the exterior world of appearances and the inner world of feeling. With his view of culture now went emphasis on the value of emotions. Seminal use of concepts – such as "citizen" to indicate the rights proper to a member of a free society – strengthened signals that could otherwise confuse as much as inspire.

Dealing with the basic relations of life, Rousseau introduced the prophetic note that was to sound through democratic rhetoric. The state of nature was a hypothesis rather than an ideal: man must seek to recover wholeness at a higher level of existence. For this to be possible he must have a new kind of education and humanity a new political constitution. *Émile; on de le'éducation* (1762 *Émile; on de l'éducation*) proposed an education to foster natural growth. His *Du contrat social ou principes du droit politique* (1762; *The Social Contract; or Principles of Political Right*) was banned, and this lent glamour to proposals for a constitution to enable the individual to develop without offending against the principle of social equality. The crucial question concerned legitimate authority. Rousseau rejected both natural law and force as its basis. He sought a form of association that would allow both security and the natural freedom in which "each man, giving himself to all, gives himself to nobody." It is realized in the form of the general will, expressed in laws to which all submit. More than the sum of individual wills, it is general in that it represents the public spirit seeking the common good, which Rousseau defined as liberty and equality, the latter because liberty cannot subsist without it. He advocated the total sovereignty of the state, a political formula which depended on the assumption that the state would be guided by the general will. Rousseau's good society was a democratic and egalitarian republic. Geneva, his birthplace, was to prove boundless in inspiration. Rousseau's influence may have been slight in his lifetime, though some were proud to be numbered among his admirers. His eloquence touched men of sensibility on both sides of the Atlantic.

The French writer Morelly, in the *Code de la nature* (1755), attacked property as the parent of crime and proposed that every man should contribute according to ability and receive according to need. Two decades later, another radical abbé, Gabriel de Mably, started with equality as the law of nature and argued that the introduction of property had destroyed the golden age of man. In England, William Godwin, following Holbach in obeisance to reason, condemned not only property but even the state of marriage: according to Godwin, man freed from the ties of custom and authority could devote himself to the pursuit of universal benevolence. To the young poets William Wordsworth and Percy Bysshe Shelley it was a beguiling vision; those less radical might fear for social consequences, as did the French draftsmen of the *Declaration of the Rights of Man and of the Citizen* of 1789, who were careful to proclaim the sacred right of property.

Thomas Jefferson made the rights of man the foundation of his political philosophy as well as of the US Constitution, but he remained a slave owner. The idea of "de-natured" man was as potent for the unsettling of the ancien régime as loss of the sense of God had been for the generation of Martin Luther and St Ignatius. It struck home to the educated young who might identify with Rousseau's self-estrangement and read into the image of "man everywhere in chains" their own perception of the privilege that thwarted talent. Such were Maximilien Robespierre, the young lawyer of Arras; Aleksandr Radischev, who advocated the emancipation of Russian serfs, or the Germans who felt restricted in regimented, often minuscule states. Both the severe rationalism of Kant and the idealism of German Romantics found inspiration in Rousseau. Yet Kant's *Kritik der reinen Vernunft* (1781; *Critique of Pure Reason*) and the sentimental hero portrayed by Goethe in his *Die Leiden des Jungen Werther* (1774; *Sorrows of Young Werther*) mark the end of the Enlightenment. "It came upon us so grey, so cimmerian, so corpse-like that we could hardly endure its ghost," wrote Goethe, speaking for the Romantic generation and pronouncing valediction.

In France the Enlightenment touched government circles only through individuals, such as Anne-Robert Turgot, a physiocrat, finance minister (1774–6), and frustrated reformer. The physiocrats, taking their cue from economists such as François Quesnay, author of *Tableau économique* (1758), advocated the removal of artificial obstacles to the growth of the natural economic order of a free market for the produce of the land. Even Adam Smith, who wrote *The Wealth of Nations* (1776) with a capitalist economy in mind, could see his avowed disciple, the British statesman William Pitt, move only cautiously in the direction of free trade.

Although the visionary poet William Blake could be adduced to show that there was powerful resistance to the new industrial society, the physician and scientist Erasmus Darwin, grandfather of Charles Darwin, was – with his fellow luminaries of the Lunar Society, Josiah Wedgwood and Matthew Boulton – at the heart of the entrepreneurial culture: there was no deep divide separating the English philosophes, with their sanctification of private property and individual interests, from the values and programmes of government. In France, where there was no internal common market and much to inhibit private investment, physiocratic ideas were politically naive: the gap between theory and implementation only illustrates the way in which the Enlightenment undermined confidence in the regime. Operating in a political vacuum, the philosophes could only hope that they would, like Diderot with Catherine the Great, exercise such influence abroad as might fulfil their sense of mission. In both Germany and Italy, however, circumstances favoured emphasis on the practical reforms that appealed as much to the rulers as to their advisers.

The Enlightenment in Germany

In Germany the Aufklärung found its highest expression in a science of government. One explanation lies in the importance of universities. There were nearly 50 by 1800 (24 had been founded since 1600); they were usually the product of a prince's need to have trained civil servants rather than of a patron's zeal for higher learning. Not all were as vigorous as Halle (1694) or Göttingen (1737), but others, such as Vienna in the last quarter of the 18th century, were inspired to emulate them. In general, the universities dominated intellectual and cultural life. Rulers valued them, and their teachers were influential, because they served the state by educating those who would serve. Leading academic figures held posts enabling them to advise the government: the political economist Joseph von Sonnenfels was an adviser to the Habsburgs on the serf question.

Lutheranism was another important factor in the evolution of the attitude to authority that makes the German Enlightenment so markedly different from the French. In the 18th century it was further influenced by Pietism, which was essentially a devotional movement though imbued with a reforming spirit. Nor was the earnest religious spirit confined to the Protestant confessions. In the Austria of Empress Maria Theresa, Jansenism, which penetrated Viennese circles from Austrian Flanders, was as important in influencing reforms in church and education as it was in sharpening disputes with the papacy. But there was nothing comparable, even in the Catholic south and Rhineland, to the revolt of Western intellectuals against traditional dogma. Amid all his speculations, Leibniz, who more than any other influenced German thought, had held to the idea of a personal God not subject to the limitations of a material universe. It was devotion, not indifference, that made him, with Bossuet, seek ground for Christian reunion.

Leibniz's disciple, Christian Wolff, a leading figure of the Aufklärung, was opposed to the Pietists, who secured his expulsion from Halle in 1723. Yet, though he believed that reason and revelation could be reconciled, he shared with the Pietists fundamental Christian tenets. In Halle there emerged a synthesis of Wolffism and Pietism, a scientific theology that was progressive but orthodox. Pervading all was respect for the ruler, reflecting the acceptance of the *cuius regio, eius religio* principle (which meant that the ruler of a principality determined its religion); it reduced the scope for internal conflicts, which elsewhere bred doubts about authority. In translating conservative attitudes into political doctrines, the contribution of the lawyers and the nature of the law they taught were crucial. In place of the moral vacuum in which the single reality was the power of the individual ruler, there had come into being a body of law, articulated pre-eminently by the Dutch jurist Hugo Grotius in *On the Law of War and Peace* (1625). It was grounded not only in proven principles of private law but also in the Christian spirit, though it was strengthened by Grotius' separation of natural law from its religious aspects.

As expounded by Wolff and the German historian Samuel Pufendorf, natural law endorsed absolutism. They did not wholly neglect civil rights, they advocated religious toleration, and they opposed torture, but, living in a world far removed from that of Locke or Montesquieu, they saw no need to stipulate constitutional safeguards. Wolff declared that "he who exercises the civil power has the right to establish everything that appears to him to serve the public good." Such a sovereign, comprising legislative, executive, and judicial functions, was also, as defined in Wolff's *Rational Thoughts on the Social Life of Mankind* (1756), a positive force, benevolent: he was Luther's "godly prince" in 18th-century dress, serving his people's needs. Cameralwissenschaft – the science and practice of administration – would serve the ruler by increasing revenue and also improve the lot of the people.

Envisaging progress under the sovereign who created the schools, hospitals, and orphanages and provided officials to run them, Wolff was only one among numerous writers who contributed to the ideal of benevolent bureaucratic absolutism, or Wohlfahrstaat. Although also influenced by the local school of cameralists and 17th-century writers such as Philippe Wilhelm von Hörnigk and Johann Joachim Becher, the emperor Joseph II, having the largest area to rule and the most earnest commitment to its principles, came to exemplify the Aufklärung. By his time, however, there was a growing reaction against the soulless rationality of the natural lawyers. With the exception of the Prussian critic Johann Gottfried Herder, whose ideal Volk-state would have a republican constitution, political thought was unaffected by the emphasis of the literary giants of Romanticism on freedom and spontaneity.

His contemporary Kant, an anticameralist, believed in a degree of popular participation but would not allow even the theoretical right of revolution. In *Was ist Aufklärung?* Kant drew a vital distinction between the public and private use of one's reason. With Frederick II in mind, he advanced the paradox that can be taken as a text for the Enlightenment as well as for German history. The ruler with a well-disciplined and large army could provide more liberty than a republic. A high degree of civil freedom seems advantageous to a people's intellectual freedom, yet also sets up insuperable barriers to it.

Conversely, a lesser degree of civil freedom gives intellectual freedom enough room to expand to its fullest extent.

The Enlightenment in Italy

Foreigners who came to see the monuments of Italy, or perhaps to listen to the music that they might recognize as the inspiration of some of the best of their own, were likely to return convinced that the country was backward. Its intellectual life might remain a closed book. As elsewhere, the Enlightenment consisted of small, isolated groups; measured by impact on governments, they had little obvious effect. Where there was important change, it was usually the work of a ruler, such as Leopold of Tuscany, or a minister, such as Bernardo Tanucci in Naples. The power of the church, symbolized by the listing of Galileo, a century after his condemnation, on the Index of Forbidden Books; the survival, particularly in the south, of an oppressive feudal power; and the restrictive power of the guilds were among the targets for liberals and humanitarians.

Universities like Bologna, Padua, and Naples had preserved traditions of scholarship and still provided a stimulating base for such original thinkers as Vico and Antonio Genovesi, a devout priest, professor of philosophy, and pioneer in ethical studies and economic theory. The distinctive feature of the Italian Enlightenment, however, as befitted the country that produced such scientists as Luigi Galvani and Alessandro Volta, was its practical tendency. Its proponents introduced to political philosophy utilitarianism's slogan "the greatest happiness of the greatest number". They also felt the passion of patriots seeking to rouse their countrymen.

The greatest representative of the Italian Enlightenment was Cesare Beccaria, whose work included *Dei delitti e delle pene*

(1764; *Of Crimes and Punishments*), a celebrated volume on the reform of criminal justice; in his lifetime it was translated into 22 languages. Beccaria's treatise is the first succinct and systematic statement of principles governing criminal punishment. Although many of the ideas expressed were familiar, and Beccaria's indebtedness to such writers as Montesquieu is clear, the work nevertheless represents a major advance in criminological thought. "Newtoncino", as Beccaria was called by admirers, claimed to apply the geometric spirit to the study of criminal law. "That bond which is necessary to keep the interest of individuals united, without which men would return to their original state of barbarity," may recall the pessimism of the English political philosopher Thomas Hobbes, but his formula for penalties answered to the enlightened ruler's search for what was both rational and practical: "Punishments which exceed the necessity of preserving this bond are in their nature unjust." So Beccaria condemned torture and capital punishment, questioned the treatment of sins as crimes, and stressed the value of equality before the law and of prevention having priority over punishment.

Much of the best enlightened thought comes together in Beccaria's work, in which the link between philosophy and reform is clearly evident. The treatise exerted significant influence on criminal-law reform throughout western Europe. In England, the utilitarian philosopher and reformer Jeremy Bentham advocated Beccaria's principles, and Bentham's disciple Samuel Romilly devoted his parliamentary career to reducing the scope of the death penalty. Legislative reforms in Russia, Sweden, and the Habsburg Empire were also influenced by the treatise. The legislation of several American states reflected Beccaria's thought.

Spain, Portugal, and Eastern Europe

The Enlightenment was a pan-European phenomenon: examples of enlightened thought and writing can be found in every country. There were important reforms in late 18th-century Spain under the benevolent rule of Charles III. The spirit of acceptance, however, was stronger than that of inquiry; Spain apparently was a textbook example of the philosophes' belief that religion stifled freedom of thought. It was a priest, Benito Feijóo y Montenegro, who did as much as anyone to prepare for the Spanish Enlightenment, preaching the criterion of social utility in a society still obsessed with honour and display. Conservatism was, though, well entrenched, whether expressed in the pedantic procedures of the Inquisition or in the crude mob destroying the Marqués de Squillace's new street lamps in Madrid in 1766. "It is an old habit in Spain", wrote the Count de Campomanes, "to condemn everything that is new."

So the accent in Spain was utilitarian, as in other countries where local circumstances and needs dictated certain courses of action. Johann Struensee's liberal reforms in Denmark (1771–2) represented, besides his own eccentricity, justifiable resentment at an oppressive Pietist regime. The constitutional changes that followed the first partition of Poland in 1772 were dictated as much by the need to survive as by the imaginative idealism of King Stanislaw. Despite her interest in abstract ideals, reforms in law and government in Catherine the Great's vast Russian lands represented the overriding imperative, the security of the state. In Portugal, Pombal, the rebuilder of post-earthquake Lisbon, was motivated chiefly by the need to restore vitality to a country with a pioneering maritime past. Leopold of Tuscany was able to draw on a rich humanist tradition and civic pride. Everywhere the preferences of the ruler had an idiosyncratic effect, as in the Margrave Charles Frederick of Baden's unsuccessful attempt in 1770 to introduce a land tax, or in Pombal's campaign to expel the Jesuits (copied loosely by other Catholic rulers).

Overall it may seem as easy to define the Enlightenment by what it opposed as by what it advocated. Along with some superficiality in thought and cynical expediency in action, this is the basis for conservative criticism: when reason is little more than common sense and utilitarianism so infects attitudes that progress can be measured only by material standards, then the conservative statesman Edmund Burke's lament about the age of "sophisters, economists, and calculators" is held to be justified. Some historians have followed Burke in ascribing not only radical authoritarianism but even 20th-century totalitarianism to tendencies within the Enlightenment. Indeed, it may be that the movement that helped to free man from the past and its "self-incurred tutelage" (Kant) failed to prevent the development of new systems and techniques of tyranny. This intellectual odyssey, following Shaftesbury's "mighty light which spreads itself over the world", should, however, be seen to be related to the growth of the state, the advance of science, and the subsequent development of an industrial society. For their ill effects, the Enlightenment cannot be held to be mainly responsible. Rather it should be viewed as an integral part of a broader historical process. In this light it is easier to appraise the achievements that are its singular glory. To be challenged to think harder, with greater chance of discovering truth; to be able to write, speak, and worship freely; and to experience equality under the law and relatively humane treatment if one offended against it was to be able to live a fuller life.

2

THE SCIENTIFIC REVOLUTION

The history of philosophy is intertwined with the history of the natural sciences. Long before the 19th century, when the term "science" began to be used with its modern meaning, those who are now counted among the major figures in the history of Western philosophy were often equally famous for their contributions to "natural philosophy", the bundle of inquiries now designated as sciences. Aristotle was the first great biologist; René Descartes formulated analytic geometry ("Cartesian geometry") and discovered the laws of the reflection and refraction of light; Gottfried Wilhelm Leibniz laid claim to priority in the invention of the calculus; and Immanuel Kant offered the basis of a still-current hypothesis regarding the formation of the solar system (the Kant–Laplace nebular hypothesis).

In reflecting on human knowledge, the great philosophers also offered accounts of the aims and methods of the sciences, ranging from Aristotle's studies in logic through the proposals of Francis Bacon and Descartes, which were instrumental in shaping 17th-century science. They were joined in these reflections by the most eminent natural scientists. Galileo supplemented his arguments about the motions of earthly and heavenly bodies with claims about the roles of mathematics and experiment in discovering facts about nature. Similarly, the account given by Sir Isaac Newton of his system of the natural world is punctuated by a defence of his methods and an outline of a positive programme for scientific inquiry. The French chemist Antoine-Laurent Lavoisier and others continued this tradition, offering their own insights into the character of the scientific enterprise.

Sir Isaac Newton, the English physicist and mathematician, was one of the greatest figures of the movement now known as the scientific revolution. In optics, his discovery of the composition of white light integrated the phenomena of colours into the science of light and laid the foundation for modern physical optics. In mechanics, his three laws of motion, the basic principles of modern physics, resulted in the formulation of the law of universal gravitation. In mathematics, he was one of the original discoverers of the infinitesimal calculus. Newton's *Philosophiae Naturalis Principia Mathematica* (1687; *Mathematical Principles of Natural Philosophy*, commonly called the *Principia*) was one of the most important single works in the history of modern science.

When Newton arrived in Cambridge in 1661, the scientific revolution was well advanced, and many of the works basic to modern science had already appeared. Astronomers from Copernicus to Johannes Kepler had elaborated the heliocentric system of the universe. Galileo had proposed the foundations of a new mechanics built on the principle of inertia. Led by Descartes, philosophers had begun to formulate a new conception of nature as an intricate, impersonal, and inert machine. Yet as far as the universities of Europe, including Cambridge, were concerned, all this might well have never happened. They continued to be the strongholds of outmoded Aristotelianism, which rested on a geocentric view of the universe and dealt with nature in qualitative rather than quantitative terms.

The Position of the Earth

In 1543, as he lay on his deathbed, Copernicus finished reading the proofs of his great work *De revolutionibus orbium coelestium libri VI* (*Six Books Concerning the Revolutions of the Heavenly Orbs*); he died just as it was published. His was the opening shot in a revolution whose consequences were greater than those of any other intellectual event in the history of humankind. The scientific revolution radically altered the conditions of thought and of material existence in which the human race lived, and its effects have not yet been exhausted. Copernicus' daring lay in placing the Sun, not the Earth, at the centre of the cosmos. In the century and a half following Copernicus, two easily discernible scientific movements – the first critical, the second innovative and synthetic – worked together to bring the old cosmos into disrepute and, ultimately, to replace it with a new one.

The Danish astronomer Tycho Brahe measured stellar and planetary positions more accurately than had anyone before him, yet insisted that the Earth was motionless. Copernicus did persuade Tycho to move the centre of revolution of all other planets to the Sun. Perhaps the most serious critical blows, however, were delivered by Galileo after the invention of the telescope. In quick succession, he announced that there were mountains on the Moon, satellites circling Jupiter, and spots upon the Sun. Moreover, the Milky Way was composed of countless stars whose existence no one had suspected until

Galileo saw them. Here was criticism that struck at the very roots of Aristotle's system of the world.

At the same time, in Germany, Tycho's precise observations permitted Kepler to discover that Mars (and, by analogy, all the other planets) did not revolve in a circle at all, but in an ellipse, with the Sun at one focus. Ellipses tied all the planets together in grand Copernican harmony. Galileo attacked the problems of the Earth's rotation and its revolution by logical analysis. Bodies do not fly off the Earth because they are not really revolving rapidly, even though their speed is high. Bodies fall to the base of towers from which they are dropped because they share with the tower the rotation of the Earth. Hence, bodies already in motion preserve that motion when another motion is added. Hence, Galileo concluded, the planets, once set in circular motion, continue to move in circles forever. Therefore, Copernican orbits exist. Galileo never acknowledged Kepler's ellipses; to do so would have meant abandoning his solution to the Copernican problem.

Kepler realized that there was a real problem with planetary motion. He sought to solve it by appealing to the one force that appeared to be cosmic in nature, namely magnetism. The Earth had been shown to be a giant magnet by William Gilbert in England in 1600, and Kepler seized upon this fact. A magnetic force, Kepler argued, emanated from the Sun and pushed the planets around in their orbits, but he was never able to quantify this rather vague and unsatisfactory idea.

New Philosophies

By the end of the first quarter of the 17th century Aristotelianism was rapidly dying, but there was no satisfactory system to take its place. The result was a mood of scepticism and unease.

It was this void that accounted largely for the success of a rather crude system proposed by Descartes. Matter and motion were taken by Descartes to explain everything by means of mechanical models of natural processes, even though he warned that such models were not the way nature probably worked. They provided merely "likely stories", which seemed better than no explanation at all.

According to Descartes, and expounded in his *Discours de la méthode* (1637; *Discourse on Method*), the material universe consists of an indefinitely large plenum of infinitely divisible matter, which is separated into the subtle matter of space and the denser matter of bodies by a determinate quantity of motion that is imparted and conserved by God. Bodies swirl like leaves in a whirlwind in vortices as great as that in which the planets sweep around the Sun and as small as that of tiny spinning globes of light. All bodily joinings and separations are mechanical, resulting from the collisions of other moving bodies. Because the amount of motion is conserved according to the laws of nature, the Cartesian material world exhibits a kind of determinism. After the initial impulse, the world evolves lawfully. If the speeds and positions of all the whirling portions of matter in the universe at any one moment could be completely described, then a complete description of their speeds and positions at any later time could be deduced through calculations based on the laws of motion.

Armed with matter and motion, Descartes attacked the basic Copernican problems. Bodies once in motion, Descartes argued, remain in motion in a straight line unless and until they are deflected from this line by the impact of another body. All changes of motion are the result of such impacts. Hence, the ball falls at the foot of the mast because, unless struck by another body, it continues to move with the ship. Planets move around the Sun because they are swept around by whirlpools of a subtle matter filling all space. Similar models could be constructed to account for all phenomena; the Aristotelian system could be replaced by the Cartesian.

There was one major problem, however, and it sufficed to bring down Cartesianism. Cartesian matter and motion had no purpose, nor did Descartes' philosophy seem to need the active participation of a deity. Although God is the primary cause of the existence of the material universe and of the laws of nature, all physical events – all movements and interactions of bodies – result from secondary causes, that is, from bodies colliding with each other. God stands merely for the uniformity and consistency of the laws of nature. The Cartesian cosmos, as Voltaire later put it, was like a watch that had been wound up at the creation and continues ticking to eternity.

The core of Descartes' near contemporary Francis Bacon's philosophy of science is the account of inductive reasoning given in Book II of his *Novum Organum* (1620). The defect of all previous systems of beliefs about nature, he argued, lay in the inadequate treatment of the general propositions from which the deductions were made. Either they were the result of precipitate generalization from one or two cases, or they were uncritically assumed to be self-evident on the basis of their familiarity and general acceptance.

In order to avoid hasty generalization Bacon urged a technique of "gradual and unbroken ascent", that is, the patient accumulation of well-founded generalizations of steadily increasing degrees of generality. This method would have the beneficial effect of loosening the hold of ill-constructed everyday concepts that obliterate important differences and fail to register important similarities.

The crucial point, Bacon realized, is that induction must work by elimination not, as it does in common life and the defective scientific tradition, by simple enumeration.

Bacon presented tables of presence, of absence, and of degree. Tables of presence contain a collection of cases in which one specified property is found. They are then compared to each other to see what other properties are always present. Any property not present in just one case in such a collection cannot be a necessary condition of the property being investigated. Second, there are tables of absence, which list cases that are as alike as possible to the cases in the tables of presence except for the property under investigation. Any property that is found in the second case cannot be a sufficient condition of the original property. Finally, in tables of degree proportionate variations of two properties are compared to see if the proportion is maintained.

There are, however, more serious difficulties. An obvious one is that Bacon assumed both that every property natural science can investigate actually has some other property which is both its necessary and sufficient condition (a very strong version of determinism) and also that the conditioning property in each case is readily discoverable. What he had himself laid down as the task of metaphysics in his sense (theoretical natural science in contemporary terms), namely the discovery of the hidden "forms" that explain what is observed, ensured that the tables could not serve for that task since they are confined to the perceptible accompaniments of what is to be explained. This point is implied by critics who accused Bacon of failing to recognize the indispensable role of hypotheses in science. In general he adopted a naive and unreflective view about the nature of causes, ignoring their possible complexity and plurality as well as the possibility that they could be at some distance in space and time from their effects.

The conception of a scientific research establishment, which Bacon developed in his utopia, *The New Atlantis* (1627), may be a more important contribution to science than his theory of

induction. Here the idea of science as a collaborative under-
taking, conducted in an impersonally methodical fashion and
animated by the intention to give material benefits to humankind, is set out with literary force.

Isaac Newton and the Rise of Modern Science

It was Isaac Newton who was finally to discover the way to a
new synthesis in which truth was revealed and God was
preserved. Newton was both an experimental and a mathematical genius, a combination that enabled him to establish
both the Copernican system and a new mechanics. His method
was simplicity itself: "from the phenomena of motions to
investigate the forces of nature, and then from these forces
to demonstrate the other phenomena". Newton's genius
guided him in the selection of phenomena to be investigated,
and his creation of a fundamental mathematical tool – the
calculus (simultaneously invented by Leibniz) – permitted him
to submit the forces he inferred to calculation. The result was
the *Principia*, which appeared in 1687. Here was a new
physics that applied equally well to terrestrial and celestial
bodies. Copernicus, Kepler, and Galileo were all justified by
Newton's analysis of forces. Descartes was utterly routed.

Newton's three laws of motion and his principle of universal
gravitation sufficed to regulate the new cosmos, but only,
Newton believed, with the help of God. Gravity, he more
than once hinted, was direct divine action, as were all forces
for order and vitality. Absolute space, for Newton, was
essential, because space was the "sensorium of God", and
the divine abode must necessarily be the ultimate coordinate
system. Finally, Newton's analysis of the mutual perturbations
of the planets caused by their individual gravitational fields

predicted the natural collapse of the solar system unless God acted to set things right again.

The first work which would make Newton's reputation was Book I of the *Opticks*. Beginning with Kepler's *Paralipomena* in 1604, the study of optics had been a central activity of the scientific revolution. Descartes' statement of the sine law of refraction, relating the angles of incidence and emergence at interfaces of the media through which light passes, had added a new mathematical regularity to the science of light, supporting the conviction that the universe is constructed according to mathematical regularities. Descartes had also made light central to the mechanical philosophy of nature; the reality of light, he argued, consists of motion transmitted through a material medium. Newton fully accepted the mechanical nature of light, though he chose the atomistic alternative and held that light consists of material corpuscles in motion. The corpuscular conception of light was always a speculative theory on the periphery of his optics, however. The core of Newton's contribution had to do with colours. An ancient theory extending back at least to Aristotle held that a certain class of colour phenomena, such as the rainbow, arises from the modification of light, which appears white in its pristine form. Descartes had generalized this theory for all colours and translated it into mechanical imagery.

Through a series of experiments performed in 1665 and 1666, in which the spectrum of a narrow beam was projected on to the wall of a darkened chamber, Newton denied the concept of modification and replaced it with that of analysis. Basically, he denied that light is simple and homogeneous – stating instead that it is complex and heterogeneous and that the phenomena of colours arise from the analysis of the heterogeneous mixture into its simple components. The ultimate source of Newton's conviction that light is corpuscular was his recognition that individual rays of light have immutable properties; in his view, such properties imply immutable particles of matter. He held that individual rays (that is, particles of given size) excite sensations of individual colours when they strike the retina of the eye. He also concluded that rays refract at distinct angles – hence, the prismatic spectrum, a beam of heterogeneous rays, i.e., alike incident on one face of a prism, separated or analysed by the refraction into its component parts – and that phenomena such as the rainbow are produced by refractive analysis. Because he believed that chromatic aberration could never be eliminated from lenses, Newton turned to reflecting telescopes; he constructed the first ever built. The heterogeneity of light has been the foundation of physical optics since his time. In 1671 Newton was asked to show his telescope to the Royal Society; he then volunteered a paper on light and colours early in 1672.

In 1675, he brought forth a second paper, an examination of the colour phenomena in thin films, later published as Book II of the *Opticks*. The purpose of the paper was to explain the colours of solid bodies by showing how light can be analysed into its components by reflection as well as refraction. Since they provided the principal basis for subsequent investigations, Newton's optical views were subject to close consideration until well into the 19th century. By the mid-18th century the Swiss mathematician Leonhard Euler and others had theoretical arguments against Newton, but Newton's theory continued to dominate the century, due partly to its successful direct application by Newton and his followers and partly to the comprehensiveness of Newton's thought.

At the turn of the 19th century, Thomas Young, an English physician studying optics was able to explain both interference and the various colour phenomena observed by Newton by means of a wave theory of light. This theory was developed from 1815 onward in a series of brilliant mathematical and experimental memoirs of the French physicist Augustin-Jean Fresnel but was countered by adherents of the corpuscular theory, most notably a group of other French scientists, Pierre-Simon Laplace, Siméon-Denis Poisson, Étienne Malus, and Jean-Baptiste Biot, and most strikingly in connection with Malus' discovery (1808) of the polarization of light by reflection. Following Young's suggestion in 1817, Fresnel was able to render polarization effects comprehensible by means of a wave theory that considered light to be a transverse rather than a longitudinal wave, as the analogy with sound had suggested.

The *Principia*

In the 1670s Newton began to work on the idea of attractions and repulsions in terrestrial phenomena – chemical affinities, the generation of heat in chemical reactions, surface tension in fluids, capillary action, the cohesion of bodies, and the like – but late in 1679, Robert Hooke, the inventor and subsequent curator of experiments for the Royal Society, mentioned in a letter his analysis of planetary motion – in effect, the continuous diversion of a rectilinear motion by a central attraction. Newton began to describe experiments to demonstrate the rotation of the Earth – the dropping of a body from a tower and the path it would follow – and the correspondence with Hooke led him to demonstrate that the elliptical orbit described entails an inverse square attraction to one focus – one of the two crucial propositions on which the law of universal gravitation would ultimately rest. What is more, Hooke's definition of orbital motion – in which the constant action of an attracting body continuously pulls a planet away from its inertial path – suggested a cosmic application for Newton's concept of force and an explanation of planetary paths employing it. In 1679 and 1680, Newton dealt only with orbital dynamics; he had not yet arrived at the concept of universal gravitation.

Nearly five years later, in August 1684, Newton was visited by the astronomer Edmond Halley, who was also troubled by the problem of orbital dynamics. Upon learning that Newton had solved the problem, he extracted Newton's promise to send the demonstration. Three months later he received a short tract entitled *De Motu* (*On Motion*). In two and a half years, *De Motu* grew into the *Principia*, which is not only Newton's masterpiece but also the fundamental work for the whole of modern science. By quantifying the concept of the action of forces between bodies in the second of his three laws of motion, Newton completed the exact quantitative mechanics that has been the paradigm of natural science ever since.

The mechanics of the *Principia* rested on Newton's three laws of motion: (1) that a body remains in its state of rest unless it is compelled to change that state by a force impressed on it; (2) that the change of motion (the change of velocity times the mass of the body) is proportional to the force impressed; (3) that to every action there is an equal and opposite reaction. The analysis of circular motion in terms of these laws yielded a formula of the quantitative measure, in terms of a body's velocity and mass, of the centripetal force necessary to divert a body from its rectilinear path into a given circle. When Newton substituted this formula into Kepler's third law, he found that the centripetal force holding the planets in their given orbits about the Sun must decrease with the square of the planets' distances from the Sun. Because the satellites of Jupiter also obey Kepler's third law, an inverse square centripetal force must also attract them to the centre of their orbits.

Newton was able to show that a similar relation holds between the Earth and the Moon. The distance of the Moon is approximately 60 times the radius of the Earth. Newton compared the distance by which the Moon, in its orbit of known size, is diverted from a tangential path in one second with the distance that a body at the surface of the Earth falls from rest in one second. When the latter distance proved to be 3,600 (60 x 60) times as great as the former, he concluded that one and the same force, governed by a single quantitative law, is operative in all three cases, and from the correlation of the Moon's orbit with the measured acceleration of gravity on the surface of the Earth, he applied the ancient Latin word *gravitas* (literally, "heaviness" or "weight") to it. The law of universal gravitation, which he also confirmed from such further phenomena as the tides and the orbits of comets, states that every particle of matter in the universe attracts every other particle with a force that is proportional to the product of their masses and inversely proportional to the square of the distance between their centres.

The *Principia* immediately raised Newton to international prominence. In their continuing loyalty to the mechanical ideal, continental scientists rejected the idea of action at a distance for a generation, but even in their rejection they could not withhold their admiration for the technical expertise revealed by the work. The publication of the *Principia* marks the culmination of the movement begun by Copernicus and, as such, has always stood as the symbol of the scientific revolution.

There were, however, similar attempts to criticize, systematize, and organize natural knowledge that did not lead to such dramatic results. In the same year as Copernicus' great volume, there appeared an equally important book on anatomy: *De humani corporis fabrica* (1543; *On the Fabric of the Human Body*, called the *De fabrica*), by the Flemish physician Andreas Vesalius, a critical examination of Galen's anatomy in which Vesalius drew on his own studies to correct many of Galen's errors. Vesalius, like Newton a century later, emphasized the phenomena, i.e., the accurate description of natural facts. Vesalius' work touched off a flurry of anatomical work in Italy and elsewhere that culminated in the discovery of the circulation of the blood by William Harvey, whose (*Exercitatio Anatomica de Motu Cordis et Sanguinis in Animalibus, An Anatomical Exercise Concerning the Motion of the Heart and Blood in Animals*) was published in 1628. This was the *Principia* of physiology that established anatomy and physiology as sciences in their own right.

In other sciences the attempt to systematize and criticize was not so successful. In chemistry, for example, the work of the medieval and early modern alchemists had yielded important new substances and processes, such as the mineral acids and distillation, but had obscured theory in almost impenetrable mystical argot. Robert Boyle in England tried to clear away some of the intellectual underbrush by insisting upon clear descriptions, reproducibility of experiments, and mechanical conceptions of chemical processes.

In many areas there was little hope of reducing phenomena to comprehensibility, simply because of the sheer number of facts to be accounted for. New instruments like the microscope and the telescope vastly multiplied the worlds that had to be reckoned with. The voyages of discovery brought back a flood of new botanical and zoological specimens that overwhelmed ancient classificatory schemes. The best that could be done was to describe new things accurately and hope that someday they could all be fitted together in a coherent way.

The Dissemination of Scientific Knowledge

The growing flood of information put heavy strains upon old institutions and practices. It was no longer sufficient to publish scientific results in an expensive book that few could buy; information had to be spread widely and rapidly. Scientific societies sprang up, beginning in Italy in the early years of the 17th century and culminating in the two great national scientific societies that mark the zenith of the scientific revolution: the Royal Society of London for the Promotion of Natural Knowledge, created by royal charter in 1662, and the Académie des Sciences of Paris, formed in 1666.

The Royal Society had originated on November 28 1660, when 12 men met after a lecture at Gresham College, London, by Christopher Wren (then professor of astronomy at the college) and resolved to set up "a Colledge for the promoting of Physico-Mathematicall Experimentall Learning". Those present included the scientists Robert Boyle and Bishop John Wilkins and the courtiers Sir Robert Moray and William, 2nd Viscount Brouncker. From the outset, the society aspired to combine the role of research institute with that of clearing house for knowledge and forum for arbitration, though the latter function became dominant after the society's earliest years.

A key development was the establishment in 1665 of a periodical that acted as the society's mouthpiece (though it was actually published by the secretary, initially Henry Oldenburg, and was only officially adopted by the society in 1753): this was the *Philosophical Transactions*, which still flourishes today as the oldest scientific journal in continuous publication. It was soon copied in France by the Academy of Science's *Mémoires*, which won equal importance and prestige. In the late 18th century the society played an active role in encouraging scientific exploration, particularly under its longest-serving president, Sir Joseph Banks, who earlier had accompanied James Cook on his great voyage of discovery of 1768–71. In these societies and others like them all over the world, natural philosophers could gather to examine, discuss, and criticize new discoveries and old theories.

Celestial Mechanics and Astronomy

Eighteenth-century theoretical astronomy in large measure derived both its point of view and its problems from the *Principia*. The test of Newtonian mechanics was its congruence with physical reality. At the beginning of the 18th century it was put to a rigorous test. Cartesians insisted that the Earth, because it was squeezed at the Equator by the etherial vortex causing gravity, should be somewhat pointed at the poles, a shape rather like that of an American football; Newtonians, arguing that centrifugal force was greatest at the Equator, calculated an oblate sphere that was flattened at the poles and bulged at the Equator. The Newtonians were proved correct after careful measurements of a degree of the meridian were made on expeditions to Lapland and to Peru.

The final touch to the Newtonian edifice was provided by the French mathematician Pierre-Simon, Marquis de Laplace, whose masterly *Traité de mécanique céleste* (1798–1827; *Celestial Mechanics*) systematized everything that had been done in the field under Newton's inspiration. Laplace went beyond Newton by showing that the perturbations of the planetary orbits caused by the interactions of planetary gravitation are in fact periodic and that the solar system is, therefore, stable, requiring no divine intervention.

The 18th century witnessed various attempts to extend Newtonian theories to the problem of determining the motion of three bodies – two planets and the Sun or the Sun–Earth–Moon system – affected only by their mutual gravitation (the three-body problem). An illustrious group of continental

mathematicians (including Alexis Clairaut, Jean le Rond
d'Alembert, Joseph-Louis, Comte de Lagrange, and the Marquis de Laplace of France as well as the Bernoulli family and
Euler of Switzerland) attacked this problem, as well as related
ones in Newtonian mechanics, by developing and applying the
calculus of variations – "a branch of mathematics concerned
with the problem of finding a function for which the value of a
certain integral is either the largest or the smallest possible" –
as it had been formulated by Leibniz, in 1675.

Certain of the three-body problems, most notably that of the
secular acceleration of the Moon, defied early attempts at
solution but finally yielded to the increasing power of the
calculus of variations in the service of Newtonian theory.
Newtonian theory was also employed in much more dramatic
discoveries that captivated the imagination of a broad and
varied audience. Within 40 years of the discovery of the planet
Uranus in 1781 by the German-born British astronomer
William Herschel, it was recognized that the planet's motion
was somewhat anomalous. In the next 20 years the gravitational attraction of an unobserved planet was suspected to be
the cause of Uranus' persisting deviations. In 1845 Urbain-
Jean-Joseph Le Verrier of France and John Couch Adams of
England independently calculated the position of this unseen
body; the visual discovery (at the Berlin Observatory in 1846)
of Neptune in just the position predicted constituted an immediately engaging and widely understood confirmation of
Newtonian theory.

Astronomy of the 18th and 19th centuries was not completely Newtonian, however. Herschel's discovery of Uranus,
for example, was not directly motivated by gravitational
considerations. Nine years earlier, a German astronomer,
Johann D. Titius, had announced a purely numerical sequence,
subsequently refined by another German astronomer, Johann

E. Bode, that related the mean radii of the planetary orbits – a relation entirely outside gravitational theory.

Regularities in the structure of the solar system, such as the Bode–Titius law, and the fact that all planets move in the same direction around the Sun suggested that the system might originally have been formed by a simple mechanistic process. Laplace proposed that this process was driven by the cooling of the hot, extended, rotating atmosphere of the primitive Sun. As the atmosphere contracted, it would have to rotate faster (to conserve angular momentum), and when centrifugal force exceeded gravity at the outside, a ring of material would be detached, later to condense into a planet. The process would be repeated several times and might also produce satellites. After Herschel suggested that the nebulas he observed in the sky were condensing to stars, the theory became known as the "nebular hypothesis", or the Kant–Laplace nebular hypothesis. It was to remain the favoured theory of the origin of the solar system throughout the 19th century.

The Development of Mathematics

Many physical problems were reduced to mathematical ones that proved amenable to solution by increasingly sophisticated analytical methods. D'Alembert and Lagrange succeeded in completely mathematizing mechanics, reducing it to an axiomatic system requiring only mathematical manipulation. Euler was one of the most fertile and prolific workers in mathematics and mathematical physics. His development of the calculus of variations provided a powerful tool for dealing with highly complex problems. Euler also developed the theory of trigonometric and logarithmic functions, reduced analytical operations to a greater simplicity, and threw new light on nearly all parts of pure mathematics.

At the invitation of Frederick II of Prussia in 1741, he became a member of the Berlin Academy, where for 25 years he produced a steady stream of publications. In 1748, he developed the concept of function in mathematical analysis, through which variables are related to each other and in which he advanced the use of infinitesimals and infinite quantities. He did for modern analytic geometry and trigonometry what the *Elements* of Euclid had done for ancient geometry, and the resulting tendency to render mathematics and physics in arithmetical terms has continued ever since.

Euler's textbooks in calculus, *Institutiones calculi differentialis* in 1755 and *Institutiones calculi integralis* in 1768–70, have served as prototypes because they contain formulas of differentiation and numerous methods of indefinite integration, many of which he invented himself, for determining the work done by a force and for solving geometric problems. He also made advances in the theory of linear differential equations, which are useful in solving problems in physics.

After Frederick II became less cordial toward him, Euler in 1766 accepted the invitation of Catherine II to return to Russia, where he had been an associate of the St Petersburg Academy of Sciences from 1727 to 1741. Soon after his arrival at St Petersburg, a cataract formed in his remaining good eye, and he spent the last years of his life in total blindness. Despite this tragedy, his productivity continued undiminished. Euler devoted considerable attention to developing a more perfect theory of lunar motion, which was particularly troublesome, since it involved the three-body problem which is still unsolved. His partial solution, published in 1753, assisted the British Admiralty in calculating lunar tables, of importance then in attempting to determine longitude at sea. Throughout his life Euler was much absorbed by problems dealing with the theory of numbers, which treats of the properties and relationships of integers, or whole numbers (0, 1, 2, etc.); in this, his greatest discovery, in 1783, was the law of quadratic reciprocity.

In his effort to replace synthetic methods by analytic ones, Euler was succeeded by Lagrange. By 1761 Lagrange was already recognized as one of the greatest living mathematicians. In 1764 he was awarded a prize offered by the French Academy of Sciences for an essay on the libration of the Moon (i.e., the apparent oscillation that causes slight changes in the position of lunar features on the face that the Moon presents to the Earth). In this essay he used the equations that now bear his name.

In 1766, on the recommendation of Euler and the French mathematician d'Alembert, Lagrange went to Berlin to fill the post at the academy vacated by Euler, at the invitation of Frederick II, who expressed the wish to have "the greatest mathematician in Europe" at his court. Lagrange stayed in Berlin until 1787. His productivity in those years was prodigious: he published papers on the three-body problem; differential equations; prime number theory; the fundamentally important number-theoretic equation that has been identified (incorrectly by Euler) with the English mathematician John Pell; probability; mechanics; and the stability of the solar system. In his long paper *Réflexions sur la résolution algébrique des équations* (1770; *Reflections on the Algebraic Resolution of Equations*), he inaugurated a new period in algebra.

When Frederick died, Lagrange preferred to accept Louis XVI's invitation to Paris. From the Louvre he published his classic *Mécanique analytique* (*Analytic Mechanics*), a lucid synthesis of the one hundred years of research in mechanics since Newton. When the École Centrale des Travaux Publics (later renamed the École Polytechnique) was opened in 1794, he became, with Gaspard Monge, its leading professor of mathematics. His lectures published as *Théorie des fonctions analytiques* (1797; *Theory of Analytic Functions*) and *Leçons sur le calcul des fonctions* (1804; *Lessons on the Calculus of Functions*) became the first textbooks on real analytic functions. He and Euler are regarded as the greatest mathematicians of the 18th century.

A Chemical Revolution

Eighteenth-century chemistry took many of its problems and much of its viewpoint from the *Opticks*. Newton's suggestion of a hierarchy of clusters of unalterable particles formed by virtue of the specific attractions of its component particles led directly to comparative studies of interactions and thus to the tables of affinities of the Dutch physician Herman Boerhaave and others early in the century. This work culminated at the end of the century in work by the Swedish chemist Torbern Bergman, whose table of elements gave quantitative values of the affinity of elements both for reactions when "dry" and when in solution, and that considered double as well as simple affinities.

Seventeenth-century investigations of "airs" or gases, combustion and calcination, and the nature and role of fire were incorporated by the chemists Johann Joachim Becher of Speyer and Georg Ernst Stahl of Sweden into a theory of phlogiston. According to this theory, which was most influential after the middle of the 18th century, the fiery principle, phlogiston, was released into the air in the processes of combustion, calcination, and respiration. The theory explained that air was simply the receptacle for phlogiston, and any combustible or calcinable substance contained phlogiston as a principle or element and thus could not itself be elemental. Iron, in rusting, was considered to lose its compound nature and to assume its elemental state as the calx of iron by yielding its phlogiston into the ambient air.

In 1659 Boyle and Hooke completed the construction of their famous air pump and used it to study pneumatics. Their resultant discoveries regarding air pressure and the vacuum appeared in *New Experiments Physico-Mechanicall, Touching the Spring of the Air and its Effects* (1660). Boyle and Hooke discovered several physical characteristics of air, including its role in combustion, respiration, and the transmission of sound. One of their findings, published in 1662 and later known as "Boyle's law", expresses the inverse relationship that exists between the pressure and volume of a gas; it was determined by measuring the volume occupied by a constant quantity of air when compressed by differing weights of mercury. Other natural philosophers, including Henry Power and Richard Towneley, concurrently reported similar findings.

Boyle's scientific work is characterized by its reliance on experiment and observation and its reluctance to formulate general theories. His contributions to chemistry were based on a mechanical "corpuscularian hypothesis" – a brand of atomism which claimed that everything was composed of minute (but not indivisible) particles of a single universal matter and that these particles were differentiable only by their shape and motion. Among his most influential writings were *The Sceptical Chymist* (1661), which assailed the then-current Aristotelian and especially Paracelsian notions about the composition of matter and methods of chemical analysis, and the *Origine of Formes and Qualities* (1666), which used chemical phenomena to support the corpuscularian hypothesis.

In France the mathematician Blaise Pascal reproduced and amplified experiments on atmospheric pressure in order to test the theories of Galileo and Evangelista Torricelli (an Italian physicist who discovered the principle of the barometer) by constructing mercury barometers and measuring air pressure. These tests paved the way for further studies in hydrodynamics and hydrostatics. While experimenting, Pascal invented the syringe and created the hydraulic press, an instrument based upon the principle that became known as Pascal's law: pressure applied to a confined liquid is transmitted undiminished through the liquid in all directions regardless of the area to which the pressure is applied. His publications on the problem of the vacuum (1647–8) added to his reputation. In what has been described as Pascal's "worldly period" (1651–4) but was, in fact, primarily a period of intense scientific work, he composed treatises on the equilibrium of liquid solutions and on the weight and density of air.

Although the role of air, and of gases generally, in chemical reactions had been glimpsed in the 17th century, it was not fully seen until the classic experiments of the English chemist Joseph Black on magnesia alba (basic magnesium carbonate) in the 1750s. It was one of the major advances in chemistry in the 18th century. By extensive and careful use of the chemical balance, Black showed that an air with specific properties could combine with solid substances like quicklime and be recovered. This discovery served to focus attention on the properties of "air", which was soon found to be a generic, not a specific, name. Chemists discovered a host of specific gases and investigated their various properties: some were flammable, others put out flames; some killed animals, others made them lively.

Joseph Priestley began intensive experimental investigations into chemistry in 1767. Between 1772 and 1790, he published six volumes of *Experiments and Observations on Different Kinds of Air* and more than a dozen articles in the Royal Society's *Philosophical Transactions* describing his experiments on gases. English pneumatic chemists had previously identified three types of gases: air, carbon dioxide (fixed air), and hydrogen (inflammable air). Priestley incorporated an explanation of the chemistry of these gases into the phlogiston theory, according to which combustible substances released phlogiston during burning.

Priestley discovered ten new gases: nitric oxide (nitrous air), nitrogen dioxide (red nitrous vapour), nitrous oxide (inflammable nitrous air, later called "laughing gas"), hydrogen chloride (marine acid air), ammonia (alkaline air), sulphur dioxide (vitriolic acid air), silicon tetrafluoride (fluor acid air), nitrogen (phlogisticated air), oxygen (dephlogisticated air, independently codiscovered by Carl Wilhelm Scheele), and a gas later identified as carbon monoxide. Priestley's experimental success resulted predominantly from his ability to design ingenious apparatuses and his skill in manipulating them.

Priestley's lasting reputation in science, however, is founded upon the discovery he made in August 1774, when he obtained a colourless gas by heating red mercuric oxide. Finding that a candle would burn and that a mouse would thrive in this gas, he called it "dephlogisticated air", based upon the belief that ordinary air became saturated with phlogiston once it could no longer support combustion and life. Priestley was not yet sure, however, that he had discovered a "new species of air". The following October, he accompanied his patron, Shelburne, on a journey through Belgium, Holland, Germany, and France, where in Paris he informed Lavoisier how he obtained the new "air". This meeting between the two scientists was highly significant for the future of chemistry. Lavoisier immediately repeated Priestley's experiments and, between 1775 and 1780, conducted intensive investigations from which he derived the elementary nature of oxygen, recognized it as the "active" principle in the atmosphere, interpreted its role in combustion and respiration, and gave it its name.

Priestley did not, however, accept all of Lavoisier's conclusions and continued, in particular, to uphold the phlogiston theory: in 1803 he published the *Doctrine of Phlogiston*, a detailed account of what he envisioned to be the empirical, theoretical, and methodological shortcomings of the oxygen theory. Priestley called for a patient, humble, experimental approach to God's infinite creation. Chemistry could support piety and liberty only if it avoided speculative theorizing and encouraged the observation of God's benevolent creation.

Lavoisier's oxygen theory of combustion, on the other hand, explained combustion not as the result of the liberation of phlogiston, but rather as the result of the combination of the burning substance with oxygen. This transformation, coupled with the reform in nomenclature at the end of the 18th century (due to Lavoisier and others) – a reform that reflected the new conceptions of chemical elements, compounds, and processes – constituted the revolution in chemistry. It was as much a revolution in method as in conception. Gravimetric methods made possible precise analysis, and this, Lavoisier insisted, was the central concern of the new chemistry. Only when bodies were analysed into their constituent substances was it possible to classify them and their attributes logically and consistently.

Very early in the 19th century, another study of gases, this time in the form of a persisting Newtonian approach to certain meteorological problems by the English chemist John Dalton, led to the enunciation of a chemical atomic theory. From this theory, Dalton was able to calculate definite atomic weights by assuming the simplest possible ratio for the numbers of combining atoms. Beginning at the turn of the century, the English scientist Humphry Davy and many others had employed the strong electric currents of voltaic piles for the analysis of compound substances and the discovery of new elements. From these results, it appeared obvious that chemical forces were essentially electrical in nature. It was not until the development in the 20th century of a quantum-mechanical theory of the chemical bond, however, that bonding was to be satisfactorily explained.

Electricity and Magnetism

The Newtonian method of inferring laws from close observation of phenomena and then deducing forces from these laws was applied with great success to phenomena in which no ponderable matter figured. Light, heat, electricity, and magnetism were all entities that were not capable of being weighed, i.e., imponderable. In the *Opticks*, Newton had assumed that particles of different sizes could account for the different refrangibility of the various colours of light. Clearly, forces of some sort must be associated with these particles if such phenomena as diffraction and refraction are to be accounted for. During the 18th century heat, electricity, and magnetism were similarly conceived as consisting of particles with which were associated forces of attraction or repulsion.

Early in the 18th century, Stephen Gray in England and Charles François de Cisternay DuFay in France studied the direct and induced electrification of various substances by the two kinds of electricity (then called vitreous and resinous and now known as positive and negative), as well as the capability of these substances to conduct the "effluvium" of electricity. By about mid-century, the use of Leyden jars (to collect

charges) and the development of large static electricity machines brought the experimental science into the drawing
room, while the theoretical aspects were being cast in various
forms of the single-fluid theory (by Benjamin Franklin and the
German-born physicist Franz Aepinus, among others) and the
two-fluid theory.

By the end of the century, Priestley had noted that no electric
effect was exhibited inside an electrified hollow metal contain-
er and had brilliantly inferred from this similarity that the
inverse-square law (of gravity) must hold for electricity as well.
In the 1780s, Charles-Augustin de Coulomb in France was
able to measure electrical and magnetic forces, using a delicate
torsion balance of his own invention, and to show that these
forces follow the general form of Newtonian universal attraction. Only light and heat failed to disclose such general force
laws, thereby resisting reduction to Newtonian mechanics.

The Romantic Revolt

Perhaps inevitably, the triumph of Newtonian mechanics
elicited a reaction, one that had important implications for
the further development of science. Its origins are many and
complex, and it is possible here to focus on only one, that
associated with Kant. Kant challenged the Newtonian confidence that the scientist can deal directly with subsensible
entities such as atoms, the corpuscles of light, or electricity.
Instead, he insisted, all that the human mind can know is
forces. This epistemological axiom freed Kantians from having
to conceive of forces as embodied in specific and immutable
particles. It also placed new emphasis on the space between
particles; indeed, if one eliminated the particles entirely, there
remained only space containing forces. From these two con-

siderations were to come powerful arguments, first, for the transformations and conservation of forces and, second, for field theory as a representation of reality. What makes this point of view Romantic is that the idea of a network of forces in space tied the cosmos into a unity in which all forces were related to all others, so that the universe took on the aspect of a cosmic organism. The whole was greater than the sum of all its parts, and the way to truth was contemplation of the whole, not analysis.

What Romantics, or nature philosophers, as they called themselves, could see that was hidden from their Newtonian colleagues was demonstrated by the Danish physicist Hans Christian Ørsted. He found it impossible to believe that there was no connection between the forces of nature. Chemical affinity, electricity, heat, magnetism, and light must, he argued, simply be different manifestations of the basic forces of attraction and repulsion. In 1820 he showed that electricity and magnetism were related, for the passage of an electrical current through a wire affected a nearby magnetic needle. This fundamental discovery was explored and exploited by the English physicist Michael Faraday, who spent his whole scientific life converting one force into another. By concentrating on the patterns of forces produced by electric currents and magnets, Faraday laid the foundations for field theory, in which the energy of a system was held to be spread throughout the system and not localized in real or hypothetical particles.

The transformations of force necessarily raised the question of the conservation of force. Is anything lost when electrical energy is turned into magnetic energy, or into heat or light or chemical affinity or mechanical power? Faraday, again, provided one of the early answers in his two laws of electrolysis, based on experimental observations that quite specific amounts of electrical "force" decomposed quite specific amounts of chemical substances. This work was followed by that of James Prescott Joule, Robert Mayer, and Hermann von Helmholtz, each of whom arrived at a generalization of basic importance to all science, the principle of the conservation of energy.

The submicroscopic world of material atoms became similarly comprehensible. Beginning with Dalton's fundamental assumption that atomic species differ from one another solely in their weights, chemists were able to identify an increasing number of elements and to establish the laws describing their interactions. Order was established by arranging elements according to their atomic weights and their reactions. The result was the periodic table, devised by the Russian chemist Dmitry Mendeleyev, which implied that some kind of subatomic structure underlay elemental qualities. Thus was laid the basis for the development of modern atomic theory in the 19th and 20th centuries.

3

MAN AND EVOLUTION

Human Nature

The Enlightenment was characterized by an optimistic faith in the ability of human beings to develop progressively by using reason. By coming to know both themselves and the natural world better they would be able to develop morally and materially, increasingly dominating both their own animal instincts and the natural world that formed their environment. The writings of the Scottish philosopher David Hume give a clear statement of the implications of empiricist epistemology for the study of human nature. Hume argued first that scientific knowledge of the natural world can consist only of conjectures as to the laws, or regularities, to be found in the sequence of natural phenomena. Not only must the causes of the phenomenal regularities remain unknown but the whole idea of a reality behind and productive of experience must be discounted as making no sense, for experience can afford nothing on the basis of which to understand such talk. Given that this is so, and given that man also observes regularities in human behaviour, the sciences of human nature are possible and can be put on exactly the same footing as the natural sciences. The observed regularities of human conduct can be systematically recorded and classified, and this is all that any science can or should aim to achieve.

Human beings thus become an object of study by natural history in the widest possible sense. All observations – whether of physiology, behaviour, or culture – contribute to the empirical knowledge of humans. There is no need, beyond one of convenience, to compartmentalize these observations, since the method of study is the same whether marital customs or skin colour is the topic of investigation; the aim is to record observations in a systematic fashion making generalizations where possible. Such investigations into the natural history of humans were undertaken by Linnaeus, Buffon, and Blumenbach, among others.

In his *Systema Naturae* (1735), the Swedish naturalist Carolus Linnaeus (Carl von Linné) gave a very precise description of human beings, placing them among the mammals in the order of primates, alongside the apes and the bat. But the distinguishing characteristic of humans remains their use of reason, something that is not dependent on any physiological characteristics. Moreover, the variations that are to be found within the genus homo sapiens are the product of culture and climate. In later editions of *Systema Naturae*, Linnaeus presented a summary of the diverse varieties of the human species. The Asian, for example, is "yellowish, melancholy, endowed with black hair and brown eyes", and has a character that is "severe, conceited, and stingy. He puts on loose clothing. He is governed by opinion." The African is recognizable by the colour of his skin, by his kinky hair, and by the structure of his face. "He is sly, lazy, and neglectful. He rubs his body with oil or grease. He is governed by the arbitrary will of his masters." As for the white European, "he is changeable, clever, and inventive. He puts on tight clothing. He is governed by laws." Here mentality, clothes, political order, and physiology are all taken into account.

The French naturalist Georges Leclerc, Comte de Buffon, devoted two of the 44 volumes of his *Histoire naturelle, générale et particulière* (1749–1804; *Natural History, General and Particular*) to humans as a zoological species. Buffon criticized Linnaeus' system and all other systems of classification that depended only on external characteristics; to force individual objects into a rational set of categories was to impose an artificial construct on nature. He was echoing arguments that Locke had used, arguments based on the conception of the Great Chain of Being as a continuum, not as a sequence of discrete steps. An artificial taxonomy came from the mind, not from nature, and achieved precision at the expense of verisimilitude. Buffon's answer was to determine species not by characteristics but by their reproductive history. Two individual animals or plants are of the same species if they can produce fertile offspring. Species as so defined necessarily have a temporal dimension: a species is known only through the history of its propagation.

This means that it is absurd to use the same principles for classifying living and non-living things. Rocks do not mate and have offspring, so the taxonomy of the mineral kingdom cannot be based on the same principles as that of the animal and vegetable kingdom. Similarly, according to Buffon, there is "an infinite distance" between animals and humans, for "man is a being with reason, and the animal is one without reason." Thus, "the most stupid of men can command the most intelligent of animals . . . because he has a reasoned plan, an order of actions, and a series of means by which he can force the animal to obey him." The ape, even if in its external characteristics it is similar to a human, is deprived of thought and all that is distinctive of humans. Ape and human differ in temperament, in gestation period, in the rearing and growth of the body, in length of life, and in all the habits that Buffon regarded as constituting the nature of a particular being. Most important, apes and other animals lack the ability to speak. This is significant in that Buffon saw the rise of human intelligence as a product of development of an articulated language. But this linguistic ability is the primary manifestation of the presence of reason and is not merely dependent on physiology. Animals lack speech not because they cannot produce articulated sound sequences, but because, lacking minds, they have no ideas to give meaning to these sounds.

The German scholar Johann Friedrich Blumenbach is recognized as the father of physical anthropology for his work *De Generis Humani Varietate Nativa* (*On the Natural Variety of Mankind*), published in 1775 or 1776. He also regarded language as an important distinguishing characteristic of humans, but added that only humans are capable of laughing and crying. Perhaps most important is the suggestion, also made by Benjamin Franklin, that only humans have hands that make them capable of fashioning tools. This was a suggestion that broke new ground in that it opened up the possibility of speculating on a physiological origin for the development of intellectual capacities.

The great German philosopher Immanuel Kant credited Hume with having wakened him from his dogmatic slumbers. But while Kant concurred with Hume in rejecting the possibility of taking metaphysics as a philosophical starting point (dogmatic metaphysics), he did not follow him in dismissing the need for metaphysics altogether. Instead he returned to the French philosopher René Descartes' project of seeking to find in the structure of consciousness itself something that would point beyond it.

Thus, Kant started from the same point as the empiricists, but with Cartesian consciousness – the experience of the individual considered as a sequence of mental states. But instead of asking the empiricists' question of how it is that humans acquire such concepts as number, space, or colour, he inquired into the conditions under which the conscious awareness of mental states is possible. The empiricist simply takes the character of the human mind – consciousness and self-consciousness – for granted as a given of human nature and then proceeds to ask questions concerning how experience, presumed to come in the form of sense perceptions, gives rise to all of one's various ideas and ways of thinking. The methods proposed for this investigation are observational, and thus the study is continuous with natural history. The enterprise overlaps with what would now be called cognitive psychology but includes introspection regarded simply as self-observation. But this clearly begs a number of questions, in particular, how the empiricist can claim knowledge of the human mind and of the character of the experience that is the supposed origin of all ideas.

Even Hume was forced to admit that self-observation, or introspection, given the supposed model of experience as a sequence of ideas and impressions, can yield nothing more than an impression of current or immediately preceding mental states. Experiential self-knowledge, on this model, is impossible. The knowing subject, by his effort to know himself, is already changing himself so that he can only know what he was, not what he is. Thus, any empirical study, whether it be of human beings or of the natural world, must be based on foundations that can only be provided by a non-empirical, philosophical investigation into the conditions of the possibility of the form of knowledge sought. Without this foundation an empirical study cannot achieve any unified conception of its object and never will be able to attain that systematic, theoretically organized character that is demanded of science.

The method of such philosophical investigation is that of critical reflection – employing reason critically – not that of introspection or inner observation. It is here that the origin of what has come to be regarded as philosophical anthropology in the strict sense can be identified, since there is an insistence that studies of the knowing and moral subject must be founded in a philosophical study. But there remain questions about the humanity of Kant's subject. Kant's position was still firmly dualist; the conscious subject constitutes itself through the opposition between experience of itself as free and active (in inner sense) and of the thoroughly deterministic, mechanistic, and material world (in the passive receptivity of outer sense). The subject with which philosophy is thus concerned is finite and rational, limited by the constraint that the content of its knowledge is given in the form of sense experience rather than pure intellectual intuition.

Humanist thought is anthropocentric in that it places humans at the centre and treats them as the point of origin. There are different ways of doing this, however, two of which are illustrated in the works of the English philosopher John Locke and Kant, respectively. The first, realist, position assumes at the outset a contrast between an external, independently existing world and the conscious human subject. In this view humans are presented as standing "outside" of the physical world that they observe. This conception endorses an instrumental view of the relation between humans and the nonhuman, natural world and is therefore most frequently found to be implicit in the thought of those enthusiastic about modern technological science. Nature, from this viewpoint, exists for humans, who by making increasingly accurate conjectures as to the laws governing the regular succession of natural events are able to increase their ability to predict them and so to control his environment.

The second, idealist, position argues that the world exists only in being an object of human thought; it exists only by virtue of humans' conceptualization of it. In the form in which Kant expressed this position, the thought that constitutes the material, physical world is that of a transcendent mind, of which the actual minds of humans are merely vehicles.

There is also a third, dialectical, form of anthropocentrism, which, although it did not emerge fully until the 19th century, was prefigured in the works of the Italian philosopher Giambattista Vico and the German critic Johann Gottfried von Herder. From this standpoint the relation between humans and nature is regarded as an integral part to the dynamic whole of which it is a part. The world is what it is as a result of being lived in and transformed by human beings, while people, in turn, acquire their character from their existence in a particular situation within the world. Any thought about the world is concerned with a world as lived through a subject, who is also part of the world about which he thinks. There is no possibility of transcendence in thought to some external, non-worldly standpoint. Such a position wants both to grant the independent existence of the world and to stress the active and creative role of human beings within it. It is within this relatively late form of humanism – which arose from a synthesis of elements of the Kantian position, with the insights of Vico and Herder – that philosophical anthropology in the strict sense can be located.

Vico's *Scienza nuova* (1725; *New Science*) announced not so much a new science as the need to recognize a new form of scientific knowledge. He argued (against empiricists) that the study of humanity must differ in its method and goals from that of the natural world. This is because the nature of humans is not static and unalterable; a person's own efforts to under-stand the world and adapt it to his needs, physical and spiritual, continuously transform that world and himself. Each individual is both the product and the support of a collective consciousness that defines a particular moment in the history of the human spirit. Each epoch interprets the sum of its traditions, norms, and values in such a way as to impose a model for behaviour on daily life as well as on the more specialized domains of morals and religion and art.

Given that those who make or create something can under-stand it in a way in which mere observers of it cannot, it follows that if, in some sense, people make their own history, they can understand history in a way in which they cannot understand the natural world, which is only observed by them. The natural world must remain unintelligible to man; only God, as its creator, fully understands it. History, however, being concerned with human actions, is intelligible to humans. This means, moreover, that the succession of phases in the culture of a given society or people cannot be regarded as governed by mechanistic, causal laws. To be intelligible these successions must be explicable solely in terms of human, goal-directed activity. Such understanding is the product neither of sense perception nor of rational deduction but of imaginative reconstruction. Here Vico asserted that, even though a per-son's style of thought is a product of the phase of culture in which he participates, it is nonetheless possible for him to understand another culture and the transitions between cul-tural phases. He assumed that there is some underlying com-monality of the needs, goals, and requirement for social organization that makes this possible.

Herder denied the existence of any such absolute and universally recognized goals. This denial carried the disturbing implication that the specific values and goals pursued by various human cultures may not only differ but also may not all be mutually compatible. Hence, not only may cultural transitions not all be intelligible, but conflict may not be an attribute of the human condition that can be eliminated. If this is so, then the notion of a single code of precepts for the harmonious, ideal way of life, which underlies mainstream Western thought and to which – whether they know it or not – all human beings aspire, could not be sustained. There will be many ways of living, thinking, and feeling, each self-validating but not mutually compatible or comparable nor capable of being integrated into a harmonious pluralistic society.

Mercantilism and Population Theories

From the 16th through the 18th centuries, mercantilism, the theory that governments should regulate national economies to augment state power, dominated European economic and political thought. Mercantilists and the absolute rulers who dominated many states of Europe saw each nation's population as a form of national wealth: the larger the population, the richer the nation. Large populations provided a larger labour supply, larger markets, and larger (and hence more powerful) armies for defence and for foreign expansion. Moreover, since growth in the number of wage earners tended to depress wages, the wealth of the monarch could be increased by capturing this surplus. In the words of Frederick II of Prussia, "the number of the people makes the wealth of states." Similar views were held by mercantilists in Germany, France, Italy, and Spain. For the mercantilists, accelerating the growth of the population by encouraging fertility and discouraging emigration was consistent with increasing the power of the nation or the king. Most mercantilists, confident that any number of people would be able to produce their own subsistence, had no worries about harmful effects of population growth.

By the 18th century the physiocrats were challenging the intensive state intervention that characterized the mercantilist system, urging instead the policy of laissez-faire. Their targets included the pronatalist strategies of governments; physiocrats such as François Quesnay argued that human multiplication should not be encouraged to a point beyond that sustainable without widespread poverty. For the physiocrats, economic surplus was attributable to land, and population growth could therefore not increase wealth. In their analysis of this subject matter the physiocrats drew upon the techniques developed in England by John Graunt, Edmond Halley, Sir William Petty, and Gregory King, which for the first time made possible the quantitative assessment of population size, the rate of growth, and rates of mortality.

In another development, the optimism of mercantilists was incorporated into a very different set of ideas, those of the so-called utopians. Their views, based upon the idea of human progress and perfectibility, led to the conclusion that once perfected, humankind would have no need of coercive institutions such as police, criminal law, property ownership, and the family. In a properly organized society, in their view, progress was consistent with any level of population, since population size was the principal factor determining the amount of resources. Such resources should be held in common by all persons, and if there were any limits on population growth, they would be established automatically by the normal functioning of the perfected human society. Principal proponents of such views included the Marquis de Condorcet, the English philosopher William Godwin, and Daniel Malthus, the father of the English economist and demographer Thomas Malthus. Through his father the younger Malthus was introduced to such ideas relating human welfare to population dynamics.

In 1798 Thomas Malthus published *An Essay on the Principle of Population*. In this pamphlet he argued that infinite human hopes for social happiness must be vain, for population will always tend to outrun the growth of production. The increase of population will take place, if unchecked, in a geometric progression, while the means of subsistence will increase in only an arithmetic progression. Population will always expand to the limit of subsistence and will be held there by famine, war, and ill health. "Vice" (which included, for Malthus, contraception), "misery", and "self-restraint" alone could check this excessive growth. In this, Malthus echoed the much earlier arguments of Robert Wallace in his *Various Prospects of Mankind, Nature, and Providence* (1761), which posited that the perfection of society carried with it the seeds of its own destruction, in the stimulation of population growth such that "the earth would at last be overstocked, and become unable to support its numerous inhabitants."

Not many copies of Malthus' essay were published, but it nonetheless came under attack. This criticism stimulated Malthus to pursue additional data and other evidence. He collected information on one country that had plentiful land (the United States) and estimated that its population was doubling in less than 25 years. He attributed the far lower rates of European population growth to "preventive checks", giving special emphasis to the characteristic late marriage pattern of western Europe, which he called "moral restraint". The other preventive checks to which he alluded were birth control, abortion, adultery, and homosexuality, all of which as an Anglican minister he considered immoral.

In one sense, Malthus reversed the arguments of the mercantilists that the number of people determined the nation's resources, adopting the contrary argument of the physiocrats that the resource base determined the numbers of people. From this he derived an entire theory of society and human history, leading inevitably to a set of provocative prescriptions for public policy. Those societies that ignored the imperative for moral restraint – delayed marriage and celibacy for adults until they were economically able to support their children – would suffer the deplorable "positive checks" of war, famine, and epidemic, the avoidance of which should be every society's goal. From this humane concern about the sufferings due to positive checks arose Malthus' admonition that poor laws (i.e., legal measures that provided relief to the poor) and charity must not cause their beneficiaries to relax their moral restraint or increase their fertility, lest such humanitarian gestures become perversely counterproductive. Having stated his position, Malthus was denounced as a reactionary, though he favoured free medical assistance for the poor, universal education, and democratic institutions at a time of elitist alarums about the French Revolution. Malthus was accused of blasphemy by the conventionally religious. Nevertheless his ideas had important effects upon public policy (such as reforms in the poor laws) and upon the ideas of the classical and neoclassical economists, demographers, and evolutionary biologists, led by Charles Darwin. Moreover, the evidence and analyses produced by Malthus dominated scientific discussion of population during his lifetime.

The Idea of Progress

The belief in unbounded human progress, was central to the Enlightenment, particularly in France among philosophers such as Condorcet and Denis Diderot and scientists such as Georges-Louis Leclerc, Comte de Buffon.

Condorcet was one of the major revolutionary formulators of the idea of progress, or the indefinite perfectibility of humankind. He was the friend of almost all the distinguished men of his time and a zealous propagator of the progressive views then current among French men of letters. A protégé of the French mathematician d'Alembert, he took an active part in the preparation of Diderot's *Encyclopédie*.

During the French Revolution, he was elected to represent Paris in the Legislative Assembly and became its secretary. He was active in the reform of the educational system, and in 1792 he presented a scheme for a system of state education, which was the basis of the system ultimately adopted. But in the wake of the revolution, his opposition to the arrest of members of the Girondin factions led to his being outlawed.

It was while he was in hiding that he wrote the work by which he is best known, the *Esquisse d'un tableau historique des progrès de l'esprit humain* (1795; *Sketch for a Historical Picture of the Progress of the Human Mind*). Its fundamental idea is the continuous progress of the human race to an ultimate perfection. He represents humans as starting from the lowest stage of savagery with no superiority over other animals save that of bodily organization and as advancing uninterruptedly toward enlightenment, virtue, and happiness. The human race has already gone through nine stages, or nine great epochs of history.

There is an epoch of the future – a tenth epoch – and the most original part of Condorcet's treatise is devoted to it. After insisting that general laws regulative of the past warrant general inferences as to the future, he argues that the three tendencies that the entire history of the past shows will be characteristic features of the future are: (1) the destruction of inequality between nations; (2) the destruction of inequality between classes; and (3) the improvement of individuals, the indefinite perfectibility of human nature itself – intellectually, morally, and physically. The equality to which he represents nations and individuals as tending is not absolute equality but equality of freedom and of rights. Nations and individuals, he asserts, are equal if equally free and are all tending to equality because all are tending to freedom.

As to indefinite perfectibility, he nowhere denies that progress is conditioned both by the constitution of humanity and by the character of its surroundings. But he affirms that these conditions are compatible with endless progress and that the human mind can assign no fixed limits to its own advancement in knowledge and virtue or even to the prolongation of bodily life.

Diderot, in his philosophical works *L'Entretien entre d'Alembert et Diderot* (written 1769, published 1830; *Conversation Between d'Alembert and Diderot*), *Le Rêve de d'Alembert* (written 1769, published 1830; *D'Alembert's Dream*), and the *Eléments de physiologie* (1774–80; *Elements of Physiology*) speculated on the origins of life without divine intervention and put forth a strikingly prescient picture of the cellular structure of matter. Buffon is now remembered for his comprehensive work on natural history, *Histoire naturelle, générale et particulière*, which he began in 1749. Appointed keeper of the Jardin du Roi (the royal botanical garden, now the National Museum of Natural History) and its museum in 1739, and charged to catalogue the royal collections in natural history, the ambitious Buffon produced an account of the whole of nature. This was the first modern attempt to present systematically all existing knowledge in the fields of natural history, geology, and anthropology in a single publication.

Buffon's *Histoire naturelle* was translated into various languages and widely read throughout Europe. Buffon interspersed descriptions of animals with philosophical discussions of nature, the degeneration of animals, the nature of birds, and other topics. While his great project opened up vast areas of knowledge that were beyond his powers to encompass, the *Natural History* was the first work to present the previously isolated and apparently disconnected facts of natural history in a generally intelligible form.

Although theologians were aroused by his conceptions of geological history and others criticized his views on biological classification, in some areas of natural science Buffon had a lasting influence. He was the first to reconstruct geological history in a series of stages, in *Époques de la nature* (1778; *Epochs of Nature*). His notion of lost species opened the way to the development of paleontology.

The Emergence of Modern Geological Thought

With the exception of a few prescient individuals such as the 13th-century philosopher Roger Bacon and Leonardo da Vinci, no one stepped forward to champion an enlightened view of the natural history of the Earth until the mid-17th century. Leonardo recognized that the marine organisms now found as fossils in rocks exposed in the Tuscan hills were simply ancient animals that lived in the region when it had been covered by the sea and were eventually buried by muds along the seafloor.

In spite of this, little or no attention was given to the history – namely, the sequence of events in their natural progression – that might be preserved in the rocks. In 1669 the Danish-born natural scientist Nicolaus Steno published his noted treatise *De Solido intra Solidum Naturaliter Contento Dissertationis Prodromus* (*The Prodromus of Nicolaus Steno's Dissertation*

Concerning a Solid Body Enclosed by Process of Nature Within a Solid). This seminal work laid the essential framework for the science of geology by showing in very simple fashion that the layered rocks of Tuscany exhibit sequential change – that they contain a record of past events – and that rocks deposited first lie at the bottom of a sequence, while those deposited later are at the top – the crux of what is now known as the principle of superposition.

With the publication of the *Prodromus* and the ensuing widespread dissemination of Steno's ideas, other natural scientists of the late 17th and early 18th centuries applied them to their own work. The English geologist John Strachey, for example, produced in 1725 what may well have been the first modern geological maps of rock strata. He also described the succession of strata associated with coal-bearing sedimentary rocks in Somerset, the same region of England where he had mapped the rock exposures.

Others soon followed in the classification of stratified rocks. In 1756 Johann Gottlob Lehmann of Germany reported on three distinct rock assemblages in the southern part of his country and the Alps. In the Tuscan hills, Giovanni Arduino, regarded by many as the father of Italian geology, proposed a four-component rock succession. In 1773, Georg Christian Füchsel also applied Lehmann's earlier concepts of superposition to another sequence of stratified rocks in southern Germany, using nearly nine categories of sedimentary rocks. And the German naturalist Peter Simon Pallas reported on rock sequences exposed in the southern Urals of eastern Russia. Nevertheless, there remained to be answered a number of fundamental questions relating to the temporal and lateral relationships that seemed to exist among these disparate European sites. Were these various sites of rock succession contemporary? Did they record the same series of geological events in the Earth's past? Were the various layers at each site similar to those of other sites? In short, was correlation among these various sites now possible?

Inherent in many of the assumptions underlying the early attempts at interpreting natural phenomena in the latter part of the 18th century was the ongoing controversy between the biblical view of Earth processes and history and a more direct approach based on what could be observed and understood from various physical relationships demonstrable in nature. A substantial amount of information about the compositional character of many rock sequences was beginning to accumulate at this time. Abraham Gottlob Werner, a German scholar of wide repute, was very successful in reaching a compromise between what could be said to be scientific "observation" and biblical "fact".

Werner's theory was that all rocks (including the sequences being identified in various parts of Europe at that time) and the Earth's topography were the direct result of either of two processes: (1) deposition in the primeval ocean, represented by the Noachian flood (his "Universal", or primary, rock series), or (2) sculpturing and deposition during the retreat of this ocean from the land (his "Partial", or disintegrated, rock series). Werner's interpretation, which came to represent the so-called Neptunist conception of the Earth's beginnings, found widespread and nearly universal acceptance owing in large part to its theological appeal and to Werner's own personal charisma.

One result of Werner's approach to rock classification was that each unique lithology in a succession implied its own unique time of formation during the Noachian flood and a universal distribution. As more and more comparisons were made of diverse rock outcroppings, it began to become apparent that Werner's interpretation did not "universally" apply. Thus arose an increasingly vocal challenge to the Neptunist theory.

In the late 1780s the Scottish scientist James Hutton launched an attack on much of the geological dogma that had its basis in either Werner's Neptunist approach or its corollary that the prevailing configuration of the Earth's surface is largely the result of past catastrophic events which have no modern counterparts. Perhaps the quintessential spokesman for the application of the scientific method in solving problems presented in the complex world of natural history, Hutton instead used deductive reasoning to explain what he saw.

By Hutton's account, the Earth could not be viewed as a simple, static world not currently undergoing change. Ample evidence from Hutton's Scotland provided the key to unravelling the often thought but still rarely stated premise that events occurring today at the Earth's surface – namely erosion, transportation and deposition of sediments, and volcanism – seem to have their counterparts preserved in the rocks. The rocks of the Scottish coast and the area around Edinburgh proved the catalyst for his argument that the Earth is indeed a dynamic, ever-changing system, subject to a sequence of recurrent cycles of erosion and deposition and of subsidence and uplift. Hutton's formulation of the principle of uniformitarianism, which holds that Earth processes occurring today had their counterparts in the ancient past, while not the first time that this general concept was articulated, was probably the most important geological concept developed out of rational scientific thought of the 18th century. The publication of Hutton's two-volume *Theory of the Earth* in 1795 firmly established him as one of the founders of modern geological thought.

It was not easy for Hutton to popularize his ideas, however. The *Theory of the Earth* certainly did set the fundamental principles of geology on a firm basis, and several of Hutton's colleagues, notably John Playfair with his *Illustrations of the Huttonian Theory of the Earth* (1802), attempted to counter the entrenched Wernerian influence of the time. Nonetheless, another 30 years were to pass before Neptunist and catastrophist views of Earth history were finally replaced by those grounded in a uniformitarian approach.

This gradual unseating of the Neptunist theory resulted from the accumulated evidence that increasingly called into question the applicability of Werner's Universal and Partial formations in describing various rock successions. Clearly, not all assignable rock types would fit into Werner's categories, either superpositionally in some local succession or as a unique occurrence at a given site. Also, it was becoming increasingly difficult to accept certain assertions of Werner that some rock types (e.g., basalt) are chemical precipitates from the primordial ocean.

It was this latter observation that finally rendered the Neptunist theory unsustainable. Hutton observed that basaltic rocks exposed in the Salisbury Craigs, just on the outskirts of Edinburgh, seemed to have baked adjacent enclosing sediments lying both below and above the basalt. This simple observation indicated that the basalt was emplaced within the sedimentary succession while it was still sufficiently hot to have altered the sedimentary material. Clearly, basalt could not form in this way as a precipitate from the primordial ocean as Werner had claimed. Furthermore, the observations at Edinburgh indicated that the basalt intruded the sediments from below – in short, it came from the Earth's interior, a process in clear conflict with Neptunist theory.

While explaining that basalt may be intrusive, the Salisbury Craigs observations did not fully satisfy the argument that some basalts are not intrusive. Did the Neptunist approach have some validity after all? The resolution of this latter problem occurred at an area of recent volcanism in the Auvergne area of central France. Here, numerous cinder cones and fresh lava flows composed of basalt provided ample evidence that this rock type is the solidified remnant of material ejected from the Earth's interior, not a precipitate from the primordial ocean.

Hutton's words were not lost on the entire scientific community. Charles Lyell, another Scottish geologist, was a principal proponent of Hutton's approach, emphasizing gradual change by means of known geological processes. In his own observations on rock and faunal successions, Lyell was able to demonstrate the validity of Hutton's doctrine of uniformitarianism and its importance as one of the fundamental philosophies of the geological sciences. He realized from his studies of geological formations that the relative ages of deposits could be estimated by means of the proportion of living and extinct molluscs.

Lyell, however, imposed some conditions on uniformitarianism that perhaps had not been intended by Hutton: he took a literal approach to interpreting the principle of uniformity in nature by assuming that all past events must have conformed to controls exerted by processes that behaved in the same manner as those processes behave today. No accommodation was made for past conditions that did not have modern counterparts.

Lyell's contribution enabled the doctrine of uniformitarianism finally to hold sway, even though it did impose for the time being a somewhat limiting condition on the uniformity principle. This, along with the increased recognition of the utility of fossils in interpreting rock successions, made it possible to begin addressing the question of the meaning of time in Earth history.

An 1812 study by the French zoologist Georges Cuvier was prescient in its recognition that fossils do in fact record events in the Earth's history and serve as more than just "follies" of nature. Cuvier's thesis, based on his analysis of the marine invertebrate and terrestrial vertebrate fauna of the Paris Basin, showed conclusively that many fossils, particularly those of terrestrial vertebrates, had no living counterparts. Indeed, they seemed to represent extinct forms, which, when viewed in the context of the succession of strata with which they were associated, constituted part of a record of biological succession punctuated by numerous extinctions. These, in turn, were followed by a seeming renewal of more advanced but related forms and were separated from each other by breaks in the associated rock record. Many of these breaks were characterized by coarser, even conglomeratic strata following a break, suggesting "catastrophic" events that may have contributed to the extinction of the biota. Whatever the actual cause, Cuvier felt that the evidence provided by the record of faunal succession in the Paris Basin could be interpreted by invoking recurring catastrophic geologic events, which in turn contributed to recurring massive faunal extinction, followed at a later time by biological renewal.

As Cuvier's theory of faunal succession was being considered, William Smith, a civil engineer from the south of England, was also coming to realize that certain fossils can be found consistently associated with certain strata. In the course of evaluating various natural rock outcroppings, quarries, canals, and mines during the early 1790s, Smith increasingly utilized the fossil content as well as the lithological character of various rock strata to identify the successional position of different rocks, and he made use of this information to effect a correlation among various localities he had studied. The consistency of the relationships that Smith observed eventually led him to conclude that there is indeed faunal succession and that there appears to be a consistent progression of forms from more primitive to more advanced.

As a result of this observation, Smith was able to begin what was to amount to a monumental effort at synthesizing all that was then known of the rock successions outcropping throughout parts of Great Britain. This effort culminated in the publication of his *Geologic Map of England, Wales and Part of Scotland* (1815), a rigorous treatment of diverse geological information resulting from a thorough understanding of geological principles, including those of original horizontality, superposition, and faunal succession. With this, it now became possible to assume within a reasonable degree of certainty that correlation could be made between and among widely separated areas. It also became apparent that many sites that had previously been classified according to the then-traditional views of Arduino, Füchsel, and Lehmann did not conform to the new successional concepts of Smith.

The seminal work of Smith at clarifying various relationships in the interpretation of rock successions and their correlations elsewhere resulted in an intensive look at what the rock record and, in particular, the fossil record had to say about past events in the long history of the Earth. A testimony to Smith's efforts in producing one of the first large-scale geological maps of a region is its essential accuracy in portraying what is now known to be the geological succession for the particular area of Britain covered.

The application of the ideas of Lyell, Smith, Hutton, and others led to the recognition of lithological and paleontological successions of similar character from widely scattered areas. It also gave rise to the realization that many of these similar sequences could be correlated.

Evolutionary Theory
and Classification of Species

The theory of evolution is one of the fundamental key-stones of modern biological theory. Yet the Enlightenment belief in progress did not inevitably lead to the development of a theory of evolution. Buffon, for example, explicitly considered – and rejected – the possible descent of several species from a common ancestor. He postulated that organisms arise from organic molecules by spontaneous generation, so that there could be as many kinds of animals and plants as there are viable combinations of organic molecules.

Pierre-Louis Moreau de Maupertuis proposed the spontaneous generation and extinction of organisms as part of his theory of origins, but he advanced no theory of evolution. However, in the researches for his *Système de la nature* (1751), Maupertuis produced the first scientifically accurate record of the transmission of a dominant hereditary trait in humans. It contained theoretical speculations on the nature of biparental heredity based on his careful study of the occurrences of polydactyly, or extra fingers, in several generations of a Berlin family. He demonstrated that polydactyly could be transmitted by either the male or the female parent, and he presciently explained the trait as the result of a mutation in the "hereditary particles" possessed by them. He also calculated the mathematical probability of the trait's future occurrence in new members of the family.

The English physician Erasmus Darwin, grandfather of Charles Darwin, offered in his *Zoonomia; or, The Laws of Organic Life* (1794–6) some evolutionary speculations, concluding that species descend from common ancestors and that there is a struggle for existence among animals, but they were not further developed and had no real influence on subsequent theories.

Although Linnaeus insisted on the fixity of species, his classification system eventually contributed much to the acceptance of the concept of common descent. His hierarchical system of plant and animal classification is still in use in a modernized form. Prior to Linnaeus, most taxonomists started their classification systems by dividing all the known organisms into large groups and then subdividing these into progressively smaller groups.

Unlike his predecessors, Linnaeus began with the species, organizing them into larger groups or genera, then arranging analogous genera to form families and related families to form orders and classes. Probably utilizing the earlier work of the English botanist Nehemiah Grew and others, Linnaeus chose the structure of the reproductive organs of the flower as a basis for grouping the higher plants. Thus he distinguished between plants with real flowers and seeds (phanerogams) and those lacking real flowers and seeds (cryptogams), subdividing the former into hermaphroditic (bisexual) and unisexual forms. For animals, Linnaeus relied upon teeth and toes as the basic characteristics of mammals; he used the shape of the beak as the basis for bird classification. Having demonstrated that a binomial classification system based on concise and accurate descriptions could be used for the grouping of organisms, Linnaeus established taxonomic biology as a discipline.

Probably the most important of the 18th-century evolutionists was the great French naturalist Jean-Baptiste de Monet, Chevalier de Lamarck. He recognized the role of isolation in species formation; he also saw the unity in nature and conceived the idea of the evolutionary tree and the idea that acquired traits are inheritable. Lamarck's first publication was a three-volume flora of France in 1778 which, while it did not adhere slavishly to the methods of Linnaeus, won for him appointment to the Academy of Sciences. Just as Linnaeus brought order to classification of species, Lamarck was also one of the originators of the modern concept of the museum collection, an array of objects whose arrangement constitutes a classification under institutional sponsorship.

After the revolution of 1789 the royal collection of natural history was discontinued. Lamarck addressed a memoir to the National Assembly urging that collections be applied to the progress of science through the establishment of a great museum of natural history. Within such a collection objects "ought to be arranged in methodical or properly systematic order", not for display at random: each division of nature (animal, vegetable, and mineral) should be subdivided by classes, and those in turn by orders, and so to genera, with a written catalogue that would be the basis for systematic knowledge. When the National Museum of Natural History was founded in 1793, Lamarck was placed in charge of the invertebrates, of which he had already made an important collection. He seems to have been the first to relate fossils to the living organisms to which they corresponded most closely.

Lamarck held the enlightened view of his age that living organisms represent a progression, with humans as the highest form. From this idea he proposed, in the early years of the 19th century, the first broad theory of evolution. Lamarck imagined a vast sequence of life forms extending like a series of staircases from the simplest to the most complex. Impelled by "excitations" and "subtle and ever-moving fluids", the organs of animals became more complex and took their place on successively higher levels. This was the summary view of the relationship between physical energy and the overall organization of life set forth in *Research on the Organization of Living Bodies* (1802) and the *Zoological Philosophy* (1809). In the latter work he stated two "laws" that he held to govern the ascent of life to higher stages: first, that organs are improved with repeated use and weakened by disuse; and second, that such environmentally determined acquisitions or losses of organs "are preserved by reproduction to the new individuals which arise". Although this assumption, later called the inheritance of acquired characteristics (or Lamarckism), was to be thoroughly disproved in the 20th century, Lamarck made important contributions to the gradual acceptance of biological evolution. A complete theory of evolution was not announced until the publication in 1859 of Charles Darwin's *On the Origin of Species by Means of Natural Selection or the Preservation of Favoured Races in the Struggle for Life*.

The Rise of Medicine

The study of living matter moved slowly, largely because organisms are so complex. In the 17th century the natural sciences had moved forward on a broad front, the supreme achievement being William Harvey's explanation of the circulation of the blood. In 1628 he published *Exercitatio Anatomica de Motu Cordis et Sanguinis in Animalibus* (*An Anatomical Exercise Concerning the Motion of the Heart and Blood in Animals*), in which he demonstrated that the heart expands passively and contracts actively. By measuring the amount of blood flowing from the heart, Harvey concluded that the body could not continuously produce that amount. Having shown that blood was returned to the heart through the veins, he postulated a connection (the capillaries) between the arteries and veins that was not to be discovered for another century.

Harvey's discovery was a landmark of medical progress; the new experimental method by which the results were secured was as noteworthy as the work itself. Following the method described by the English philosopher Francis Bacon, he drew the truth from experience and not from authority. There was one gap, however, in Harvey's argument: he was obliged to assume the existence of the capillary vessels that conveyed the blood from the arteries to the veins. This link in the chain of evidence was supplied by Marcello Malpighi of Bologna. With a primitive microscope, Malpighi saw a network of tiny blood vessels in the lung of a frog. Harvey also failed to show why the blood circulated. After Robert Boyle had shown that air is essential to animal life, it was Richard Lower who traced the interaction between air and the blood. Eventually the importance of oxygen was revealed, though it was not until the late 18th century that Antoine-Laurent Lavoisier discovered the essential nature of oxygen and clarified its relation to respiration.

Harvey's book made him famous throughout Europe, though the overthrow of so many time-hallowed beliefs attracted virulent attacks and much abuse. Harvey's second great book, *Exercitationes de Generatione Animalium* (*Experiments Concerning Animal Generation*), published in 1651, laid the foundation of modern embryology. He suggested that there is a stage (the egg) in the development of all animals during which they are undifferentiated living masses. A biological dictum, *ex ovo omnia* ("everything comes from the egg"), is a summation of this concept.

Although the compound microscope had been invented slightly earlier, probably in Holland, its development was the work of Galileo. He was the first to insist upon the value of measurement in science and in medicine, thus replacing theory and guesswork with accuracy. The great Dutch microscopist Antonie van Leeuwenhoek devoted his long life to microscopical studies and was probably the first to see and describe bacteria, reporting his results to the Royal Society of London. Isolating bacteria and protozoa from different sources, such as rainwater, pond and well water, and the human mouth and intestine, he calculated their sizes. His observations helped lay the foundations for the sciences of bacteriology and protozoology, and the dramatic nature of his discoveries made him world famous.

In England, Robert Hooke, who was Boyle's assistant and curator to the Royal Society, published his *Micrographia* in 1665, which discussed and illustrated the microscopic structure of a variety of materials. He included in the book his studies and illustrations of the crystal structure of snowflakes, discussed the possibility of manufacturing artificial fibres by a process similar to the spinning of the silkworm, and first used the word "cell" to name the microscopic honeycomb cavities in cork.

Several attempts were made in the 17th century to discover an easy system that would guide the practice of medicine. Although a substratum of superstition still remained – even the learned English physician Thomas Browne stated that witches really existed – there was a general desire to discard the past and adopt new more enlightened ideas.

The view of the French philosopher René Descartes that the human body is a machine and that it functions mechanically had its repercussions in medical thought. One group adopting this explanation called themselves the iatrophysicists; another school, preferring to view life as a series of chemical processes, were called iatrochemists. Santorio Santorio, working at Padua, was an early exponent of the iatrophysical view and a pioneer investigator of metabolism. He was especially concerned with the measurement of what he called "insensible perspiration", described in his book *De statica medicina* (1614; *On Medical Measurement*). Another Italian researcher, who developed the idea still further, was Giovanni Alfonso Borelli, a professor of mathematics at Pisa University, who gave his attention to the mechanics and statics of the body and to the physical laws that govern its movements.

The iatrochemical school was founded at Brussels by Jan Baptist van Helmont, whose writings are tinged with the mysticism of the alchemist. A more logical and intelligible view of iatrochemistry was advanced by Franciscus Sylvius, at Leiden; and in England a leading exponent of the same school was Thomas Willis, who is better known for his description of the brain in his *Cerebri Anatome Nervorumque Descriptio et Usus* (*Anatomy of the Brain and Descriptions and Functions of the Nerves*), published in 1664 and illustrated by Christopher Wren.

It soon became apparent that no easy road to medical knowledge and practice was to be found along these channels and that the best method was the age-old system of straightforward clinical observation initiated by Hippocrates. The need for a return to these views was strongly urged by Thomas Sydenham, recognized as a founder of clinical medicine and epidemiology, and well regarded as the "the English Hippocrates" for his emphasis on detailed observations of patients and the maintainance of accurate records. Sydenham was not a voluminous writer and, indeed, he had little patience with book learning in medicine; nevertheless he gave excellent descriptions of the phenomena of disease. He made an exacting study of epidemics, which formed the basis of his book on fevers (1666), later expanded into *Observationes Medicae* (1676), a standard textbook for two centuries. His treatise on gout (1683) is considered his masterpiece. He was among the first to describe scarlet fever – differentiating it from measles and naming it – and to explain the nature of hysteria and St Vitus' dance (Sydenham's chorea). Sydenham introduced laudanum (alcohol tincture of opium) into medical practice, was one of the first to use iron in treating iron-deficiency anaemia, and helped popularize quinine in treating malaria. His greatest service, however, was to divert physicians' minds from speculation and lead them back to the bedside, where the true art of medicine could be studied.

In the 18th century the search for a simple way of healing the sick continued. In Edinburgh the writer and lecturer John Brown expounded his view that there were only two diseases, sthenic (strong) and asthenic (weak), and two treatments, stimulant and sedative; his chief remedies were alcohol and opium. Lively and heated debates took place between his followers, the Brunonians, and the more orthodox Cullenians (followers of William Cullen, a professor of medicine at Glasgow), and the controversy spread to the medical centres of Europe.

At the same time, Samuel Hahnemann of Leipzig originated homeopathy, a system of treatment involving the administration of minute doses of drugs whose effects resemble those of the disease being treated. In 1790, while translating William Cullen's *Lectures on the Materia Medica* into German, he was struck by the fact that the symptoms produced by quinine on the healthy body were similar to those of the disordered states that quinine was used to cure. This observation led him to assert the theory that "likes are cured by likes," *similia similibus curantur* – i.e., diseases are cured (or should be treated) by those drugs that produce in healthy persons symptoms similar to the diseases. He promulgated his principle in a paper published in 1796; and, four years later, convinced that drugs in small doses effectively exerted their curative powers, he advanced his doctrine of their "potentization of dynamization". His chief work, *Organon der rationellen Heilkunst* (1810; *Organon of Rational Medicine*), contains an exposition of his system, which he called *Homöopathie,* or homeopathy. His *Reine Arzneimittellehre* (1811; *Pure Pharmacology*) detailed the symptoms produced by "proving" a large number of drugs – i.e., by systematically administering them to healthy subjects. His ideas had a salutary effect upon medical thought at a time when prescriptions were lengthy and doses were large.

By the 18th century medical education had been increasingly incorporated into the universities of Europe, and Edinburgh became the leading academic centre for medicine in Britain. In London, Scottish doctors were the leaders in surgery and obstetrics. John Hunter conducted extensive researches in comparative anatomy and physiology, and founded surgical pathology. He also attained for surgery the dignity of a scientific profession, basing its practice on a vast body of general biological principles. His brother William Hunter, an eminent teacher of anatomy, became famous as an obstetrician. William Smellie, the leading obstetrician in London, whose *Treatise on the Theory and Practice of Midwifery*, published in three volumes in 1752–64, contained the first systematic discussion on the safe use of obstetrical forceps, placed midwifery on a sound scientific footing, and helped to establish obstetrics as a recognized medical discipline.

The science of modern pathology also had its beginnings at this time. Giovanni Battista Morgagni, of Padua, in 1761 published his massive work *De Sedibus et Causis Morborum per Anatomen Indagatis* (*The Seats and Causes of Diseases Investigated by Anatomy*), a description of the appearances found by postmortem examination of almost 700 cases, in which he attempted to correlate the findings after death with the clinical picture in life.

One highly significant medical advance achieved late in the century was vaccination. Smallpox, disfiguring and often fatal, was widely prevalent. Inoculation was popularized in England in 1721–2 by Lady Mary Wortley Montagu, who is best known for her letters. She observed the practice in Turkey, where it produced a mild form of the disease, thus securing immunity, although not without danger. The next step was taken by Edward Jenner, a country practitioner who had been a pupil of John Hunter.

Jenner had been impressed by the fact that a person who had suffered an attack of cowpox – a relatively harmless disease that could be contracted from cattle – could not become infected with smallpox. Pondering this phenomenon, Jenner concluded that cowpox not only protected against smallpox but could be transmitted from one person to another as a deliberate mechanism of protection. The story of the great breakthrough is well known. In May 1796 Jenner found a young dairymaid, Sarah Nelmes, who had fresh cowpox lesions on her hand. On May 14, using matter from Sarah's lesions, he inoculated an eight-year-old boy, James Phipps, who had never had smallpox. Phipps became slightly ill over the course of the next nine days but was well on the tenth. On July 1 Jenner inoculated the boy again, this time with smallpox matter. No disease developed; protection was complete. In 1798 Jenner, having added further cases, published privately a slender book entitled *An Inquiry into the Causes and Effects of the Variolae Vaccinae*. The reaction to the publication was not immediately favourable. Jenner went to London seeking volunteers for vaccination but, in a stay of three months, was not successful. In London vaccination became popularized through the activities of others, particularly the surgeon Henry Cline, to whom Jenner had given some of the inoculant, and the doctors George Pearson and William Woodville. Difficulties arose; Pearson tried to take credit from Jenner, and Woodville, a physician in a smallpox hospital, contaminated the cowpox matter with smallpox virus. Vaccination rapidly proved its value, however, and Jenner received worldwide recognition. The procedure spread rapidly to America and the rest of Europe and soon was carried around the world.

Public health and hygiene were receiving more attention during the 18th century. Population statistics began to be kept, and suggestions arose concerning health legislation. Hospitals were established for a variety of purposes. In Paris, the physician Philippe Pinel initiated bold reforms in the care of the mentally ill, releasing them from their chains and discarding the long-held notion that insanity was caused by demon possession.

In the latter part of the century, however, two pseudoscientific doctrines relating to medicine emerged from Vienna and attained wide notoriety. Mesmerism, a belief in "animal magnetism" sponsored by Franz Anton Mesmer, probably owed any therapeutic value it had to suggestions given while the patient was under hypnosis. Phrenology, propounded by Franz Joseph Gall, held that the contours of the skull were a guide to an individual's mental faculties and character traits; this theory remained popular well into the 20th century.

Despite these mistakes, sound scientific thinking was making steady progress, and advances in physics, chemistry, and the biological sciences were converging to form a rational scientific basis for every branch of clinical medicine. New knowledge disseminated thoughout Europe and travelled across the sea to America, where centres of medical excellence were established.

4

CULTURE AND EDUCTATION

The Cultural Climate

Europe at the dawn of the 18th century was a confused and disturbed place. England had survived a Civil War and the Glorious Revolution and edged into the new century with caution yet would become the most powerful nation in Europe. Elsewhere on the Continent, the wages of continuous war were taking their toll. France was entering the last years of the reign of the absolutist Louis XIV who had sapped the country's wealth to conduct his dynastic wars. The Dutch Republic, latter-day Holland, was also suffering the costs of aggressive foreign policy and was losing its predominance as Europe's leading trading nation. The new century offered opportunities for change.

The cultural climate in England during the Enlightenment period was to a large extent focused on and guided by the capital. By 1700 London had overtaken Paris in population. By 1820, when George IV succeeded to the throne, many of the villages and hamlets that in the 17th and 18th centuries had been the destination of summer outings from the heart of the city had been covered by a tide of bricks and mortar.

Socially, commercially, and financially, London was the hub of the kingdom. It was also the centre of the world economy from the late 18th century to 1914, having taken over that role from Amsterdam. As a corollary to its great wealth, fed by the profits of the trade with the East and West Indies and with the Americas – indeed with most of the world – it reigned supreme in matters of the theatre, literature, and the arts. Eighteenth-century London was the city of the actor David Garrick, the playwright and essayist Oliver Goldsmith, the critic and wit Samuel Johnson, and the portraitist Sir Joshua Reynolds; of great furniture makers and silversmiths; and of renowned foreign composers, including George Frideric Handel, Franz Joseph Haydn, and Wolfgang Amadeus Mozart. A contemporary description of the metropolis is given in the third edition (1788–97) of *Encyclopædia Britannica*:

> London, then, in its large sense, including Westminster, Southwark, and part of Middlesex, forms one great metropolis, of vast extent and of prodigious wealth. When considered with all its advantages, it is now what ancient Rome once was; the seat of liberty, the encourager of arts, and the admiration of the whole world. It is the centre of trade; has an intimate connection with all the counties in the kingdom; and is the grand mart of the nation, to which all parts send their commodities, from whence they are again sent back into every town in the nation and to every part of the world.

Cultural activity in France also remained largely centred on the capital, but smaller cities such as Aix-les-Bains, Grenoble, and Lyon were vital in their own right. The culture of the

Enlightenment was built on reason and analytic argumentation, mirrored, as political scientist Alexis de Tocqueville remarked, in the French Revolution's

> attraction for general theories, for general systems of legislation, the exact symmetry of laws . . . the same desire to remake the entire constitution at once following the rules of logic and in accordance with a single plan, instead of seeking ways to amend its parts.

Among its tenets was the idea of meritocracy, or an aristocracy of ability and intelligence, which accorded a central place to intellectuals unknown in most other societies and opened France's schools to students from the provinces without regard for social class.

The Age of the Academies

The role of the academies was significant during this period. Academies had begun to be formed in medieval Italy, for the study first of classical and then of Italian literature, but their influence was greatest during the 17th and 18th centuries.

Academies of fine arts, music, social sciences, medicine, mining, and agriculture were formed from the 18th century onward. The French Academy, which would become Europe's best-known literary academy, began in 1635. The Royal Spanish Academy was founded in 1713 to preserve the Spanish language, and it published a landmark Spanish dictionary for that purpose. However, the United States, like Great Britain, Canada, and other English-speaking countries, had no state-established academies of science or literature – a fact reflective of English beliefs that culture should basically be a matter for private initiative. The first learned society in what would become the United States was founded by Benjamin Franklin in 1743 and was called the American Philosophical Society. The rival American Academy of Arts and Sciences was founded in 1779. Russia's Imperial Academy of Sciences was founded by Peter the Great in St Petersburg in 1724 and renamed the Academy of Sciences in 1925.

In the visual arts there was a tradition of academies being institutions for the instruction of artists but they were often endowed with other functions too, most significantly that of providing a place of exhibition for students and mature artists accepted as members. The first true academy for instruction, the Accademia del Disegno ("Academy of Design"), was established in 1563 in Florence by the grand duke Cosimo I de' Medici at the instigation of the painter and art historian Giorgio Vasari. When Vasari's academy fell into disorganization, his ideas were taken up by the Accademia di San Luca. With its emphasis on instruction and exhibition, the Accademia di San Luca was the prototype for the modern academy. Among its functions, much-imitated in later academies, was the sponsorship of lectures given by members of the academy and later published and made available to the general public. The secondary aims of the institution – to obtain important commissions, to enhance the prestige of the members, and to practice exclusionary policies against those who were not members – were avidly pursued.

In France the Académie Royale de Peinture et de Sculpture was founded in 1648 as a free society of members all entitled to the same rights and granted admission in unlimited numbers. Under the sponsorship of the powerful minister Jean Baptiste Colbert and the direction of the painter Charles Le Brun, however, the Académie Royale began to function as an authoritarian arm of the state. As such, it assumed almost total control of French art and began to exercise considerable influence on the art of Europe. For the first time, the concept of aesthetic orthodoxy obtained official endorsement. The Académie achieved a virtual monopoly of teaching and exhibition in France, beginning in 1667 the long-lived series of periodic official art exhibitions called Salons. Thus, the idea, born of the Enlightenment, that aesthetic matters could be universally subjected to reason led to a rigid imposition of a narrow set of aesthetic rules on all art that came within the Académie's jurisdiction. This approach found especially fertile ground in the neoclassical style, which arose in the second half of the 18th century and which the Académie espoused with enthusiasm.

Numerous academies, usually state-supported and similar in structure and approach to the French Académie, were established throughout Europe and in America. By 1790 there were more than 80 such institutions. One of the most important was the Royal Academy of Arts in London, established in 1768 by George III with Sir Joshua Reynolds as its first president. There had been no public exhibitions of contemporary artists in London before 1760, when Reynolds helped found the Society of Artists and the first of many successful exhibitions was held. Reynolds guided the policy of the Royal Academy with such skill that the pattern he set has been followed with little variation ever since. Reynolds' *Discourses Delivered at the Royal Academy* (1769–91) is among the most important art criticism of the time. In it he outlined the essence of grandeur in art and suggested the means of achieving it through rigorous academic training and study of the old masters of art. Despite this, the Royal Academy never dominated art as completely as academies on the European continent.

A Revolution in Print

One of the most dramatic cultural advances during the Enlightenment came in the form of the printed word. London's first daily newspaper appeared in 1702. By 1760 the city had four dailies and six tri-weekly evening papers that circulated in the country at large as well as in the capital. But the provinces also generated their own newspapers, and their own books, dictionaries, magazines, printed advertisements, and primers. In 1695 Parliament passed legislation allowing printing presses to be established freely outside London. Between 1700 and 1750 presses were founded in 57 English provincial towns, and they proliferated at an even faster rate in the last third of the 18th century. By 1725 no fewer than 22 provincial newspapers had emerged. By 1760 there were 37 such papers and by 1780, 50. In Scotland seven newspapers and periodicals were in existence by 1750, including the monthly *Scots Magazine*, which was printed in Edinburgh but could also be purchased from booksellers at Aberdeen, Glasgow, Dundee, Perth, and Stirling. Wales had no English-language newspaper until 1804, but many English papers found their way there.

By 1760 more than nine million newspapers were sold in Britain every year. Because they were expensive by the standards of the time (three or four pennies), one copy of a paper may have been shared and read by as many as 20 different people. There is little doubt that this explosion of newsprint helped to integrate the nation. All provincial newspapers and periodicals were parasitic on the London press. They borrowed large extracts from the more popular and controversial London papers and pamphlets. Increasingly, too, they broke the law and reprinted London journalists' accounts of debates in the House of Commons and House of Lords (printing parliamentary debates was illegal until 1770). Consequently, by the time of the Seven Years War (1756–63), larger numbers of Britons than ever before had some access to political information. They were more aware of their country's military victories and defeats and more conscious of political scandals and protest. Politics was no longer just the preserve of the politicians at court, in Parliament, and in the country houses.

At the same time, the book trade expanded and moved gradually toward its modern form. The key functions of publishing shifted from the printer to the bookseller and from him to the publisher in his own right; the author, too, at last came into his own. The battle with the censor became increasingly fierce before any measure of freedom of the press was allowed.

The great increase in available reading matter after about 1650 both resulted from and promoted the spread of education to the middle classes, especially to women. The wider readership is reflected among the middle classes by the rich development of the prose novel in the 18th century and, among the less well-to-do, by the large sales of almanacs and chapbooks. Growth in the book trade led naturally to growth in libraries. Some of the oldest collections of books developed into national "copyright libraries". Sir Thomas Bodley opened his famous library (the Bodleian Library) at Oxford in 1602, and in 1610 the Stationers' Company undertook to give it a copy of every book printed in England. Later, Acts of Parliament required the delivery of copies of every book to a varying number of libraries, the most important being the library of the British Museum, founded in 1759. This idea of a definitive collection was adopted elsewhere; e.g., in the United States, where the librarian of the Library of Congress (founded in 1800) was appointed copyright officer in 1870.

Successful books became highly profitable, and the author's right to a proper share was more widely recognized. By the

1750s patronage was virtually at an end: "We have done with patronage," said Samuel Johnson. In its place came the public at large, to whom Henry Fielding dedicated his satirical piece for the theatre, *The Historical Register for the Year 1736*, on its publication in the following year.

In Britain the final separation of publisher and bookseller was marked – and fostered – by the passing of the Copyright Act of 1709, the first of its kind in any country. It was "An Act for the encouragement of Learning, by vesting the copies of printed books in the authors or purchasers of such copies during the times therein mentioned" – in other words, it gave authors a monopoly on the reproduction of their work: for books printed before the Act, 21 years, for works not yet published, 14 years. The terms it set were amended when they came to be regarded as too short; but in setting any term at all, and in focusing attention on the author as prime producer, it was revolutionary.

In France, Louis XIII had also tried to regulate the trade in books. By an ordinance of 1618, a body called the Chambre des Syndicats was established. It was organized along lines similar to the Stationers' Company in England, but because it contained two royal nominees, its control was even more absolute. The power of censorship, though it remained for a time with the Sorbonne, also passed eventually to officials of the crown. Under these conditions, publishers were inclined to exercise caution; as in other strictly regulated areas, more controversial works first appeared outside the country (often in Holland or Geneva) or under a false imprint. A remarkable publishing feat of the 18th century was the 70-volume collected edition of the works of Voltaire (François-Marie Arouet), produced from 1784 to 1789 at Kehl, in Baden, by Pierre-Augustin Caron de Beaumarchais, the author of *The Barber of Seville* and *The Marriage of Figaro*.

Beaumarchais bought the printing equipment (especially for the purpose) from the widow of the great English typographer John Baskerville.

Although Frankfurt continued to be important for the production of type and illustrated books in Germany, the centre of the trade shifted decisively to Leipzig. There, an enlightened government and a celebrated university favoured cultural life and patronized book publishing. Philipp Erasmus Reich, a partner of Moritz Georg Weidmann, which was founded in 1682, was known in the 18th century as "the prince of the German book trade". He could be said to have invented the net-price principle, under which publishers allow a trade discount to booksellers only on condition that the book is sold to the public at not less than its "net published price" as fixed by the publisher. Reich also invented the idea of a booksellers' association (1765), which in 1825 became the Börsenverein der Deutschen Buchhändler, a unique organization of publishers, wholesalers, and retailers.

Censorship and Freedom of the Press

From the 18th century censorship in most Western countries diminished. It was abolished in Sweden in 1766, in Denmark in 1770, and in Germany in 1848. The clearest statement, to which lip service, at least, is now almost universally paid, came from the French National Assembly in 1789: "The free communication of thought and opinion is one of the most precious rights of man; every citizen may therefore speak, write and print freely." In the United States, no formal censorship has ever been established; control over printed matter has always been exercised through the courts under the law of libel. This was also the case in England after the lapsing of the Licensing

Act in 1694; but two important steps had yet to be taken: in 1766, Parliament put an end to general warrants (i.e., for the arrest of unnamed persons and for the seizure of unspecified papers); and in 1792, the Libel Act finally gave the jury the right to decide the issue, which had previously depended mainly on the judge.

It was John Wilkes, the politician and editor of the *North Briton*, who in the mid-18th century brought the issue of the freedom of the press to the fore in England. He came to be regarded as a champion of liberty. In 1762, in the *North Briton,* he began to give rancorous support to Earl Temple's campaign against the ministry of Lord Bute, not hesitating to write libellous innuendos about Bute's relations with George III's mother. His incitement of antiministerial feeling was partly responsible for Bute's decision to retire.

Temple, equally hostile to the new ministry formed by George Grenville, encouraged Wilkes to publish the now famous "No. 45" of the *North Briton* on April 23 1763, a devastating attack upon ministerial statements in the King's Speech, which Wilkes described as false. The new ministers instituted immediate proceedings against him. A general warrant was issued and 48 people were seized in the search for evidence before Wilkes himself was arrested. He was thrown into the Tower of London, but a week later, to the public delight, was released on the ground that his arrest was a breach of parliamentary privilege. Wilkes and others instituted actions for trespass against the secretary of state, the Earl of Halifax, and his underlings that led to awards of damages and established the illegality of general warrants. Assuming his immunity, Wilkes prepared to continue his campaign. Asked by a French acquaintance how far liberty of the press extended in England, he said: "I cannot tell, but I am trying to find out."

A second attack on him was now more carefully prepared, and in 1763, the House of Commons, on a government motion, declared "No. 45" a seditious libel. During the Christmas vacation Wilkes stole off to Paris to visit his daughter and decided not to return to face prosecution. In due course he was pronounced an outlaw for impeding royal justice. For the next four years Wilkes was on the Continent. Then, in 1768, in desperation, his indebtedness making a longer stay in Paris unsafe, he staked all on the hazardous chance of securing re-election to Parliament and determined to stand for London as an opponent of the government in the name of public liberty. He was elected for Middlesex.

In the following months he published inflammatory squibs against the ministers' use of the military against rioters, and he attempted to reopen the whole question of his conviction by a petition to the Commons. He was expelled again from the Commons on February 3 1769. His popularity nevertheless ensured his re-election for Middlesex on February 16, and again on March 16 after a further expulsion, but after a last re-election, on April 13, the Commons declared his defeated opponent, Henry Luttrell, the duly elected member. Wilkes was finally expelled by a method fraught with danger to the constitution, since it set aside in the name of parliamentary privilege the right of the elector to choose his representative.

Friends and sympathizers of Wilkes early in 1769 formed the Society for the Defence of the Bill of Rights to uphold his cause and pay his debts. Shut out of Parliament, he pursued his ambitions, becoming lord mayor of London in 1774. It may be that expediency rather than principle made him embrace the radical programme adopted in 1771 by the Bill of Rights men, which called for shorter Parliaments, a wider franchise, and the abolition of aristocratic "pocket boroughs". In 1771 he successfully exploited the judicial privileges of the city to prevent the arrest for breach of privilege of printers who reported parliamentary debates. He was subsequently elected a further three times for Middlesex on a radical programme, but his popularity waned in later years.

His real achievement lay, however, in extending the liberties of the press. His challenge led to the court findings that general warrants as hitherto used by government against the press were illegal, and he effectively destroyed the power of the Houses of Parliament to exact retribution for the reporting of parliamentary debates.

Political and Other Literature in England

Although the 18th century is called the Age of Reason, it is more accurate to say that the period was marked by two main impulses: reason and passion. The respect paid to reason was shown in pursuit of order, symmetry, decorum, and scientific knowledge; the cultivation of the feelings stimulated philanthropy, exaltation of personal relationships, religious fervour, and the cult of sentiment, or sensibility. In literature the rational impulse fostered satire, argument, wit, plain prose; the other inspired the psychological novel and the poetry of the sublime.

The cult of wit, satire, and argument is evident in England in the writings of Alexander Pope, Jonathan Swift, and Samuel Johnson. The novel was established as a major art form in English literature partly by a rational realism shown in the works of Henry Fielding, Daniel Defoe, and Tobias Smollett and partly by the psychological probing of the novels of Samuel Richardson and of Laurence Sterne's *Tristram Shandy*.

The expiry of the Licensing Act in 1695 had halted state censorship of the press. During the next 20 years there were to be ten general elections. These two factors combined to produce an enormous growth in the publication of political literature. Senior politicians, especially Robert Harley, saw the potential importance of the pamphleteer in wooing the support of a wavering electorate, and numberless hack writers produced copy for the presses. Harley instigated Defoe's work on the *Review* (1704–13), which consisted, in essence, of a regular political essay defending, if often by indirection, current governmental policy. He also secured Swift's polemical skills for contributions to *The Examiner* (1710–11). Swift's most ambitious intervention in the paper war, again overseen by Harley, was *The Conduct of the Allies* (1711), a devastatingly lucid argument against any further prolongation of the War of the Spanish Succession.

The avalanche of political writing whetted the contemporary appetite for reading matter generally and, in the increasing sophistication of its ironic and fictional manoeuvres, assisted in preparing the way for the astonishing growth in popularity of narrative fiction during the subsequent decades. It also helped fuel the other great new genre of the 18th century: periodical journalism. After Defoe's *Review* the great innovation in this field came with the achievements of Richard Steele and Joseph Addison in *The Tatler* (1709–11) and then *The Spectator* (1711–12). In a familiar, urbane style they tackled a great range of topics, from politics to fashion, from aesthetics to the development of commerce. They aligned themselves with those who wished to see a purification of manners after the laxity of the Restoration and wrote extensively, with descriptive and reformative intent, about social and family relations. Their political allegiances were Whig, and in their creation of Sir Roger de Coverley they painted a wry portrait of the landed Tory squire as likable, possessed of good qualities, but feckless and anachronistic. Contrariwise, they spoke admiringly of the positive and honourable virtues bred by a healthy, and expansionist, mercantile community.

Later in the century other periodical forms developed. Edward Cave invented the idea of the "magazine", founding the hugely successful *Gentleman's Magazine* in 1731. One of its most prolific early contributors was the young Samuel Johnson. The practice and the status of criticism were transformed in mid-century by the *Monthly Review* (founded 1749) and the *Critical Review* (founded 1756), the latter edited by Smollett. From this period the influence of reviews began to shape literary output, and writers began to acknowledge their importance.

Alexander Pope contributed to *The Spectator* and moved for a time in Addisonian circles; but from about 1711 onward, his more influential friendships were with Tory intellectuals. The mock-heroic *The Rape of the Lock* (final version published in 1714) is an astonishing feat and a delicately ironic commentary upon the contemporary social world. His *Essay on Man* (1733–4) was a grand systematic attempt to buttress the notion of a God-ordained, perfectly ordered, all-inclusive hierarchy of created things.

Ambitious debates on society and human nature ran parallel with explorations of a literary form finding new popularity with a large audience, the novel. Jonathan Swift, perhaps the greatest prose satirist in the English language, is most famous for *Gulliver's Travels* (1726). At its heart is a radical critique of human nature in which subtle ironic techniques work to part the reader from any comfortable preconceptions and challenge him to rethink from first principles his notions of humanity. Daniel Defoe's *Robinson Crusoe* (1719), an immediate success, is a unique fictional blending of the traditions of Puritan spiritual autobiography with an insistent scrutiny of the nature of humans as social creatures and it displays Defoe's extraordinary ability to invent a sustaining modern myth.

The enthusiasm prompted by Defoe's best novels demonstrated the growing readership for innovative prose narrative. Samuel Richardson, a prosperous London printer, created *Pamela; or, Virtue Rewarded* (1740, with a less-happy sequel in 1741). Using the epistolary form, it tells the story of an employer's attempted seduction of a young servant woman, her subsequent victimization, and her eventual reward in virtuous marriage with the penitent exploiter. As well as being popular, it was the first such work of prose fiction to aspire to respectability, indeed moral seriousness. For contemporaries, the so-called "rise of the novel" began here. Pamela's frank speaking about the abuses of masculine and gentry power sounds the sceptical note more radically developed in Richardson's masterpiece, *Clarissa; or, The History of a Young Lady* (1747–8), which has a just claim to being considered the greatest of all English tragic novels. It was admired and imitated throughout Europe.

An experiment of a radical and seminal kind is Laurence Sterne's *Tristram Shandy* (1759–67), which, drawing on a tradition of learned wit from Erasmus and Rabelais to Burton and Swift, provides a brilliant comic critique of the progress of the English novel to date. Sterne's *A Sentimental Journey Through France and Italy* (1768) similarly defies conventional expectations of what a travel book might be. It mingles affecting vignettes with episodes in a heartier, comic mode, but coherence of imagination is secured by the delicate insistence with which Sterne ponders how the impulses of sentimental and erotic feeling are psychologically interdependent. Sensuality and sentiment are also seen in other works of the period: John Cleland's *Memoirs of a Woman of Pleasure* (1748–9; known as *Fanny Hill*); Henry Mackenzie's *The Man of Feeling* (1771); and Fanny Burney's *Evelina* and *Camilla* (1796).

In poetry, Thomas Gray's *The Bard* (1757) is part of a larger movement of taste, of which the contemporary enthusiasm for James Macpherson's alleged translations (1760–63) of the Irish warrior-poet Ossian is a further indicator. The 1780s brought publishing success to Robert Burns for his *Poems, Chiefly in the Scottish Dialect* (1786). Born a poor tenant farmer's son, Burns made himself well-versed in English literary traditions, and his innovations were fully premeditated. His work bears the imprint of the revolutionary decades in which he wrote, and recurrent in much of it are a joyful hymning of freedom, both individual and national, and an instinctive belief in the possibility of a new social order. Oliver Goldsmith's *The Deserted Village* describes the experience of enforced exile, as an idealized village community is ruthlessly broken up in the interests of landed power.

While Samuel Johnson was known for his poetry, and for his twice-weekly essays for *The Rambler* (1750–52), it was the successful completion of two major projects, his innovative *Dictionary of the English Language* (1755) and the great edition of Shakespeare's plays (1765), which brought him lasting fame. The latter played a major part in the establishment of Shakespeare as the linchpin of a national literary canon.

The *Life of Johnson*, by his friend James Boswell, may be regarded as a representative psychological expression of the Enlightenment; it certainly epitomizes several typical characteristics of that age: devotion to urban life, confidence in common sense, emphasis on humans as social beings. Yet in its extravagant pursuit of the life of one individual, in its laying bare the eccentricities and suggesting the inner turmoil of personality, it may be thought of as part of that revolution in self-awareness, ideas, and aspirations exemplified in the French philosopher Jean-Jacques Rousseau's *Confessions*, the French Revolution,

the writings of the German philosopher Immanuel Kant, the
political tracts of the American revolutionary Thomas Paine,
and the poetical works of Burns, William Blake, and William
Wordsworth – a revolution in its concern with the individual
psyche and with human freedom.

Writing in France

In France the major characteristic of the Enlightenment lies in
philosophical and political writings, which had a profound
influence throughout the rest of Europe and foreshadowed the
French Revolution. Voltaire, Rousseau, the Baron Montesquieu, Diderot and d'Alembert all devoted much of their
writing to controversies about social and religious matters,
often involving direct conflict with the authorities.

Two important precursors were Pierre Bayle, whose *Dictionnaire historique et critique* (1697; *Historical and Critical
Dictionary*) became an arsenal of knowledge and critical ideas
for the 18th century, and Bernard de Fontenelle whose *Entretiens sur la pluralité des mondes* (1686; *Conversations on the
Plurality of Worlds*) explains the Copernican universe in
simple terms. Both promoted the Enlightenment principle that
the pursuit of verifiable knowledge was a central human
activity. Bayle was concerned with the problem of evil, which
seemed to him a mystery understandable by faith alone. But
such unknowable matters did not at all invalidate the search
for hard facts, as the *Dictionary* abundantly shows. Fontenelle, for his part, saw that the furtherance of truth depended
upon the elimination of error, arising as it did from human
laziness in unquestioningly accepting received ideas or from
human love of mystery.

Montesquieu, the first of the great Enlightenment authors,

demonstrated a liberal approach to the world fitting in with an innovative pluralist and relativist view of society. His *Lettres persanes* (1721; *Persian Letters*) established his reputation. A fictional set of correspondences centred on two Persians making their first visit to Europe, they depict satirically a Paris in transition between the old dogmatic absolutes of monarchy and religion and the freedoms of a new age. At their centre is the condition of women – trapped in the private space of the harem, emancipated in the Salons of Paris. The personal experience of the Persians generates debate on a wide range of crucial moral, political, economic, and philosophical issues, all centring on the link between the public good and the regulation of individual desire.

Montesquieu's interest in social mechanisms and causation is pursued further in the *Considérations sur les causes de la grandeur des Romains et de leur décadence* (1734; *Considerations on the Causes of the Grandeur and the Decadence of the Romans*). To explain Rome's greatness and decline, he invokes the notion of an *esprit général* ("general spirit"), a set of secondary causes underlying each society and determining its developments. Herein are the seeds of *De l'esprit des lois* (1748; *The Spirit of the Laws*), the preparation of which took 14 years. This great work brought political discussion into the public arena in France.

Voltaire, on any count, bestrides the Enlightenment. Whether as dramatist, historian, reformer, poet, storyteller, philosopher, or correspondent, for 60 years he remained an intellectual leader in France. A stay in England (1726–8) led to the *Lettres philosophiques* or *Lettres sur les Anglais* (1734; *Philosophical Letters,* or *Letters on England*), which – taking England as a polemical model of philosophical freedom, experimental use of reason, enlightened patronage of arts and science, and respect for the new merchant classes and their contribution to the nation's economic well-being – offered a programme for a whole civilization, as well as sharp satire of a despotic, authoritarian, and outdated France. The *Dictionnaire philosophique* (1764; *Philosophical Dictionary*) is the epitome of Voltairean attitudes, but he is best remembered for the tale *Candide* (1759), a savage denunciation of metaphysical optimism that reveals a world of horrors and folly. Candide at last renounces the search for absolute truths as futile and settles for the simple life of labours within his reach, "cultivating his garden".

Diderot and the *Encyclopédie*

Another universal genius, Denis Diderot, occupied a somewhat less exalted place in his own times, since most of his greatest works were published only posthumously. But his encylopaedic range is undeniable. He was a theorist of the bourgeois drama, the first great French art critic, a sharp observer of the psychology of repression and its political function in authoritarian society, and author of the greatest French antinovel of the century *Jacques le fataliste et son maître* (1796; *Jacques the Fatalist and his Master*). Influenced by Laurence Sterne's *Tristram Shandy*, Diderot's work anticipates in its form, techniques and language both 20th-century realism and the mode of the *nouveau roman* ("new novel"). Diderot seized on the pantheistic vision of a world materialistic and godless yet pulsating with energy and the unexpected. *Jacques the Fatalist* captures the fluidity of a disconcerting universe where nothing is ever clear-cut or under control, where history, in the form of choices already made by others, determines any individual's fate, and yet free will and responsibility are among the highest human values. The admirable servant Jacques, who sees through yet loyally serves and protects his bonehead of a master and who establishes and maintains his own humane values, following his heart as well as his head in a world given over to cruelty and chance, is the model new man of the Enlightenment.

In his own day, Diderot was best known as editor of the *Encyclopédie*, a vast work in 17 folio volumes of text and 11 of illustrations. Diderot undertook the task with the distinguished mathematician Jean le Rond d'Alembert as coeditor but soon profoundly changed the nature of the publication, broadening its scope and turning it into an important organ of radical and revolutionary opinion. He gathered around him a team of dedicated litterateurs, scientists, and even priests. All were fired with a common purpose: to further knowledge and, by so doing, strike a resounding blow against reactionary forces in church and state. As a *dictionnaire raisonné* ("rational dictionary"), the *Encyclopédie* was to bring out the essential principles and applications of every art and science. The underlying philosophy was rationalism and a qualified faith in the progress of the human mind.

The *Encyclopédie* was the most ambitious publishing enterprise of the century and its publishing history reveals much of the ambience of the Enlightenment. It appeared between 1751 and 1765, after checks and delays that would have disheartened anyone less committed than Diderot. The critical point was reached in 1759, when French military defeats made the authorities sensitive to anything that implied criticism of the regime. The publication of Claude-Adrien Helvétius' *De l'esprit* (1758; *On the Mind*), together with doubts about the orthodoxy of another contributor, the Abbé de Prades, and concern about the growth of Freemasonry, convinced government ministers that they faced a plot to subvert authority. If they had been as united as the officials of the church, the

Encyclopédie would have been throttled. It was placed on the Index of Forbidden Books, and a ban of excommunication was pronounced on anyone who should read it; but even Rome was equivocal. The knowledge that Pope Benedict XIV was privately sympathetic lessened the impact of the ban; Malesherbes, from 1750 to 1763 director of the Librairie, whose sanction was required for publication, eased the passage of volumes he was supposed to censor. Production continued, but without Rousseau, an early contributor, who became increasingly hostile to the encyclopaedists and their utilitarian philosophy.

D'Alembert introduced the first volume in 1751. Diderot edited alone from 1758 until the final volume of plates appeared in 1772. A summation of new scientific and technological knowledge and, by that very fact, a radically polemical enterprise, the *Encyclopédie* is the embodiment of the Enlightenment, disseminating practical information to improve the human lot, reduce theological superstition, and, in Diderot's words from his key article "Encyclopédie", "change the common way of thinking".

Sensibility and Jean-Jacques Rousseau

Despite official opposition and occasional censorship, the novel developed apace, with increasing emphasis on the new ethos of sensibility and realism. As the bourgeoisie acquired a more prominent place in society, the focus switched to exploring the textures of everyday life and the *roman de moeurs* ("novel of manners") became important, most notably with the novels of Alain-René Lesage. Characterization and sensibility receive greater attention in the novels of Abbé Prévost, best known for the *Histoire du chevalier des Grieux et de Manon Lescaut* (1731; *Tale of the Chevalier des Grieux and Manon Lescaut*; English translation *Manon Lescaut*). By contrast, Pierre Marivaux as novelist devoted his main energies to psychological analysis and the moral life of his characters in his two great narratives, *La vie de Marianne* (1731–41; *The Life of Marianne*) and *Le paysan parvenu* (1734–5; The Upstart Peasant).

From the middle of the century, studies of women's position in society, Salon, or family emerged from the pens of women writers. Françoise de Graffigny (*Lettres d'une Péruvienne* [1747; *Letters from a Peruvian Woman* or *Letters from a Peruvian Princess*]), Marie-Jeanne Riccoboni, and Isabelle de Charrière use the popular epistolary form of the novel to allow their heroines to voice the pain and distress of a situation of unremitting dependency. The processes of modernization were beginning to bring their own solutions to women's subordination. The educationalist Madame de Genlis (Stéphanie-Félicité du Crest), much influenced by Rousseau, found a Europe-wide readership for her treatises, plays, and, especially, the novel *Adèle et Théodore; ou, lettres sur l'éducation* (1782; *Adelaide and Theodore; or, Letters on Education*), which offered enlightened and advanced educational programmes for children and young women of all classes. The subordination of women to men was a theme emphasized in the highly popular historical and political romances she would later write in exile, during the Revolution.

The pre-eminent name associated with the sensibility of the age, however, is that of Jean-Jacques Rousseau. His work gave rise to the cult of nature, lakes, mountains, and gardens, in contrast to what he presented as the false glitter of society. He called for a new way of life attentive above all to the innate sense of pity and benevolence he attributed to human beings, rather than dependent upon what he saw as the meretricious reason prized by his fellow philosophes; he espoused untutored simplicity and declared the true equality of all, based in the capacity for feeling that all humans share; and he argued the importance of total sincerity and claimed to practise it in his confessional writings, which are seminal instances of modern autobiography. With these radical new claims for a different mode of feeling, he would foster a revolutionary new politics.

He established the modern novel of sensibility with the resounding success of his *Julie; ou la nouvelle Héloïse* (1761; *Julie; or The New Heloise*), a novel about an impossible, doomed love between a young aristocrat and her tutor. He composed a classic work of educational theory with *Émile; ou de l'éducation* (1762; *Emile; or, On Education*). Rousseau's struggle toward a morality based on transparent honesty and on values authenticated not by any external authority but by his own conscience and feelings, is made explicit in the *Confessions* (written 1764–70). Here he suggests that self-knowledge is to be achieved by a growing familiarity with the unconscious, a recognition of the importance of childhood in shaping the adult, and an acceptance of the role of sexuality – an anticipation of modern psychoanalysis.

The later 18th-century novel, preoccupied with the understanding of the tensions and dangers of a society about to wake up to the Revolution of 1789 is dominated by the masterpiece of Pierre Choderlos de Laclos, *Les liaisons dangereuses* (1782; *Dangerous Acquaintances*), and its stylish account of erotic psychology and its manipulations. The libertine Valmont and his accomplice and rival, Mme de Merteuil, plot the downfall of their victims in a Parisian society that illustrates Rousseau's strictures: natural human values have no place in a world of conformist expediency, cynicism, and vicious exploitation.

Another follower of Rousseauist ideals, the verbose and prolific Nicolas-Edme Restif, became the self-proclaimed chronicler and analyst of Parisian society, with novels which evoke vividly the manners and morals of men and especially women, in all their social ranks, from the bourgeois mistress of the house to the prostitutes in the street. A very different response to this time of radical change came from Donatien-Alphonse-François, Comte de Sade, generally known as the Marquis de Sade, whose fascination with the connections of power, pain, and pleasure, between individuals and in society's larger structures, gave rise to the word sadism. In Sade's philosophy, where the essential operation of Nature is not procreation but destruction, murder is natural and morally acceptable. The true libertine must replace soft sentiment by an energy aspiring to the total freedom of individual desire.

German Rationalism

The Enlightenment as a European movement had begun in England and Holland and spread from there to France. When it finally arrived in Germany, English authors became the models for German literature to follow during the latter half of the 18th century, after the influence of French classicism had faded.

In the middle of the 18th century, after decades of exhaustion, stagnation, and provincialization, a significant cultural and literary revival occurred, accompanied by a new understanding of humanity's ability to master nature and by a belief in the rational capacity of humans to set their own moral course.

The first literary reforms in Germany between 1724 and 1740, however, were based on French 17th-century classicism. Its primary proponent was Johann Christoph Gottsched, a professor at Leipzig whose *On the Mind* (1730) provided examples for German writers to follow. Gottsched's principal criterion for the production and reception of literature was reason. Basing his precepts on a literal interpretation of Aristotle's *Poetics*, he argued that Nature was governed by reason and that it was the task of poets to imitate reason as it manifested itself in Nature. Gottsched also edited some of the first German moral weeklies, which were patterned after English models such as *The Spectator* and *The Tatler*. Opposition to him arose on various fronts, most notably from Johann Jakob Bodmer and Johann Jakob Breitinger who called for a stronger emphasis on imagination in literary production.

The major representative of the Enlightenment in German literature was Gotthold Ephraim Lessing. He surmounted Gottsched's strictures and became, through his own impressive output of plays and theoretical writings for the theatre, the founder of modern German literature. With his play *Miss Sara Sampson* (1755), Lessing introduced to the German stage a new genre: the *bürgerliches Trauerspiel* ("bourgeois tragedy") and demonstrated that tragedy need not be limited to the highborn. Lessing reinterpreted Aristotle in his *Hamburgische Dramaturgie* (1767–9; *Hamburg Dramaturgy*), asserting that the cathartic emotions of pity and fear are felt by the audience rather than by figures in the drama. With this stress on pity and compassion, Lessing interpreted Aristotle in terms of Christian middle-class virtues and established Shakespeare as the model for German dramatists to follow.

His final, blank-verse drama, *Nathan der Weise* (1779; *Nathan the Wise*), is representative of the Enlightenment. Set in 12th-century Jerusalem during the Crusades, the play deals with religious tolerance. At the core of the play is the parable of the ring that Nathan offers as an answer to the question of which of the three religions – Judaism, Christianity, and Islam – is the true one. Lessing's use of a wise Jew was a tribute to his friend Moses Mendelssohn, a philosopher who was the central figure of German Jewish emancipation.

The foremost novelist of the German Enlightenment was Christoph Martin Wieland. He introduced the model of Miguel de Cervantes' *Don Quixote* in his *Die Abentheuer des Don Sylvio von Rosalva* (1764; *The Adventures of Don Sylvio von Rosalva*) and that of Henry Fielding's *Tom Jones* and *Joseph Andrews* in his *Geschichte des Agathon* (1766–7; *The History of Agathon*). The hero of each is a visionary dreamer who, after many failures and erotic temptations, eventually adopts an enlightened outlook on life.

The Origins of Modern Aesthetics

It was not until the end of the 17th century that the distinctive concerns of modern aesthetics were established. At that time, taste, imagination, natural beauty, and imitation came to be recognized as the central topics in aesthetics. In England the principal influences were the 3rd Earl of Shaftesbury and his disciples Joseph Addison and the philosopher Francis Hutcheson. Shaftesbury did more than any of his contemporaries to establish ethics and aesthetics as central areas of philosophical inquiry. As a naturalist, he believed that the fundamental principles of morals and taste could be established by due attention to human nature, human sentiments being so ordered that there are certain things that naturally please them and are naturally conducive to their good (*Characteristiks of Men, Manners, Opinions, Times*, 1711). Taste is a kind of balanced discernment, whereby a person recognizes that which is congenial to his sentiments and therefore an object of pleasurable contemplation.

Following the philosopher John Locke, Shaftesbury laid much emphasis on the association of ideas as a fundamental component in aesthetic experience and the crucial bridge from the sphere of contemplation to the sphere of action. Addison adopted this position in a series of influential essays, "The Pleasures of the Imagination" in *The Spectator* (1712). He defended the theory that imaginative association is the fundamental component in the experience of art, architecture, and nature, and is the true explanation of their value.

Hutcheson was perhaps the first to place the problem of aesthetic judgement among the central questions of epistemology: How can one know that something is beautiful? What guides one's judgement and what validates it? His answer was decidedly empiricist in tone: aesthetic judgements are perceptual and take their authority from a sense that is common to all who make them. In *An Inquiry into the Original of our Ideas of Beauty and Virtue* (1725), Hutcheson explained: "The origin of our perceptions of beauty and harmony is justly called a 'sense' because it involves no intellectual element, no reflection on principles and causes."

Such a statement would have been vigorously repudiated by Hutcheson's contemporary Alexander Gottlieb Baumgarten, who, in *Reflections on Poetry*, introduced the term "aesthetic" in its distinctively modern sense. Baumgarten was a pupil of Christian Wolff, the rationalist philosopher who had created the orthodox philosophy of the German Enlightenment by building into a system the metaphysical ideas of Gottfried Wilhelm Leibniz. He was thus heir to a tradition that dismissed the senses and the imagination as incapable of providing a genuine cognition of their objects and as needing always to be corrected (and replaced) by rational reflection. Baumgarten, however, argued that poetry is surely cognitive: it provides insight into the world of a kind that could be conveyed in no other way. At the same time, poetic insights are perceptual ("aesthetic") and hence imbued with the distinctive character of sensory and imaginative experience. According to Baumgarten, the ideas conveyed by poetry are "clear and confused", as opposed to the "clear and distinct" ideas of reason in the sense that they had been described by the French philosopher René Descartes and the 17th-century rationalists. Baumgarten held that the aesthetic value of a poem resides in the relative preponderance of clarity over confusion. Accordingly, his theory of the value of art was ultimately cognitive. It was some decades before Baumgarten's coinage became philosophical currency. But there is no doubt that his treatise, for all its pedantry and outmoded philosophical method, deserves its reputation as the founding work of modern aesthetics.

The development of aesthetics between the work of Baumgarten and that of Kant, who had been influenced by Baumgarten's writings, was complex and diverse, drawing inspiration from virtually every realm of human inquiry. Yet, throughout this period certain topics repeatedly received focal attention in discussions pertaining to aesthetic questions.

One such topic was the faculty of taste, the analysis of which remained the common point among German, French, and English writers. Taste was seen either as a sense (Hutcheson), as a peculiar kind of emotionally inspired discrimination (the Scottish philosopher David Hume), or as a part of refined good manners (Voltaire). In an important essay entitled "Of the Standard of Taste" (in *Four Dissertations,* 1757), Hume, following Voltaire in the *Encyclopédie,* raised the question of the basis of aesthetic judgement and argued that "it is natural for us to seek a standard of taste; a rule by which the various sentiments of men may be reconciled; at least, a decision afforded, confirming one sentiment, and condemning another." But where is this standard of taste to be found? Hume recommends an ideal of the man of taste, whose discriminations are unclouded by an emotional distemper and informed by a "delicacy of imagination . . . requisite to convey a sensibility of . . . finer emotions". For, Hume argues, there is a great resemblance between "mental" and "bodily" taste – between the taste exercised in aesthetic discrimination and that exercised in the appreciation of food and drink, which can equally be deformed by some abnormal condition of the subject. Hume proceeded to lay down various procedures for the education of taste and for the proper conduct of critical judgement.

A second major concern of 18th-century writers was the role of imagination. Addison's essays were seminal, but discussion of imagination remained largely confined to the associative theories of Locke and his followers until Hume gave to the imagination a fundamental role in the generation of common sense beliefs. Kant attempted to describe the imagination as a distinctive faculty, active in the generation of scientific judgement as well as aesthetic pleasure. Between them, Hume and Kant laid the ground for the Romantic writers on art: Johann Gottfried von Herder, Friedrich Schiller, Friedrich Schelling, and Novalis (the pseudonym of Friedrich Leopold, Freiherr von Hardenberg) in Germany, and Samuel Taylor Coleridge and William Wordsworth in England. For such writers, imagination was to be the distinctive feature both of aesthetic activity and of all true insight into the human condition. Meanwhile, Lord Kames and Archibald Alison had each provided full accounts of the role of association in the formation and justification of critical judgement. Alison, in particular, recognized the inadequacies of the traditional empiricist approach to imaginative association and provided a theory as to how the feelings aroused by a work of art or a scene of natural beauty may become part of its appearance – qualities of the object as much as of the subject (*Essays on the Nature and Principles of Taste* [1790]).

The concept of imitation, introduced into the discussion of art by Plato and Aristotle, was fundamental to the 18th-century philosophy of art. Imitation is a vague term, frequently used to cover both representation and expression in the modern sense. The thesis that imitation is the common and distinguishing feature of the arts was put forward by James Harris in *Three Treatises* (1744) and subsequently made famous by Charles Batteux in a book entitled *Les Beaux Arts réduits à un même principe* (1746; *The Fine Arts Reduced to a Single Principle*). This diffuse and ill-argued work contains the first modern attempt to give a systematic theory of art and aesthetic judgement that will show the unity of the phenomena and their common importance. "The laws of taste," Batteux argued, "have nothing but the imitation of beautiful nature as their object"; from which it follows that the arts, which are addressed to taste, must imitate nature. The distinction between the fine and useful arts (recast by the 20th-century philosopher R.G. Collingwood as the distinction between art and craft) stems from Batteux.

Still another characteristic of 18th-century aesthetics was the concern with the distinction between the sublime and the beautiful. Edmund Burke's *A Philosophical Enquiry into the Origin of Our Ideas of the Sublime and Beautiful* (1757) merged psychological and aesthetic questioning by hypothesizing that the spectator's or reader's delight in the sublime depended upon a sensation of pleasurable pain. He introduced a famous distinction between two kinds of aesthetic judgement corresponding to two orders of aesthetic experience: the judgement of the beautiful and that of the sublime. The judgement of beauty has its origin in our social feelings, particularly in our feelings toward the other sex, and in our hope for a consolation through love and desire. The judgement of the sublime has its origin in our feelings toward nature, and in our intimation of our ultimate solitude and fragility in a world that is not of our own devising and that remains resistant to our demands. In Burke's words,

> Whatever is fitted in any sort to excite the ideas of pain, and danger, that is to say, whatever is in any sort terrible, or is conversant about terrible objects, or operates in a manner analogous to terror, is a source of the sublime; that is, it is productive of the strongest emotion which the mind is capable of feeling.

Burke's distinction emerges as part of a natural philosophy of beauty: an attempt to give the origins of our sentiments rather than to explain the logic of the judgements that convey them. It inspired one of Kant's first publications, an essay on the sublime, as well as his *Kritik der Urteilskraft* (1790; *Critique of Judgement*), the first full account of aesthetic experience as a distinct exercise of rational mentality. In Kant, the distinction between the beautiful and the sublime is recast as a distinction between two categories of aesthetic experience and two separate values that attach to it. Sometimes when we sense the harmony between nature and our faculties, we are impressed by the purposiveness and intelligibility of everything that surrounds us. This is the sentiment of beauty. At other times, overcome by the infinite greatness of the world, we renounce the attempt to understand and control it. This is the sentiment of the sublime. In confronting the sublime, the mind is "incited to abandon sensibility" – to reach over to that transcendental view of things that shows to us the immanence of a supersensible realm and our destiny as subjects of a divine order. Thus, from the presentiment of the sublime, Kant extracts the ultimate ground of his faith in a supreme being, and this is for him the most important value that aesthetic experience can convey.

Schiller's *Briefe über die ästhetische Erziehung des Menschen* (1795; *On the Aesthetic Education of Man*), inspired by Kant, develops further the theory of the disinterested character of the aesthetic. Schiller argues that through this disinterested quality aesthetic experience becomes the true vehicle of moral and political education, providing human beings both with the self-identity that is their fulfilment and with the institutions that enable them to flourish: "What is man before beauty cajoles from him a delight in things for their own sake, or the serenity of form tempers the savagery of life? A monotonous round of ends, a constant vacillation of judgement; self-seeking, and yet without a self; lawless, yet without freedom; a slave, and yet to no rule."

Treatises on beauty were common in the 18th century, one of the most famous being *The Analysis of Beauty* (1753) by the painter William Hogarth, which introduces the theory that beauty is achieved through the "serpentine line".

The view that art is expression also emerged during this period. Rousseau put forth the theory of the arts as forms of emotional expression in an essay dealing with the origin of languages. This theory, regarded as providing the best possible explanation of the power of music, was widely adopted. Treatises on musical expression also proliferated during the late 18th century. One illustrative example is James Beattie's *Essay on Poetry and Music as They Affect the Mind* (1776), in which the author rejects the view of music as a representational (imitative) art form and argues that expression is the true source of musical excellence. Another example is provided by Diderot in his didactic novel *Le neveu de Rameau* (1761; *Rameau's Nephew*).

Art Criticism

At the beginning of the 18th century, the Englishman Jonathan Richardson became the first person to develop a system of art criticism. In *An Essay on the Whole Art of Criticism as It Relates to Painting* and *An Argument in Behalf of the Science of a Connoisseur* (both 1719), he developed a practical system of critical evaluation that anticipated the utilitarian calculus of the English moral philosopher Jeremy Bentham. Establishing a hierarchy of values from 1 to 20 – "sublimity" being the peak of artistic perfection – he suggested that criticism is merely a matter of ratings.

In the mid-18th century, Baumgarten, in creating the discipline of aesthetics, giving it a place as a separate philosophical study, afforded new criteria for critical judgement. In his most important work, *Aesthetica* (1750–58), he sets forth the difference between a moral and exclusively aesthetic understanding of art, a way of thinking that can be regarded as the major difference between a traditional and modern approach to art making and art criticism. Later in the century, as we have seen, Kant's *Critique of Judgement* introduced the ideas of a disinterested judgement of taste and the purposiveness of artistic form.

Parallel with these developments, art history also came into its own in the mid-18th century in the person of the German historian-critic Johann Winckelmann, who took full advantage of the new formal parameters allowed by aesthetics. Generally regarded as the first systematic art historian, he was by training an archaeologist with a deep knowledge of antiquity. In works such as *Gedancken über die Nachahmung der griechischen wercke in der Mahlerey und Bildhauer-Kunst* (1765; *Reflections on the Painting and Sculpture of the Greeks*) and *Geschichte der Kunst des Alterthums* (1764; *The History of Ancient Art*), Winckelmann idealized Greek art for its "noble simplicity and quiet grandeur", and in the process he helped bring about the rise of neoclassicism in the arts. More important for art history and art criticism, he established a model for art-historical development based on these ancient foundations. He espoused the idea of a period style, whereby a visual idea slowly but surely unfolded in an organic sequence of artistic events, growing from a primitive seed to a sturdy plant, which flowered and then decayed. More particularly, an initial "antique" (or archaic) style matured into a sublime style, whose gains were consolidated and refined into a beautiful style, which eventually collapsed into a decadent, anticlimactic, academic style of imitation. Winckelmann thought this pattern repeated in antiquity and in modern painting.

But, just as some critics in the 17th century sought to expose the lawless alternatives to standing artistic models, Richardson's and Winckelmann's enlightened efforts to put art criticism on an objective basis were opposed by another Enlightenment figure, Diderot. Aware of the increasingly "romantic", unruly, informal – seemingly methodless – character of art, Diderot was concerned with its moral message. He perceived that art seemed to have fewer and fewer clear – let alone absolute and rational – rules, which implied that it could be evaluated in a more personal, even irrational, altogether idiosyncratic way. The looser the rules, the more relative the standards by which art could be judged. He saw that the new freedom of art allowed for a new freedom of criticism. In a sense, unconventional art needed an unconventional criticism to give it a raison d'être.

Diderot reviewed Salons from 1759 to 1781. He wrote a book-length examination of the Salon of 1767, in which he not only assesses contemporary art but attempts to clarify its principles; he shows that philosophical evaluation and empirical documentation are inseparable in art criticism.

The pages Diderot devotes to seven landscape paintings by Horace Vernet are particularly exemplary of his approach. Diderot describes Vernet's landscapes with great precision, as though he were walking through them. In addition, Diderot praises Vernet because his landscapes appealed to his mind as well as his emotions. This double demand – that the critic be responsive to the spirit of a work of art so that he is able to find the truth in it – has been the essential task of the critic ever since. It also became apparent that, if successful, criticism just might elevate a subjective preference into a canonical art. Artists have always been threatened by destructive criticism. But constructive criticism, showing how emotionally rich and intellectually meaningful his art was, could give an artist immortality.

Theories of Education: Locke to Rousseau

The Enlightenment's emphasis on reason influenced the theory and practice of education in the 18th century and afterward. The writings of Locke were especially significant, both for his general theory of knowledge and for his ideas on the education of youth. In *An Essay Concerning Human Understanding*, Locke argued that ideas come from two "fountains" of experience: sensation, through which perceptions are conveyed into the mind, and reflection, whereby the mind works with perceptions, forming ideas. Locke thought of the mind as a "blank tablet" prior to experience, but he did not claim that all minds are equal. He insisted, in *Some Thoughts Concerning Education* (1693), that some minds have a greater intellectual potential than others.

For education, Locke's empiricism meant that learning comes about only through experience. Education, which Locke felt should address both character and intellect, is therefore best achieved by providing the pupil with examples of proper thought and behaviour, by training the child to witness and share in the habits of virtue that are part of the conventional wisdom of the rational and practical man. Virtue should be cultivated through proper upbringing, preparatory to "studies" in the strict sense. The child first learns to do through activity and, later, comes to understand what has been done. The intimacy between conduct and thinking is best illustrated in the title of Locke's *Of the Conduct of the Understanding,* written as an appendix to his *Essay.* There it is clear that understanding comes only with careful cultivation and practice; this means that understanding not only involves conduct but is itself a kind of conduct. If the child and the tutor share a kind of conduct, then the child will have learned the habits of character and mind that are necessary for education to continue.

Like Locke, the Italian philosopher Giambattista Vico believed that human beings are not innately rational; he argued, however, that understanding results not from sense perception but through imaginative reconstruction. Vico was professor of rhetoric at the University of Naples from 1699 to 1741. His best-known work is *Scienza nuova* (1725; *New Science*), in which he advanced the idea that human beings in their origins are not rational, like philosophers, but imaginative, like poets. The relation between imagination and reason in *New Science* is suggestive for educational theory: civilized human beings are rational, yet they came to be that way without knowing what they were doing; the first humans created institutions literally without reason, as poets do who follow their imagination rather than their reason. Only later, after they have become rational, can human beings understand what they are and what they have made. Vico's idea that early humans were nonrational and childlike prefigured Rousseau's primitivism and his conception of human development (see below).

Vico's *De Nostri Temporis Studiorum Ratione* (1709; *On the Study Methods of Our Time*) defended a humanistic programme of studies against what he took to be an encroachment by the rationalistic system of the French philosopher René Descartes on the educational methods proper for youth. Vico asserted that the influential Cartesian treatise *The Port-Royal Logic,* by Antoine Arnauld and Pierre Nicole, inverted the natural course by which children learn by insisting on a training in logic at the beginning of the educational process. He argued, instead, that young people need to have their mental powers developed and nourished by promoting their memories through the study of languages and enhancing their imaginations through reading poets, historians, and orators.

Young minds, he stated, first need the kind of reasoning that common sense provides. Common sense, acquired through the experience of poets, orators, and people of prudence, teaches the young the importance of working with probabilities prior to an education in logic. To train youth first in logic in the absence of common sense is to teach them to make judgements before they have the knowledge necessary to do so. Vico's aim was to emphasize the importance of practical judgement in education, an echo of the ideals of Locke and a prefiguring of Rousseau.

A contrasting contemporary influence was exerted by the subjective, mystical, zealous devoutness of Pietism. For the

Pietists, all education was subordinated to a simple Christian faith. This concept was realized mainly by the German religious leader and educator August Hermann Francke. In his school, the children were to be led to a living knowledge of God and Christ and to a rightly accomplished Christianity. "True godliness and Christian wisdom" were the aims – true godliness meaning a pious, moral, devout life, and Christian wisdom referring to an ability to work hard according to the Protestant ethic. Francke's style of education was consistent with this aim: the corrupted wilfulness of man must be broken, not through severe punishment but through "loving reproaches", a close supervision of the pupils, and a schooled and regimented care of the spirit. It was an all-encompassing education, Francke promoting scientific subjects, lessons in manual skills, planned field trips, and even the reading of newspapers in the classroom.

As early as 1699 Francke had conceived the idea of a school for children who were not meant for scholarship but who could serve usefully in commercial pursuits or administration. Julius Hecker, who became a teacher in Francke's *Pädagogium* was summoned by Frederick I of Prussia to Berlin in 1739, and established a *Realschule,* or "realist school", there, designed to prepare youth for the Pietistic and Calvinistic ideal of hard work and, especially, for the new technical and industrial age that was already dawning in countries such as England and France. Godliness was to be combined with a realistic and practical way of life. His school included, among other things, classes for architecture, building, manufacturing, commerce, and trade. As similar institutions were gradually opened in other cities, Hecker's school eventually became one of the main types of German secondary education.

Rousseau and his followers were intrigued by a third ideal more elusive than Enlightenment rationalism or Pietism:

naturalism. In his *Discourse on the Origin of Inequality*, Rousseau distinguished between "natural man" (man as formed by nature) and "social man" (man as shaped by society). He argued that good education should develop the nature of man. Yet Rousseau found that man has not one nature but several: man originally lived in a "pure state of nature" but was altered by changes beyond his control and took on a different nature; this nature, in turn, was changed as man became social. The creation of the arts and sciences caused man to become "less pure", more artificial, and egoistic, and man's egoistic nature prevents him from regaining the simplicity of original human nature.

Émile; ou de l'éducation (1762; *Émile; or, On Education*), Rousseau's major work on education, describes an attempt to educate a simple and pure natural child for life in a world from which social man is estranged. Émile is removed from society at large to a little society inhabited only by the child and his tutor. Social elements enter the little society through the tutor's knowledge when the tutor thinks Émile can learn something from them. Rousseau's aim throughout is to show how a natural education, unlike the artificial and formal education of society, enables Émile to become social, moral, and rational while remaining true to his original nature. Because Émile is educated to be a man, not a priest, a soldier, or an attorney, he will be able to do what is needed in any situation.

The first book of *Émile* describes the period from birth to learning to speak. The most important thing for the healthy and natural development of the child at this age is that he learn to use his physical powers, especially the sense organs. The teacher must pay special attention to distinguishing between the real needs of the child and his whims and fancies. The second book covers the time from the child's learning to speak to the age of 12. Games and other forms of amusement should be allowed at this age, and the child should by no means be overtaxed by scholarly instruction at too early an age. The child Émile is to learn through experience, not through words. The third book is devoted to the ages from 12 to 15. This is the time of learning, not from books, of course, but from the "book of the world". Émile must gain knowledge in concrete situations provided by his tutor. He learns a trade, among other things. He studies science, not by receiving instruction in its facts but by making the instruments necessary to solve scientific problems of a practical sort. Not until the age of 15, described in the fourth book, does Émile study the history of man and social experience and thus encounter the world of morals and conscience. During this stage Émile is on the threshold of social maturity and the "age of reason". Finally, he marries and, his education over, tells his tutor that the only chains he knows are those of necessity and that he will thus be free anywhere on Earth.

The final book describes the education of Sophie, the girl who marries Émile. In Rousseau's view, the education of girls was to be different from that of boys. According to Rousseau, a woman should be the centre of the family, a housewife, and a mother. She should strive to please her husband, concern herself more than he with having a good reputation, and be satisfied with a simple religion of the emotions. Because her intellectual education is not of the essence, "her studies must all be on the practical side."

At the close of *Émile,* Rousseau cannot assure the reader that Émile and Sophie will be happy when they live apart from the tutor; the outcome of his experiment is in doubt, even in his own mind. Even so, probably no other writer in modern times has inspired as many generations as did Rousseau. His dramatic portrayal of the estrangement of natural man from society jolted and influenced such contemporary thinkers as

Kant and continues to intrigue philosophers and social scientists. His emphasis on understanding the child's nature had a profound influence by creating interest in the study of child development, inspiring the work of 19th- and 20th-century psychologists such as G. Stanley Hall and Jean Piaget.

The Sensationists and the Rousseauists

Contemporary with Rousseau and paralleling in some ways the thought of both Rousseau and Locke were a group of French writers known as the sensationists, or, sometimes, the sensationist psychologists. One of them was Étienne Bonnot de Condillac, who, along with Voltaire, may be said to have introduced Locke's philosophy to France and established it there.

In the *Traité des sensations* (1754; *Treatise on Sensations*) Condillac dramatized the idea that man is nothing but what he acquires, beginning with sensory experience. Condillac rejected the notion of innate ideas, arguing instead that all faculties are acquired. The educational significance of this idea is found in Condillac's *Essai sur l'origine des connaissances humaines* (1746; *An Essay on the Origin of Human Knowledge*), where he writes of a "method of analysis", by which the mind observes "in a successive order the qualities of an object, so as to give them in the mind the simultaneous order in which they exist". The idea that there is a natural order which the mind can learn to follow demonstrates Condillac's naturalism along with his sensationism. Condillac does not begin his work *La logique* (1789; *Logic*) with axioms or principles; rather, he writes, "we shall begin by observing the lessons which nature gives us." He explains that the method of analysis is akin to the way that children learn when they acquire knowledge without the help of adults. Nature will tell man how to know, if he will but listen as children "naturally" do. Thus the way in which ideas and faculties originate is the way of logic, and to communicate a truth is to follow the order in which ideas come from the senses.

Claude-Adrien Helvétius, a countryman of Condillac's who professed much the same philosophy, was perhaps even more insistent that all human beings lack any intellectual endowment at birth and that despite differing physical constitutions each person has the potential for identical passions and ideas. What makes people different in later life are differing experiences. Hypothetically, two people brought up with the same chance experiences and education would be exactly the same. From this it followed, in education, that the teacher must attempt to control the environment of the child and guide his instruction step by step.

While Rousseau left behind no disciples in the sense of a definite academic community, hardly a single theorist of the late 18th century or afterward could avoid the influence of his ideas. One of these was the German Johann Bernhard Basedow, who agreed with Rousseau's enthusiasm for nature, with his emphasis on manual and practical skills, and with his demand for practical experience rather than empty verbalism. The teacher, in Basedow's view, should take pains over the clearness of the lesson and make use of the enjoyment of games: "It is possible to arrange nearly all playing of children in an instructive way." In another respect, however, the contrast between Rousseau and Basedow could not be sharper; Basedow tended to force premature learning and overload a child's capabilities. He promoted, in general, a pedagogic hothouse atmosphere.

Also influenced by Rousseau's educational ideas was Kant. He dealt specifically with pedagogy only within a lecture he gave as holder of the chair of philosophy in Königsberg; the main features of the lecture were collected in a short work, *Über Pädagogik* (1803; *On Pedagogy*). In it he asserted, "A man can only become a man through education. He is nothing more than what education makes him." Education should discipline the child and make him cultured and moral; its aim is ultimately the creation of a happier humankind. In general, Kant agreed with Rousseau's education according to nature; but, from his ethical posture, he insisted that restraints be put on the child's passionate impulses and that the child even be taught specific maxims of conduct. The child must learn to rule himself and come to terms with the twin necessities of liberty and constraint, the product of which is true freedom. Children, he wrote, should be educated, not with reference to the present conditions of things, but rather with regard to a possibly improved state of the human race – that is, according to the ideal of humanity and its entire destiny.

National Education and the State

Although Rousseau himself was generally concerned with humanity as such in works such as *The Social Contract* and *Émile,* his *The Government of Poland* (1782) laid out a proposal for an education with a national basis.

From the very beginning of the Enlightenment there were nationalistic tendencies to be seen in varying shades. The real starting point of national pedagogic movements was in France, where the philosophes and rationalists such as Voltaire and Diderot emphasized the development of the individual through state education as a means of creating critical, detached, responsible citizens. For the Marquis de Condorcet, people were by nature good and capable of never-ending perfection, and the goal of education was to be the "general, gradually increasing perfection of man". He drafted a democratic and liberal but at the same time somewhat socialist concept of school policy: there should be a uniform structure of public education and equal chances for all; ability and attainment should be the only standards for selection and careers; and private interests should be prevented from having influence in the educational system. Condorcet wanted "to show the world at last a nation in which freedom and equality for all was an actuality".

Many of the Rousseauists were nationalistic in a somewhat different way. They believed in a kind of "moral patriotism". They distrusted state-controlled nationalism and favoured instead a virtuous, patriotic citizen who experienced spontaneous feelings for his nation. Proper development in the family setting and in school would lead to the mastery of everyday situations and would naturally lay the foundations for this true nationalism.

Some of the French revolutionists, particularly Maximilien de Robespierre and Louis Saint-Just, who were associated with the Reign of Terror (1793–4), were concerned with an education for the revolutionary state, an education marked by an enmity toward the idea of scholarship for its own sake and by state control, collectivism, the stressing of absolute equality, and the complete integration of all.

The benevolent or enlightened despotism of the 18th century in Russia, Austria and elsewhere limited improvements in education to middle-class persons useful in civil service and other areas of state administration. Frederick II of Prussia issued general school regulations (1763) establishing compulsory schooling for boys and girls from five to 13 or 14 years of age His minister Freiherr von Zedlitz founded a chair of pedagogy at Halle (1779) and generally planned for the improved education of teachers; he supported the founding of new schools and the centralization of school administration under an *Oberschulkollegium,* or national board of education (1787); and one of his colleagues, Friedrich Gedike, was instrumental in introducing the school-leaving examination for university entrance, the *Abitur,* which still exists.

There was a guarded though increasingly liberal attempt by benevolent despots to nationalize and expand education. In Russia, a system of state-owned schools was started by Peter the Great as a state organization for purposes of administration and for the development of mining and industry. He created mathematical, navigation, artillery, and engineering schools for utilitarian purposes. These utilitarian, secular, and scientific characteristics became the dominant features of Russian education, but because of policy changes after Peter's death, a national system of education did not develop. A second attempt at nationalizing education in Russia was made by Catherine II, who issued a statute which promised a two-year course in minor schools in every district town and a five-year course in major schools in every provincial town. Catherinian schools were also to be utilitarian, scientific, and secular.

A third nationalizing attempt was made by Alexander I, influenced by the disintegration of the serf system, the development of industry and commerce, and the ideas of the French Revolution. Also utilitarian, parochial schools in rural areas were to instruct the peasantry in reading, writing, arithmetic, and elements of agriculture, while district schools in urban areas and provincial schools were to give instruction in subjects necessary for civil servants

In England the development of a "national" education was influenced not by a political but by an industrial revolution. While theorists such as Adam Smith, Thomas Paine, and Thomas Malthus proposed state organization of elementary schooling, even they wanted to see limited state influence. Not until 1802 did Parliament intervene in the development of education, when the Health and Morals of Apprentices Act required employers to educate apprentices in basic mathematics, writing, and reading.

The reluctance on the part of the state induced several philanthropists to form educational societies, principally for the education of the poor. The educators Andrew Bell and Joseph Lancaster also played a major role in progress toward an elementary-school system. Realizing that the root of the problem lay in the lack of teachers and in the lack of money to hire assistants they developed the so-called monitorial system (also called the Lancasterian system), whereby a teacher used his pupils to teach one another. The system and the publicity connected with it expanded the efforts toward mass education.

5

ECONOMICS AND INDUSTRIAL REVOLUTION

The Growth of the Social Sciences

The interests of social philosophers in the Enlightenment was not restricted to a philosophical, much less a scientific, understanding of humanity and society. The influence of the Enlightenment on the social sciences could be seen, first, in the spreading ideal of a science of society, an ideal fully as widespread by the 18th century as the ideal of a physical science. Second, there was a rising awareness of the multiplicity and variety of human experience in the world. Ethnocentrism and parochialism, as states of mind, were more and more difficult for educated people to maintain given the immense amount of information about – or, more important, interest in – non-Western peoples, the results of trade and exploration. Third, there was the spreading sense of the social or cultural character of human behaviour in society – that is, its purely historical or conventional, rather than biological, basis. A science of society, in short, was no mere appendage of biology but was

Isaac Newton, portrait by Sir Godfrey Kneller, 1689

René Descartes

Portrait of John Locke, by Herman Verelst, 1689

PHILOSOPHIÆ

NATURALIS

PRINCIPIA

MATHEMATICA.

Autore *JS. NEWTON*, *Trin. Coll. Cantab. Soc.* Matheseos
Professore *Lucasiano*, & Societatis Regalis Sodali.

IMPRIMATUR·
S. PEPYS, *Reg. Soc.* PRÆSES.
Julii 5. 1686:

LONDINI,
Jussu *Societatis Regiæ* ac Typis *Josephi Streater.* Prostant Vena-
les apud *Sam. Smith* ad insignia Principis *Walliæ* in Cœmiterio
D. *Pauli,* aliosq; nonnullos Bibliopolas. *Anno* MDCLXXXVII.

Title page from Isaac Newton's De Philosophiae Naturalis Principia
Mathematica (1686; Mathematical Principles of Natural Philosophy)

Voltaire, bronze by Jean-Antoine Houdon

Rousseau, drawing in pastels by Maurice-Quentin de La Tour, 1753

Denis Diderot by Louis-Michel van Loo, 1767

Bill of Rights

John Wilkes, engraving from a manifesto commemorating his fight against general warrants and for the liberty of the press, 1768

Declaration of Independence in Congress, at the Independence Hall, Philadelphia, July 4th, 1776
by John Trumbull, 1819

Thomas Paine, detail of a portrait by John Wesley Jarvis

Edmund Burke, detail of an oil painting from the studio of Sir Joshua Reynolds, 1771

Mary Wollstonecraft, detail of an oil painting on canvas
by John Opie, *c.* 1797

Adam Smith, paste medallion
by James Tassie, 1787

Immanuel Kant

instead a distinct discipline, or set of disciplines, with its own distinctive subject matter.

To these may be added two other very important contributions of the 17th and 18th centuries, each of great theoretical importance. The first was the idea of structure. First seen in the writings of philosophers such as Thomas Hobbes, John Locke, and Jean-Jacques Rousseau with reference to the political structure of the state, it had spread by the mid-18th century to the economic writings of the physiocrats (the champions of economic laissez-faire) and the Scottish economist Adam Smith. The idea of structure can also be seen in certain works relating to humans' psychology and, at opposite reach, to the whole of civil society. The ideas of structure that were borrowed from both the physical and biological sciences were fundamental to the conceptions of political, economic, and social structure that took shape in the 17th and 18th centuries. These conceptions of structure have in many instances, subject only to minor changes, come down to contemporary social science.

The second major theoretical idea was that of developmental change. Its ultimate roots in Western thought, like those indeed of the whole idea of structure, go back to the Greeks, if not earlier. But it is in the 18th century, above all others, that the philosophy of developmentalism took shape, forming a preview, so to speak, of the social evolutionism of the next century. What was said by writers such as the Marquis de Condorcet, Rousseau, and Smith was that the present is an outgrowth of the past, the result of a long line of development in time, and, furthermore, a line of development that has been caused, not by God or fortuitous factors, but by conditions and causes immanent in human society. Despite a fairly widespread belief that the idea of social development is a product of the prior discovery of biological evolution, the facts are the reverse. Well before any clear idea of genetic speciation existed in European biology, there was a very clear idea of what might be called social speciation – that is, the emergence of one institution from another in time and of the whole differentiation of function and structure that goes with this emergence.

These and other seminal ideas were contained for the most part in writings whose primary function was to attack the existing order of government and society in western Europe. Another way of putting the matter is to say that they were clear and acknowledged parts of political and social idealism – using that word in its largest sense. Hobbes, Locke, Rousseau, and Smith, as well as the French philosopher Montesquieu and others, had a vivid and energizing sense of the ideal – ideal state, ideal economy, ideal civil society – and were committed to visions of the good or ideal society. Their interest in the "natural" – that is, natural morality, religion, economy, or education, in contrast to the merely conventional and historically derived – sprang as much from the desire to hold a glass up to a surrounding society that they disliked as from any dispassionate urge simply to find out what humans and society are made of.

It was the weakening of the old order, or European society, under the twin blows of the French Revolution and the Industrial Revolution that brought the break-up of the old order – an order that had rested on kinship, land, social class, religion, local community, and monarchy. For a large number of social philosophers and social scientists, in all spheres, those changes were regarded as nothing less than cataclysmic. An indication of contemporary perceptions of change is the large number of words that came into being in the final decade or two of the 18th century and the first quarter of the 19th. Among these are: industry, industrialist, democracy, class, middle class, ideology, intellectual, rationalism, humanitarian, atomistic, masses, commercialism, proletariat, collectivism, equalitarian, liberal, conservative, scientist, utilitarian, bureaucracy, capitalism, and crisis. Some of these words were invented; others reflect new and very different meanings given to old ones. All alike bear witness to the transformed character of the European social landscape as it appeared to the leading minds of the age. And all these words bear witness too to the emergence of new social philosophies and the social sciences as they are known today.

The major themes that were later to emerge in social thought were almost the direct results of the great democratic and industrial revolutions. First, there was the great increase in population. Between 1750 and 1850 the population of Europe went from 140,000,000 to 266,000,000. Thomas Malthus, in his famous *Essay on Population*, first stressed that unchecked growth could only upset the traditional balance between population and food supply. Not all social scientists in the century shared his pessimistic view but few if any were indifferent to the impact of explosive increase in population on economy, government, and society.

Second, there was the condition of labour. The wrenching of large numbers of people from the older and protective contexts of village, guild, parish, and family, and their massing in the new centres of industry, forming slums, living in common squalor and wretchedness, their wages generally below the cost of living, their families growing larger, their standard of living becoming lower, as it seemed – all of this is a frequent theme in the social thought of the century.

Third, there was the transformation of property. Not only was more and more property to be seen as industrial – manifest in the factories, business houses, and workshops of the period – but also the very nature of property was changing. Whereas for most of the history of humanity property had been "hard" –

visible in concrete possessions such as land and money – now the more intangible kinds of property such as shares of stock, negotiable equities of all kinds, and bonds were assuming ever greater influence in the economy. This led, as was early realized, to the dominance of financial interests, to speculation, and to a general widening of the gulf between the propertied and the masses. The change in the character of property made easier the concentration of property, the accumulation of immense wealth in the hands of a relative few, and, not least, the possibility of economic domination of politics and culture. Starting with the conservative statesman Edmund Burke one finds both conservatives and liberals looking at the impact of this change in analogous ways.

Fourth, there was urbanization – the sudden increase in the number of towns and cities in western Europe, and the increase in the number of people living in the historic towns and cities. Whereas in earlier centuries, the city had been regarded almost uniformly as a setting of civilization, culture, and freedom of mind, now one found more and more writers aware of the other side of cities: the atomization of human relationships, broken families, the sense of the mass, of anonymity, alienation, and disrupted values. Sociology particularly among the social sciences turned its attention to the problems of urbanization.

Fifth, there was technology. With the spread of mechanization, first in the factories and then in agriculture, social thinkers could see possibilities of a rupture of the historic relation between individual human beings, between humans and nature, and even between humans and God. To some thinkers, technology seemed to lead to the dehumanization of the worker and to a new kind of tyranny over human life.

Sixth, there was the factory system. Along with urbanization and spreading mechanization, the system of work whereby masses of workers left home and family to work long hours in the factories became a major theme of social thought as well as of social reform.

Seventh, and finally, mention should be made of the development of political masses – that is, the slow but inexorable widening of the franchise and electorate, through which ever larger numbers of persons became aware of themselves as voters and participants in the political process. This too is a major theme in social thought, to be seen most luminously perhaps in the French political scientist Alex de Tocqueville's *Democracy in America*, a classic written in the 1830s that took not merely America but democracy everywhere as its subject.

It was these great changes, all of which began in the Enlightenment, that wrought the changing ideologies of the 19th century: the liberal view of society was overwhelmingly democratic, capitalist, industrial, and, of course, individualistic; conservatives, beginning with Burke, disliked both democracy and industrialism, preferring the kind of tradition, authority, and civility that had been, in their minds, displaced by the two revolutions.

These changes would result not only in new ideologies, but also in new disciplines. In the 1820s, the French philosopher Auguste Comte called for a new science, one whose subject would be human beings as social animals. He assuredly had but a single, encompassing science of society in mind – not a congeries of disciplines, each concerned with some single aspect of humans' behaviour in society. It was, however, the opposite tendency of specialization or differentiation that won out. By the end of the 19th century not one but several distinct, competitive social sciences – economics, political science, cultural anthropology, sociology – were to be found.

From Mercantalism to Commercial Capitalism

It is usual to describe the earliest stages of capitalism as mercantilism, a system in which governments regulated national economies to augment state power. The word "mercantilism" denoted the central importance of the merchant overseas traders who rose to prominence in 17th- and 18th-century England, Germany, and the Low Countries. In numerous pamphlets, these merchants defended the principle that their trading activities buttressed the interest of the sovereign power, even when this required sending "treasure" (bullion) abroad. As the pamphleteers explained, treasure used in this way became itself a commodity in foreign trade, in which, as the 17th-century merchant Thomas Mun wrote, "we must ever observe this rule; to sell more to strangers than we consume of theirs in value."

For all its trading mentality, mercantilism was only partially a market-coordinated system. The Scottish philosopher Adam Smith complained bitterly about the government monopolies that granted exclusive trading rights to groups such as the British, Dutch, and French East India companies, and modern commentators have emphasized the degree to which mercantilist economies relied on regulated, not free, prices and wages. The economic society that Smith described in *An Inquiry into the Nature and Causes of the Wealth of Nations* in 1776 is much closer to modern society.

Smith's society is recognizable as capitalist precisely because of the prominence of those elements that had been absent in its mercantilist form. For example, with few exceptions, the production and distribution of all goods and services were entrusted to market forces rather than to the rules and regulations that had abounded a century earlier. The level of wages was likewise mainly determined by the interplay of the supply of, and the demand for, labour – not by the rulings of local magistrates. A company's earnings were exposed to competition rather than protected by government monopoly.

Perhaps of greater importance in perceiving Smith's world as capitalist as well as market oriented is its clear division of society into an economic realm and a political realm. The role of government had been gradually narrowed until Smith could describe its duties as consisting of only three functions: (1) the provision of national defence; (2) the protection of each member of society from the injustice or oppression of any other; and (3) the erection and maintenance of those public works and public institutions (including education) that would not repay the expense of any private enterpriser, although they might "do much more than repay it" to society as a whole. And if the role of government in daily life had been delimited, that of commerce had been expanded. The accumulation of capital had come to be recognized as the driving engine of the system. The expansion of "capitals" – Smith's term for firms – was the determining power by which the market system was launched on its historic course. Smith also emphasized the role of individuals over that of the state and generally attacked mercantilism. He argued that state policies often were less effective in advancing social welfare than were the self-interested acts of individuals.

One further attribute of the emerging system is the tearing apart of the formerly seamless tapestry of social coordination. Under capitalism two realms of authority existed where there had formerly been only one – a realm of political governance for such purposes as war or law and order and a realm of economic governance over the processes of production and distribution. Each realm was largely shielded from the reach of the other. The capitalists who dominated the market system were not automatically entitled to governing power, and the members of government were not entrusted with decisions as to what goods should be produced or how social rewards should be distributed. This new dual structure brought with it two consequences of immense importance. The first was a limitation of political power that proved of very great importance in establishing democratic forms of government. The second was the need for a new kind of analysis intended to clarify the workings of this new semi-independent realm within the larger social order. As a result, the emergence of capitalism gave rise to the discipline of economics.

Political Economy

Political economy emerged as a distinct field of study in the mid-18th century when Smith, the Scottish philosopher David Hume, and the French economist François Quesnay began to approach this study in systematic rather than piecemeal terms. They took a secular approach, refusing to explain the distribution of wealth and power in terms of God's will and instead appealing to political, economic, technological, natural, and social factors and the complex interactions between them.

Hume's *Political Discourses* (1741–2) did not formulate a complete system of economic theory, as did Smith, but Hume introduced several of the new ideas around which the "classical economics" of the 18th century was built. His main contentions were: that wealth consists not of money but of commodities; that the amount of money in circulation should be kept related to the amount of goods in the market; that a low rate of interest is a symptom not of superabundance of money but of booming trade; that no nation can go on exporting only for bullion; that each nation has special advantages of raw materials, climate, and skill, so that a free interchange of products (with some exceptions) is mutually beneficial; and that poor nations impoverish the rest just because they do not produce enough to be able to take much part in that exchange. He welcomed advance beyond an agricultural to an industrial economy as a precondition of any but the barer forms of civilization.

The system of political economy of Quesnay, consulting physician to Louis XV, was summed up in his *Tableau économique* (1758), which diagrammed the relationship between the different economic classes and sectors of society and the flow of payments between them. Quesnay developed the notion of economic equilibrium, a concept frequently used as a point of departure for subsequent economic analysis. Of explicit importance was his identification of capital as *avances* – that is, as a stock of wealth that had to be accumulated in advance of production. His classification of these *avances* distinguished between fixed and circulating capital.

As the originator of the term "laissez-faire" ("allow to do"), Quesnay believed, in opposition to the then-dominant French mercantilists, that high taxes, high internal tolls, and high barriers to imported goods were the cause of the grinding French poverty he saw around him. Quesnay wanted Louis XV to deregulate trade and to slash taxes so that France could start to emulate wealthier Britain. Quesnay believed that his methodology and principles of policy represented a divinely appointed economic order. He was, indeed, one of the originators of the 19th-century doctrine of the harmony of class interests and of the related doctrine that maximum social satisfaction occurs under free competition.

Smith's landmark work – *The Wealth of Nations* – conveys in its title the broad scope of early political economic analysis. Although the field itself was new, some of the ideas and approaches it drew upon were centuries old. It was influenced by the individualist orientation of Hobbes and Locke, the realpolitik of the Italian political theorist Niccolò Machiavelli, and the inductive method of scientific reasoning invented by the English philosopher Francis Bacon.

Adam Smith and *The Wealth of Nations*

After more than two centuries, Adam Smith remains a towering figure in the history of economic thought. Known primarily for a single work – *The Wealth of Nations*, the first comprehensive system of political economy – he is more properly regarded as a social philosopher whose economic writings constitute only the capstone to an overarching view of political and social evolution.

In 1759 Smith published his first work, *The Theory of Moral Sentiments*. Didactic, exhortative, and analytic by turns, it lays the psychological foundation on which *The Wealth of Nations* was later to be built. In it Smith described the principles of "human nature", which, together with Hume and the other leading philosophers of his time, he took as a universal and unchanging datum from which social institutions, as well as social behaviour, could be deduced.

One question in particular interested Smith in *The Theory of Moral Sentiments*: the source of the ability to form moral judgements, including judgements on one's own behaviour, in the face of the seemingly overriding passions for self-preservation and self-interest. Smith's answer is the presence within each of us of an "inner man" who plays the role of the "impartial spectator", approving or condemning our own and others' actions with a voice impossible to disregard. The thesis of the impartial spectator, however, conceals a more important aspect of the book. Smith saw humans as creatures driven by passions and at the same time self-regulated by their ability to reason and – no less important – by their capacity for sympathy. This duality serves both to pit individuals against one another and to provide them with the rational and moral faculties to create institutions by which the internecine struggle can be mitigated and even turned to the common good. He wrote in his *Moral Sentiments* the famous observation that he was to repeat later in *The Wealth of Nations*: that self-seeking men are often "led by an invisible hand . . . without knowing it, without intending it, [to] advance the interest of the society".

Despite its renown, *The Wealth of Nations* is in fact a continuation of the philosophical theme begun in *The Theory of Moral Sentiments*. The ultimate problem to which Smith addresses himself is how the inner struggle between the passions and the "impartial spectator" – explicated in *Moral Sentiments* in terms of the single individual – works its effects in the larger arena of history itself, both in the long-term evolution of society and in terms of the immediate characteristics of the stage of history typical of Smith's own day.

The answer to this problem enters in Book V, in which Smith outlines the four main stages of organization through which society is impelled, unless blocked by wars, deficiencies of resources, or bad policies of government: the original "rude" state of hunters, a second stage of nomadic agriculture, a third stage of feudal, or manorial, "farming", and a fourth and final stage of commercial interdependence.

It should be noted that each of these stages is accompanied by institutions suited to its needs. For example, in the age of the huntsman, "there is scarce any property . . . so there is seldom any established magistrate or any regular administration of justice." With the advent of flocks there emerges a more complex form of social organization, comprising not only "formidable" armies but the central institution of private property with its indispensable buttress of law and order as well. It is the very essence of Smith's thought that he recognized this institution, whose social usefulness he never doubted, as an instrument for the protection of privilege, rather than one to be justified in terms of natural law: "Civil government," he wrote, "so far as it is instituted for the security of property, is in reality instituted for the defence of the rich against the poor, or of those who have some property against those who have none at all." Finally, Smith describes the evolution through feudalism into a stage of society requiring new institutions, such as market-determined rather than guild-determined wages and free rather than government-constrained enterprise. This later became known as laissez-faire capitalism; Smith called it the system of perfect liberty.

The theory of historical evolution, although it is perhaps the binding conception of *The Wealth of Nations*, is subordinated within the work itself to a detailed description of how the "invisible hand" actually operates within the commercial, or final, stage of society. This becomes the focus of Books I and II, in which Smith undertakes to elucidate two questions. The first is how a system of perfect liberty, operating under the drives and constraints of human nature and intelligently designed institutions, will give rise to an orderly society. The question, which had already been considerably elucidated by earlier writers, required both an explanation of the underlying orderliness in the pricing of individual commodities and an explanation of the "laws" that regulated the division of the entire "wealth" of the nation (which Smith saw as its annual production of goods and services) among the three great claimant classes – labourers, landlords, and manufacturers.

This orderliness, as would be expected, was produced by the interaction of the two aspects of human nature, its response to its passions and its susceptibility to reason and sympathy. But whereas *The Theory of Moral Sentiments* had relied mainly on the presence of the "inner man" to provide the necessary restraints to private action, in *The Wealth of Nations* one finds an institutional mechanism that acts to reconcile the disruptive possibilities inherent in a blind obedience to the passions alone. This protective mechanism is competition, an arrangement by which the passionate desire for bettering one's condition – "a desire that comes with us from the womb, and never leaves us until we go into the grave" – is turned into a socially beneficial agency by pitting one person's drive for self-betterment against another's.

It is in the unintended outcome of this competitive struggle for self-betterment that the invisible hand regulating the economy shows itself, for Smith explains how mutual vying forces the prices of commodities down to their "natural" levels, which correspond to their costs of production. Moreover, by inducing labour and capital to move from less to more profitable occupations or areas, the competitive mechanism constantly restores prices to these "natural" levels despite short-run aberrations. Finally, by explaining that wages and rents and profits (the constituent parts of the costs of production) are themselves subject to this same discipline of self-interest and competition, Smith not only provided an ultimate rationale for these "natural" prices but also revealed an underlying orderliness in the distribution of income itself among workers, whose recompense was their wages; landlords, whose income was their rents; and manufacturers, whose reward was their profits.

Smith's analysis of the market as a self-correcting mechanism was impressive. But his purpose was more ambitious than to demonstrate the self-adjusting properties of the system. Rather, it was to show that, under the impetus of the acquisitive drive, the annual flow of national wealth could be seen to grow steadily.

Smith's explanation of economic growth, although not neatly assembled in one part of *The Wealth of Nations*, is quite clear. The core of it lies in his emphasis on the division of labour (itself an outgrowth of the "natural" propensity to trade) as the source of society's capacity to increase its productivity. But this all-important division of labour does not take place unaided. It can occur only after the prior accumulation of capital (or stock, as Smith calls it), which is used to pay the additional workers and to buy tools and machines.

The drive for accumulation, however, brings problems. The manufacturer who accumulates stock needs more labourers (since labour-saving technology has no place in Smith's scheme), and, in attempting to hire them, he bids up their wages above their "natural" price. Consequently, his profits begin to fall, and the process of accumulation is in danger of ceasing. But now there enters an ingenious mechanism for continuing the advance: in bidding up the price of labour, the manufacturer inadvertently sets into motion a process that increases the supply of labour, for "the demand for men, like that for any other commodity, necessarily regulates the production of men." Specifically, Smith had in mind the effect of higher wages in lessening child mortality. Under the influence of a larger labour supply, the wage rise is moderated and profits are maintained; the new supply of labourers offers a continuing opportunity for the manufacturer to introduce a further division of labour and thereby add to the system's growth.

Here then was a "machine" for growth – a machine that operated with all the reliability of the Newtonian system with which Smith was quite familiar. Unlike the Newtonian system, however, Smith's growth machine did not depend for its operation on the laws of nature alone. Human nature drove it, and human nature was a complex rather than a simple force. Thus, the wealth of nations would grow only if individuals, through their governments, did not inhibit this growth by catering to the pleas for special privilege that would prevent the competitive system from exerting its benign effect. Consequently, much of *The Wealth of Nations*, especially Book IV, is a polemic against the restrictive measures of the "mercantile system" that favoured monopolies at home and abroad. Smith's system of "natural liberty", he is careful to point out, accords with the best interests of all but will not be put into practice if government is entrusted to, or heeds, "the mean rapacity, the monopolizing spirit of merchants and manufacturers, who neither are, nor ought to be, the rulers of mankind".

The Wealth of Nations is therefore far from the ideological tract it is often supposed to be. Although Smith preached laissez-faire (with important exceptions), his argument was directed as much against monopoly as against government. Nor did he see the commercial system itself as wholly admirable. He wrote with discernment about the intellectual degradation of the worker in a society in which the division of labour has proceeded very far; by comparison with the alert intelligence of the husbandman, the specialized worker "generally becomes as stupid and ignorant as it is possible for a human being to become".

An Industrial Revolution

Smith was writing in an age of pre-industrial capitalism and seems to have had no real presentiment of the gathering Industrial Revolution, harbingers of which were visible in the great ironworks only a few miles from Edinburgh. Yet between the 1780s and the mid-19th century an unprecedented economic transformation took place that embraced the first stages of the great Industrial Revolution and a still more general expansion of commercial activity.

Heightened commercialization showed in a number of areas. Domestic manufacturing soared, as hundreds of thousands of rural producers worked full- or part-time to make thread and cloth, nails and tools under the sponsorship of urban merchants. Production expanded, leading by the end of the 18th century to a first wave of consumerism as rural wage earners began to purchase new kinds of commercially produced clothing, while urban middle-class families began to indulge in new tastes, such as uplifting books and educational toys for children.

In this context an outright industrial revolution took shape, led by Britain, which retained leadership in industrialization well past the middle of the 19th century. In 1840, British steam engines were generating 620,000 horsepower out of a European total of 860,000. Nevertheless, though delayed by the chaos of the French Revolution and Napoleonic Wars, many western European nations soon followed suit; thus by 1860 British steam-generated horsepower made up less than half the European total, with France, Germany, and Belgium gaining ground rapidly.

Aware of their head start, the British forbade the export of machinery, skilled workers, and manufacturing techniques. The British monopoly could not last forever, however, especially since some Britons saw profitable industrial opportunities abroad, while continental European businessmen sought to lure British know-how to their countries. Two Englishmen, William and John Cockerill, brought the Industrial Revolution to Belgium by developing machine shops at

Liège (*c.* 1807), and Belgium became the first country in continental Europe to be transformed economically. Like its English progenitor, the Belgian Industrial Revolution centred on iron, coal, and textiles.

France was more slowly and less thoroughly industrialized than either Britain or Belgium. While Britain was establishing its industrial leadership, France was immersed in its Revolution, and the uncertain political situation discouraged large investments in industrial innovations. By 1848 France had become an industrial power, but, despite great growth under the Second Empire, it remained behind Britain. Other European countries lagged even further behind.

Technological change soon spilled over from manufacturing into other areas; road and canal building, steam shipping, railways, and the telegraph. Alongside this was the use of new energy sources, including both fuels and motive power – such as coal, the steam engine, electricity, petroleum, and the internal-combustion engine – and the invention of new machines, such as the spinning jenny and the power loom that permitted increased production with a smaller expenditure of human energy, and the increasing application of science to industry. These technological changes made possible a tremendously increased use of natural resources and the mass production of manufactured goods.

Factories and the Division of Labour

The new organization of business and labour was intimately linked to the new technologies. Workers in the industrialized sectors laboured in factories rather than in scattered shops or homes. Steam and water power required a concentration of labour close to the power source. Concentration of labour also allowed new discipline and specialization, which increased productivity.

The English potter Josiah Wedgwood, for example, designed his pottery works at Etruria in England "with a view to the strictest economy of labour". His plant was laid out so that the pots were first formed and then passed through the painting room, the kiln room, the account room (for inventory control), and to storage before shipping. In potteries before this time, the workers could roam from one task to another; in Wedgwood's, the employees were assigned a particular post and worked at one task only. Out of 278 men, women, and children employed by Wedgwood in 1790, only five had no assigned post; the rest were specialists.

The new machinery was expensive, and businessmen setting up even modest factories had to accumulate substantial capital through partnerships, loans from banks, or joint-stock ventures. While relatively small firms still predominated, a tendency toward expansion of the business unit was already noteworthy. Urbanization was a vital result of growing commercialization and new industrial technology. Factory centres such as Manchester grew from villages into cities of hundreds of thousands in a few short decades.

In *The Wealth of Nations*, Smith had observed the benefits of the specialization of labour in the manufacture of pins:

> One man draws out the wire; another straights it; a third cuts it; a fourth points it; a fifth grinds it at the top for receiving the head; to make the head requires two or three distinct operations; to put it on is a peculiar business; to whiten the pin is another; it is even a trade by itself to put them into the paper; and the important business of making a pin is in this manner divided into about 18 distinct operations.

According to Smith, a single worker "could scarce, perhaps with his utmost industry, make one pin in a day, and certainly could not make 20". The new methods enabled a pin factory to turn out as many as 4,800 pins a day. Although earlier observers had noted this phenomenon, Smith's writings helped foster an awareness of industrial production and broaden its appeal.

Increases in productivity depended far more upon the rational organization of processes than upon individual skill. In 1797, for example, Eli Whitney, the American inventor of the cotton gin, proposed the manufacture of flintlocks with completely interchangeable parts, in contrast to the older method under which each gun was the individual product of a highly skilled gunsmith and each part was hand-fitted.

During the same period similar ideas were being tried out in Europe. In England Marc Brunel, a French-born inventor and engineer, established a production line to manufacture blocks (pulleys) for sailing ships, using the principles of division of labour and standardized parts. Brunel's machine tools were designed and built by Henry Maudslay, who has been called the father of the machine tool industry. Maudslay recognized the importance of precision tools that could produce identical parts; he and his student, Joseph Whitworth, also manufactured interchangeable, standardized metal bolts and nuts.

Such systemization, in which work was organized to utilize power-driven machinery and produce goods on a large scale, had important social consequences: formerly, workers had been independent craftsmen who owned their own tools and designated their own working hours, but in the factory system, the employer owned the tools and raw materials and set the hours and other conditions under which the workers laboured.

Not all were enamoured by such systems, however. Jean-Jacques Rousseau's sharp hostility toward contemporary society is profoundly elaborated in the *Discours sur l'origine et les fondements de l'inégalité parmi les hommes* (1755; *Discourse on the Origin and Foundations of Inequality among Men*; English translation *Discourse on the Origin of Inequality*). Rousseau argues that social inequality has come about because men have allowed their God-given right of freedom to be usurped by the growth of competition, specialization and division of labour, and, most of all, by laws that consolidated the inequitable distribution of property. Further, he states that elegant, civilized society is a sham whose reality is endless posturing, hostility, injustice, enslavement, and alienation.

Nevertheless, by the middle of the 19th century the general concepts of division of labour, machine-assisted manufacture, and assembly of standardized parts were well established. Large factories were in operation on both sides of the Atlantic.

The Concept of Private Property

Beginning in the 17th century, developments in property law both in England and on the Continent can be related to developments in speculative jurisprudence. In the early 17th century the Dutch speculative jurist Hugo Grotius announced the theory of eminent domain (condemnation of private property). On the one hand, according to Grotius, the state did have the power to expropriate private property. On the other hand, for such a taking to be lawful, it had to be for a public purpose and had to be accompanied by the payment of just compensation to the individual whose property was taken. The idea was not original, but Grotius stated it in such a way that it became a commonplace of Western political thought.

In the late 17th century the German jurist Samuel von Pufendorf refined a theory of the origins of property rights that had been in existence since ancient times. Property, Pufendorf said, is founded in the physical power manifested in seizing the object of property (occupation). In order, however, to convert the fact of physical power into a right, the sanction of the state is necessary. But the state cannot, Pufendorf seems to suggest, make a property right where physical possession is not present. Thus, both occupation and state sanction are necessary conditions for the legitimacy of property.

Pufendorf's English contemporary John Locke had a different theory. What gives someone a right to a thing, according to Locke, is not simply his seizing of the object but rather the fact that he has mixed his labour with the thing in making it his own. It does not require state sanction in order to be valid. It should, however, be protected by the state. Indeed, property is fundamental to the contract that people make in forming the state, and for the state to deny the right to property is a breach of this contract.

Particularly in Great Britain during the late 18th and early 19th centuries, the Scottish Enlightenment gave rise to a new set of ideas about property that were influenced greatly by the English utilitarian philosopher Jeremy Bentham. Property, according to Bentham, is nothing but an expectation of protection created by the legislator and by settled practice. It is, however, an expectation that should be carefully respected. Since the function of the legislator is to maximize the sum of human felicity, he should know that rarely does any interference with property produce more felicity than it destroys. Bentham's follower John Stuart Mill associated property with liberty and suggested that security of property is essential for humankind to maximize its potential for liberty.

On the Continent, thought about property took a somewhat different turn. Building on the categorical imperative of the

German philosopher Immanuel Kant – that persons must always be treated as ends in themselves rather than as means – philosopher Georg Wilhelm Friedrich Hegel suggested that the same imperative applies to a person's property. The reason for this, according to Hegel, is that when someone extends his will to a thing, he makes that thing a part of himself. Protection of property is thus intimately connected with protection of the human will.

6

THE AGE OF REVOLUTION:
ENLIGHTENMENT POLITICS

The central problem of political philosophy is how to deploy
or limit public power so as to maintain the survival and
enhance the quality of human life. Such questions concerning
the aims of government, the grounds of political obligation,
the rights of individuals against the state, the basis of sovereignty, the relation of executive to legislative power, and the
nature of political liberty and social justice were central to the
Enlightenment.

The development of the nation-state was not easy, however,
for the monarchs or anyone else; the legacy of the Middle Ages
was so intractable that the emergence of nation-states was very
slow. The monarchs did all they could to resist the rise of
representative institutions – except in England, where Henry
VIII and the other Tudor monarchs worked with Parliament to
make laws and where the folly of their successors, the Stuarts,
ultimately ensured Parliament's supremacy.

In Europe, absolutism – a system in which the monarch was
supposed to be supreme, in both law making and policy

making – lasted into the 18th century, especially in France, Spain, Prussia, and Austria. Before that time, however, three great occurrences – the Renaissance, the Reformation, and the discovery of the Americas – had transformed Europe. Those events contributed to the eventual failure of absolute monarchy and profoundly influenced the development of future governments.

The invention of the printing press during the Renaissance, for instance, meant that laws could be circulated far more widely than ever before, and increased the size of the educated and literate classes. This also brought public opinion into being for the first time.

The Reformation was the eldest child of the press; it, too, had diffuse and innumerable consequences, the most important of which was the destruction of the Roman Catholic Church's effective claim to universality. The discovery of the Americas opened a new epoch in world history. Portuguese and Spanish explorations gave far-flung overseas empires to both countries. Other countries – France, England, the Netherlands, Sweden, and Denmark – thought it both undesirable and unsafe not to seek such empires themselves; the Iberian monarchies were thus involved in a perpetual struggle to defend their acquisitions. Those battles entailed incessant expenditure, which was more, in the end, than the kingdoms' revenues could match. Financial weakness was one of the chief causes of the decline of Spain.

Meanwhile, the republican tradition had never quite died out. The Dutch had emerged from their long struggle against Spain clinging triumphantly to their new religion and their ancient constitution, a somewhat ramshackle federation known as the United Provinces. Switzerland was another medieval confederation; Venice and Genoa were rigidly oligarchical republics. In England, the rise of Parliament introduced a republican, if not a democratic, element. The tradition of representative estates was first exploited by Henry VIII and the Tudors, and then unsuccessfully challenged by the Stuarts. The English Civil Wars (1642–51) remade all institutions and William III conceded full power of the purse to the House of Commons. Before long it became a maxim of the dominant Whig party that no man could be legally taxed without his own consent or that of his representatives. A radically new age had dawned.

The Whig party favoured a system of constitutional monarchy. The increasingly rationalist temper of the times, exemplified in the works of the philosopher John Locke, finally buried some of the more blatantly mythological theories of government, such as the divine right of kings, and Parliament finally settled the issues that had so vexed the country by passing a series of measures that gave England a written fundamental law for the first time. Henceforth the country was to be ruled by a partnership between king and Parliament.

Natural Law and the Role of Government

The modern conception of natural law as meaning or implying natural rights was elaborated primarily by thinkers of the 17th and 18th centuries. The intellectual – and especially the scientific – achievements of the 17th century encouraged a belief in natural law and universal order; and during the Enlightenment, a growing confidence in human reason and in the perfectibility of human affairs led to the more comprehensive expression of this belief. Particularly important were the writings of Locke, arguably the most important natural-law theorist of modern times, and the works of the 18th-century philosophes centred mainly in Paris, including Montesquieu, Voltaire, and Jean-Jacques Rousseau.

Locke argued in detail that certain rights self-evidently pertain to individuals as human beings (because these rights existed in "the state of nature" before humankind entered civil society); that chief among them are the rights to life, liberty (freedom from arbitrary rule), and property; that, upon entering civil society, humankind surrendered to the state – pursuant to a "social contract" – only the right to enforce these natural rights and not the rights themselves; and that the state's failure to secure these rights gives rise to a right to responsible, popular revolution. The philosophes, building on Locke and others and embracing many and varied currents of thought with a common supreme faith in reason, vigorously attacked religious and scientific dogmatism, intolerance, censorship, and social and economic restraints. They sought to discover and act upon universally valid principles governing nature, humanity, and society, including the inalienable "rights of Man", which they treated as a fundamental ethical and social gospel.

Not surprisingly, this liberal intellectual ferment exerted a profound influence. Together with the Glorious Revolution in England (1688–9)and the resulting Bill of Rights, it provided the rationale for the wave of revolutionary agitation that swept the West, most notably in North America and France. Thomas Jefferson, who had studied Locke and Montesquieu, stated that "all men are created equal." The Marquis de Lafayette, in "La déclaration des droits de l'homme et du citoyen" ("Declaration of the Rights of Man and of the Citizen") of August 26 1789, proclaimed that "the aim of every political association is the preservation of the natural and imprescriptible rights of man."

The idea of natural rights was not without its detractors, however. In the first place, because it was frequently associated with religious orthodoxy, the doctrine of natural rights became less attractive to philosophical and political liberals. Additionally, because they were conceived in essentially absolutist terms, natural rights were increasingly considered to conflict with one another. Most importantly, the doctrine of natural rights came under powerful philosophical and political attack from both the right and the left.

In England, for example, conservative political thinkers such as Edmund Burke and David Hume united with liberals such as Jeremy Bentham to condemn the doctrine, the former out of fear that public affirmation of natural rights would lead to social upheaval, the latter out of concern lest declarations and proclamations of natural rights substitute for effective legislation. In his *Reflections on the Revolution in France* (1790), Burke – a believer in natural law who nonetheless denied that the "rights of Man" could be derived from it – criticized the drafters of the Declaration of the Rights of Man and of the Citizen for proclaiming the "monstrous fiction" of human equality, which, he argued, serves but to inspire "false ideas and vain expectations in men destined to travel in the obscure walk of laborious life".

Bentham, one of the founders of utilitarianism, was no less scornful. "Rights", he wrote, "is the child of law; from real law come real rights; but from imaginary laws, from 'law of nature', come imaginary rights . . . Natural rights is simple nonsense; natural and imprescriptible rights . . . [is] rhetorical nonsense, nonsense upon stilts." Agreeing with Bentham, Hume insisted that natural law and natural rights were unreal metaphysical phenomena.

Hobbes and the Law of Nature

In the 17th century Thomas Hobbes had entered the debate on natural law. Hobbes started from an assumption of basic human folly, competitiveness, and depravity. He believed that the fundamental physical law of life was motion and that the predominant human impulses were fear and, among those above the poverty level, pride and vanity. Men, Hobbes argued, are strictly conditioned and limited by these laws, and he tried to create a science of politics that would reflect them. "The skill of making, and maintaining Commonwealths", therefore, "consisteth in certain Rules, as doth Arithmetique and Geometry; not (as Tennis play) on Practise onely: which Rules, neither poor men have the leisure, nor men that have had the leisure, have hitherto had the curiosity, or the method to find out."

Following René Descartes's practical method of investigation, he stated plainly that power creates law, not law power. Starting from the assumption of a savage "state of nature" in which each man was at war with every other, Hobbes defined the right of nature (*jus naturale*) to be "the liberty each man hath to use his own power for the preservation of his own nature, that is to say, of life", and a law of nature (*lex naturalis*) as "a precept of general rule found out by reason, by which a man is forbidden to do that which is destructive of his life". He then enumerated the elementary rules on which peace and society could be established.

The true law of nature, Hobbes argued, is self-preservation, which can be achieved only if the citizens make a compact among themselves to transfer their individual power to the "leviathan" (ruler), who alone can preserve them in security. Such a commonwealth has no intrinsic supernatural or moral sanction: it derives its original authority from the people and can command loyalty only so long as it succeeds in keeping the peace. He thus used both the old concepts of natural law and contract, often invoked to justify resistance to authority, as a sanction for it.

Hobbes contradicted Aristotle's assumption that man is by nature a "political animal". On the contrary, he is naturally antisocial; and, even when men meet for business and profit, only "a certain market-fellowship" is engendered. All society is only for gain or glory, and the only true equality among men is their power to kill each other. Hobbes sees and desires no other equality. Indeed, he specifically discouraged "men of low degree from a saucy behaviour towards their betters".

The *Leviathan; or, The Matter, Form, and Power of a Commonwealth, Ecclesiastical and Civil* (1651) horrified most of his contemporaries; Hobbes was accused of atheism and of "maligning the Human Nature". But, if his remedies were tactically impractical, in political philosophy he had gone very deep by providing the sovereign nation-state with a pragmatic justification and directing it to utilitarian ends.

Political Power and the State

The 17th-century Dutch-Jewish philosopher Benedict de Spinoza also tried to make a scientific political theory. His was more humane and more modern. Like Hobbes, he was Cartesian, aiming at a scientific basis for political philosophy; but, whereas Hobbes was dogmatic and authoritarian, Spinoza desired toleration and intellectual liberty, by which alone he believed human life achieves its highest quality. Spinoza, reacting against the ideological wars of religion and sceptical of both metaphysics and religious dogma, was a scientific humanist who justified political power solely by its usefulness.

If state power breaks down and can no longer protect him or if it turns against him, frustrates, or ruins his life, then anyone is justified in resisting it, since it no longer fulfils its purpose. It has no intrinsic divine or metaphysical authority.

In his *Tractatus Theologico-Politicus* (1670; *Theologico-Political Treatise*) and the *Tractatus Politicus* (1677; *Political Treatise*) Spinoza develops this theme. He holds that governments should not try to "change men from rational beings into beasts or puppets, but enable them to develop their minds and bodies in security and to employ their reason unshackled". The more life is enjoyed, he declares, the more the individual participates in the divine nature. God is immanent in the entire process of nature, in which all creatures follow the laws of their own being to the limit of their powers. All are bound by their own consciousness, and man creates his own values. Spinoza was thus a pioneer of a scientific humanist view of government and of the neutrality of the state in matters of belief.

During the Reformation and Counter-Reformation, Protestant and Catholic dogmatists denounced each other and even attacked the authority of princes who, from interest or conviction, supported one side or the other. Political assassination became endemic, for both Protestant and Catholic divines declared that it was legitimate to kill a heretical ruler. Appeal was made to rival religious authority as well as to conscience. Men would resist authority and suffer execution rather than risk damnation, and in the resulting welter Hobbes and Spinoza advocated a sovereign state as the remedy.

Other political philosophers salvaged St Thomas Aquinas' concept of a divine cosmic order and of natural and human laws sanctioning the state. They also put forth the classical and medieval idea of the derivation of public power from the commonwealth as a whole and the responsibility of princes to the law. When Hobbes wrote that might makes right, he outraged such critics, who continued to assert that public power was responsible to God and the laws and that it was right to resist a tyrant who declared that the laws were in his own breast. This political theory was most influentially developed in England, where it inspired the constitutionalism that would also predominate in the United States.

Richard Hooker, an Anglican divine who wrote *Of the Laws of Ecclesiastical Polity* (incomplete at his death in 1600), reconciled Thomist doctrines of transcendent and natural law, binding on all men, with the authority of the Elizabethan Anglican Church, which he defended against the Puritan appeal to conscience. Society, he argued, is itself the fulfilment of natural law, of which human and positive law are reflections, adapted to society. And public power is not something personal, for it derives from the community under law. Thus,

> The lawful power of making laws to command whole politic societies of men belongeth so properly unto the same entire societies, that for any prince . . . to exercise the same of himself . . . is no better than mere tyranny.

Such power can derive either directly from God or else from the people. The prince is responsible to God and the community; he is not, like Hobbes' ruler, a law unto himself. Law makes the king, not the king law. Hooker, indeed, insisted that "the prince has a delegated power, from the Parliament of England, together with the convocation (of clergy) annexed thereto . . . whereupon the very essence of all government doth depend." This is the power of the crown in Parliament in a balanced constitution.

It was Locke, politically the most influential English philosopher, who further developed this doctrine. His *Two Treatises of Government* (1690) were written to justify the

Glorious Revolution. His first *Treatise* was devoted to confuting the Royalist doctrine of patriarchal divine right by descent from Adam, an argument then taken very seriously and reflecting the idea of government as an aspect of a divinely ordained chain of being. Locke tried to provide an answer by defining a limited purpose for political power, which he considered to be

> a right of making laws with penalties of death, and consequently all less penalties, for the regulating and preserving of property, and of employing the force of the community in execution of such laws, and in the defence of the commonwealth from foreign injury, and all this only for the public good.

The authority of government derives from a contract between the rulers and the people, and the contract binds both parties. It is thus a limited power, proceeding according to established laws and "directed to no other end but the peace, safety, and public good of the people".

Whatever its form, government, to be legitimate, must govern by "declared and reasoned laws", and, since every man has a "property" in his own person and has "mixed his labour" with what he owns, government has no right to take it from him without his consent. It was the threat of attack on the laws, property, and the Protestant religion that had roused resistance to King James II. Locke was expressing the concerns and interests of the landed and moneyed men by whose consent James' successor, William III, came to the throne, and his commonwealth is strictly conservative, limiting the franchise and the preponderant power to the propertied classes. Like Hooker, Locke assumed a conservative social hierarchy with a relatively weak executive power and defended the propertied classes both against a ruler by divine right and against radicals. In advocating toleration in religion he was more liberal: freedom of conscience, like property, he argued, is a natural right of all men.

Within the possibilities of the time, Locke thus advocated a constitutional mixed government, limited by parliamentary control of the armed forces and of supply. Designed mainly to protect the rights of property, it was deprived of the right of arbitrary taxation or imprisonment without trial and was in theory responsible to all the people through the politically conscious minority who were thought to represent them. Although he was socially conservative, Locke's writings are very important in the rise of liberal political philosophy. He vindicated the responsibility of government to the governed, the rule of law through impartial judges, and the toleration of religious and speculative opinion. He was an enemy of the totalitarian state, drawing on medieval arguments and deploying them in practical, modern terms.

The Irish statesman Edmund Burke espoused the theory of natural law. He held that society and state make possible the full realization of human potentiality, embody a common good, and represent a tacit or explicit agreement on norms and ends. While reiterating that government is responsible to the governed, and distinguishing between a political society and a mere mob, he thought that governments were trustees for previous generations and for posterity. In his *Vindication of Natural Society* (1756), Burke is critical of the sufferings imposed by government, but his *Thoughts on the Cause of the Present Discontents* (1770) defined and defended the principles of the Whig establishment. Responding to George III's demand to reassert a more active role for the crown, Burke argued that George's actions were against not the letter but the spirit of the constitution. The choice of ministers purely on personal grounds was favouritism; public approbation by the people through Parliament should determine their selection.

This pamphlet includes Burke's famous, and new, justification of party, defined as a body of men united on public principle, which could act as a constitutional link between king and Parliament, providing consistency and strength in administration, or principled criticism in opposition.

Elected a member of Parliament for Bristol in 1774, Burke made his well-known statement on the role of the member of Parliament. The elected member should be a representative, not a mere delegate pledged to obey undeviatingly the wishes of his constituents. The electors are capable of judging his integrity, and he should attend to their local interests; but, more importantly, he must address himself to the general good of the entire nation, acting according to his own judgement and conscience, unfettered by mandates or prior instructions from those he represents.

Burke's main concern as a Parliamentarian was the curtailment of the crown's powers. He made a practical attempt to reduce this influence as one of the leaders of the movement that pressed for parliamentary control of royal patronage and expenditure. When the Rockingham Whigs took office in 1782, bills were passed reducing pensions and emoluments of offices. Burke was specifically connected with an act regulating the civil list, the amount voted by Parliament for the personal and household expenses of the sovereign.

Burke set great store by ordered liberty and denounced the arbitrary power of the Jacobins who had captured the French Revolution. In his *Reflections on the Revolution in France* (1790) and *An Appeal from the New to the Old Whigs* (1791), he discerned in the doctrine of sovereignty of the people, in whose name the revolutionaries were destroying the old order, another and worse form of arbitrary power. No single generation has the right to destroy the agreed and inherited fabric of society, and "Neither the few nor the many have the right to govern by their will." A country is not a mere physical locality, he argued, but a community in time into which men are born, and only within the existing constitution and by the consent of its representatives can changes legitimately be made. Once the frame of society is smashed and its law violated, the people become a "mere multitude told by the head", at the mercy of any dictator who can seize power.

In France, the Baron de Montesquieu argued that natural laws were presocial and superior to those of religion and the state, His *De l'esprit des lois* (1748; *The Spirit of the Laws*, English translation 1750) won immense influence. Abandoning the classical divisions of his predecessors into monarchy, aristocracy, and democracy, Montesquieu produced his own analysis and assigned to each form of government an animating principle: the republic, based on virtue; the monarchy, based on honour; and despotism, based on fear. His definitions show that this classification rests not on the location of political power but on the government's manner of conducting policy; it involves a historical and not a narrow descriptive approach.

His most noted argument, the theory of the separation of powers, divides political authority into the legislative, executive, and judicial powers. He asserts that, in the state that most effectively promotes liberty, these three powers must be confided to different individuals or bodies, acting independently. His model of such a state was England, which he saw from the point of view of the Tory opposition to the Whig leader, Robert Walpole, as expressed in Bolingbroke's polemical writings. The chapter in which he expressed this doctrine at once became perhaps the most important piece of political writing of the 18th century. Though its accuracy has in more recent times been disputed, in its own century it was admired and held authoritative, even in England; it inspired the Declaration of the Rights of Man and the Constitution of the United States.

Rousseau and the Social Contract

The revolutionary romanticism of the French philosopher Jean-Jacques Rousseau may be interpreted in part as a reaction to the analytic rationalism of the Enlightenment. He was trying to escape the aridity of a purely empirical and utilitarian outlook and attempting to create a substitute for revealed religion. Rousseau proclaimed a secular egalitarianism and a romantic cult of the common man. His famous sentence, "man is born free, but he is everywhere in chains," called into question the traditional social hierarchy: hitherto, political philosophers had thought in terms of elites, but now the mass of the people had found a champion and were becoming politically conscious.

Casting about to reconcile his artificial antithesis between man's purported natural state of freedom and his condition in society, Rousseau utilized the old theories of contract and transformed them into the concept of the "general will". This general will, a moral will that aims at the common good and in which all participate directly, reconciles the individual and the community by representing the will of the community as deriving from the will of moral individuals, so that to obey the laws of such a community is in a sense to follow one's own will, assuming that one is a moral individual.

Commentators have differed widely in their readings of *Du contrat social ou principes du droit politique* (1762; *The Social Contract; or Principles of Political Right*) as either a liberal or a totalitarian document, and ideas similar to that of the general will became accepted as a basis for both the social-democratic welfare state and for totalitarian dictatorships. Rousseau, however, saw himself as unambiguously defending freedom from despotism; from 1789 to 1917, revolutionaries throughout the world took him as an icon.

The incursion of this revolutionary romantic into political philosophy changed the climate of political opinion.

Jeremy Bentham and Utilitarianism

A major force in the political and social thought of the 19th century was utilitarianism, the doctrine that actions (of individuals or of governments) should be judged simply by the extent to which they promote "the greatest happiness of the greatest number". The founder of the utilitarian school, Jeremy Bentham, elaborated a utilitarian political philosophy in *A Fragment, on Government* (1776) and *An Introduction to the Principles of Morals and Legislation* (1789). His influence spread widely abroad.

Bentham himself was influenced by the scientist Joseph Priestley, who argued in *An Essay on the First Principles of Government* (1768) that scientific progress and human perfectibility required freedom of speech, worship, and education. As a proponent of laissez-faire economics, developed by the Scottish economist Adam Smith, Priestley sought to limit the role of government and to evaluate its effectiveness solely in terms of the welfare of the individual. Bentham acknowledged that Priestley's influential book inspired the phrase used, as above, to depict his own movement, "the greatest happiness of the greatest number".

At first a simple reformer of law, Bentham attacked notions of contract and natural law as superfluous, "The indestructible prerogatives of mankind", he wrote, "have no need to be supported upon the sandy foundation of a fiction." The justification of government is pragmatic, its aim improvement, and to release the free choice of individuals and the play of market forces that will create prosperity. He thought society could advance by calculation of pleasure and pain. He also thought of punishment purely as a deterrent, not as retribution, and graded offences on the harm they did to happiness, not on how much they offended God or tradition.

For Bentham, the greatest happiness of the greatest number would play a role primarily in the art of legislation, in which the legislator would seek to maximize the happiness of the entire community by creating an identity of interests between each individual and his fellows. By laying down penalties for mischievous acts, the legislator would make it unprofitable for a person to harm his neighbour. With Bentham, utilitarianism became the ideological foundation of a reform movement, later known as "philosophical radicalism", that would test all institutions and policies by the principle of utility.

In 1809 Bentham wrote a tract, *A Catechism of Parliamentary Reform*, advocating annual elections, equal electoral districts, a wide suffrage, and the secret ballot, which was, however, not published until 1817. He drafted a series of resolutions based on this tract that were introduced in the House of Commons in 1818. A volume of his *Constitutional Code,* which he did not live to complete, was published in 1830.

Bentham's disciple, James Mill, postulated an economic actor whose decisions, if freely taken, would always be in his own interest, and he believed that universal suffrage, along with utilitarian legislation by a sovereign parliament, would produce the kind of happiness and well-being that Bentham desired. In his *Essay on Government* (1828) Mill thus showed a doctrinaire faith in a literate electorate as the means to good government and in laissez-faire economics as a means to social harmony. This utilitarian tradition was humanized by James Mill's son, John Stuart Mill, who expressed the still optimistic and progressive views of an intellectual elite and believed that the masses could be educated into accepting the values of liberal civilization.

In evaluating what kind of government could best attain their objectives, the utilitarians generally supported representative democracy, asserting that it was the best way to make the interest of government coincide with the general interest. Taking their cue from the notion of a free-market economy, the utilitarians called for a political system that would guarantee its citizens the maximum degree of individual freedom of choice and action consistent with efficient government and the preservation of social harmony. They also developed a doctrine of individual rights – including the rights to freedom of religion, freedom of speech, freedom of the press, and freedom of assembly – that lies at the heart of modern democracy.

Anarchism and Utopianism

While a liberal political philosophy within a framework of capitalistic free trade and constitutional self-government dominated the greatest Western powers, mounting criticism developed against centralized government itself. Radical utopian and anarchist views, previously expounded mainly by religious sects, became secularized in such works as William Godwin's *An Enquiry Concerning Political Justice, and Its Influence on General Virtue and Happiness* (1793), Robert Owen's *New View of Society* (1813), and Pierre-Joseph Proudhon's voluminous and anticlerical writings.

The English philosopher William Godwin, an extreme individualist, shared Bentham's confidence in the reasonableness of mankind. He denounced the wars accepted by most political philosophers and all centralized coercive states. The tyranny of demagogues and of "multitudes drunk with power" he regarded as being as bad as that of kings and oligarchs. The remedy, he thought, was not violent revolution, which produces tyranny, but education and freedom, including sexual freedom. His was a programme of high-minded, atheistic anarchism.

Godwin's idealistic liberalism was based on the principle of the absolute sovereignty and competence of reason to determine right choice. An optimist regarding humanity's future perfectibility, he combined cultural determinism with a doctrine of extreme individualism. The object of his principal work, *Political Justice*, was to reject conventional government by demonstrating the corrupting evil and tyranny inherent in its power of manipulation. He proposed in its place small self-subsisting communities. He argued that social institutions fail because they impose generalized thought categories and preconceived ideas, which make it impossible to see things as they are. His most powerful personal belief was that "everything understood by the term cooperation is in some sense an evil", from which proceeded his most influential anarchist doctrines.

The English socialist Robert Owen, a cotton spinner who had made a fortune, also insisted that bad institutions, not original sin or intrinsic folly, caused the evils of society, and he sought to remedy them by changing the economic and educational system. He thus devised a scheme of model cooperative communities that would increase production, permit humane education, and release the naturally benevolent qualities of mankind.

The French moralist and advocate of social reform Pierre-Joseph Proudhon attacked the "tentacular" nation-state and aimed at a classless society in which major capitalism would be abolished. Self-governing producers, no longer slaves of bureaucrats and capitalists, would permit the realization of an intrinsic human dignity, and federation would replace the accepted condition of war between sovereign states. Proudhon tried to transform society by rousing the mass of the people to cooperative humanitarian consciousness.

The Rise of Classical Liberalism

For liberalism the central problem of government is the abuse of power, and thus the freedom of the individual. For liberals, power is most importantly abused by governments, but it may also be abused by the wealthy and by monarchs, aristocrats, and others with inherited authority and privileges.

In the 17th century the ambitions of national rulers and the requirements of expanding industry and commerce led to greater state intervention in the economy, on the mercantilist assumption that this was necessary to increase state wealth and power. However, as such intervention increasingly served established interests and inhibited enterprise, it was challenged by members of the newly emerging middle class. This challenge was a significant factor in the great revolutions that rocked England and France in the 17th and 18th centuries – most notably the English Civil Wars from 1642 to 1651, the Glorious Revolution of 1688–9, the American Revolution from 1775 to 1783, and the French Revolution of 1789. Classical liberalism as an articulated creed is a product of those great collisions. The political ideas that helped to inspire these revolts were given formal expression by Hobbes and Locke.

If the political foundations of liberalism were laid in Great Britain, so too were its economic foundations. By the 18th century British monarchs were constrained by Parliament from pursuing the schemes of national aggrandizement favoured by most rulers on the Continent. These rulers fought for military supremacy, which required a strong economic base. Because the prevailing mercantilist theory understood international trade as a zero-sum game – in which gain for one nation meant loss for another – national governments intervened to determine prices, protect their industries from foreign competition, and avoid the sharing of economic information. These practices were challenged by Adam Smith, who argued in *An Inquiry into the Nature and Causes of the Wealth of Nations* (1776) that free trade would benefit all parties.

According to this view, if individuals are left free to pursue their self-interest in an exchange economy based upon a division of labour, the welfare of the group as a whole necessarily will be enhanced. The self-seeking individual becomes harnessed to the public good because in an exchange economy he must serve others in order to serve himself. But it is only in a genuinely free market, according to Smith, that this positive consequence is possible; any other arrangement, whether state control or monopoly, must lead to regimentation, exploitation, and economic stagnation.

In concrete terms, classical liberal economists called for several major changes in British and European economic organization. The first was the abolition of the host of feudal and mercantilist restrictions on nations' manufacturing and internal commerce. The second was an end to the tariffs and restrictions that governments imposed on foreign imports to protect domestic producers. In rejecting the government's regulation of trade, classical economics was based firmly on a belief in the superiority of a self-regulating market.

Inspired by the need to remove the state from destructive interference with economic life, and by the actual wealth generated by the Industrial Revolution, the guiding political principle of classical liberalism became an undeviating insistence on limiting the power of government.

Bentham cogently summarized this view in his sole advice to the state – "Be quiet"; the American statesman Thomas Jefferson similarly asserted that that government is best that governs least. Politically, liberalism ultimately aspired to a system of government based on majority rule – i.e., one in which government executed the expressed will of a majority of the electorate. The chief institutional devices for attaining this goal were the periodic election of legislators by popular vote and the election of a chief executive by popular vote or by a legislative assembly. But in answering the crucial question of who is to be the electorate, classical liberalism fell victim to ambivalence, torn between the great emancipating tendencies generated by the revolutions with which it was associated and middle-class fears that a wide or universal franchise would undermine private property.

Benjamin Franklin spoke for the Whig liberalism of the founding fathers of the United States when he stated, "As to those who have not landed property the allowing them to vote is an impropriety." John Adams, in his *Defence of the Constitutions of Government of the United States of America* (1787), was more explicit, finding that, if the majority were to control all branches of government, "Debts would be abolished first; taxes laid heavy on the rich, and not at all on others; and at last a downright equal division of everything be demanded and voted." Most 18th- and 19th-century liberal spokesmen thus feared popular sovereignty, and for a long time suffrage was limited to property owners.

The liberal solution to the problem of limiting the power of a democratic majority rested on various devices. The first was the separation of powers – i.e., the distribution of power between such functionally differentiated agencies of government as the legislature, the executive, and the judiciary. This arrangement, and the system of checks and balances by which it was accomplished, was given its classic embodiment in the Constitution of the United States and its political justification in *The Federalist* (1788), by Alexander Hamilton, James Madison, and John Jay. Of course, such a separation of powers also could have been achieved through a "mixed constitution" – i.e., one by which a monarch, a hereditary chamber, and an elected assembly share power with some appropriate differentiation of function. This was in fact the system of government in Great Britain at the time of the American Revolution. But it was despotic kings and function-less aristocrats (more functionless in France than in England) who thwarted the interests and ambitions of the middle class, which turned, therefore, to the principle of majoritarianism.

The second part of the solution lay in using staggered periodic elections to make the decisions of any given majority subject to the concurrence of other majorities distributed over time. In the United States, for example, presidents are elected every four years and members of the House of Representatives every two years, and one-third of the Senate is elected every two years for terms of six years. In Britain an act of Parliament immediately becomes part of the unwritten constitution; how-ever, before acting on a highly controversial issue, Parliament must seek a mandate from the people, which represents a majority other than the one that elected it. Thus, in a con-stitutional democracy, the power of a current majority is checked by the verdicts of majorities that precede and follow it.

The third part of the solution was related to liberalism's basic commitment to the autonomy and integrity of the individual, which the limitation of power is, after all, intended to preserve. In the liberal understanding, the individual is not only a citizen who shares a social compact with his fellows but also a person with rights upon which the state may not encroach if majoritarianism is to be meaningful. A majority verdict can come about only if individuals are free to some extent to exchange their views. This involves, beyond the right to speak and write freely, the freedom to associate and organize and, above all, the freedom from fear of reprisal. But the individual also has rights apart from his role as citizen. These rights secure his personal safety and hence his protection from arbitrary arrest and punishment. Beyond these rights are those that preserve large areas of privacy. In a liberal democracy there are affairs – such as the practice of religion, or how children are raised by their parents – that do not concern the state. For liberals of the 18th and 19th centuries they included, above all, most of the activities through which individuals engage in production and trade.

Eloquent and persuasive declarations affirming such rights were embodied in the English Bill of Rights of 1689, the United States Declaration of Independence and Constitution (1776 and 1788, respectively), the French Declaration of the Rights of Man and of the Citizen of 1789, and the basic documents of nations throughout the world that later used these declarations as their models. Freedom thereby became more than the right to make a fractional contribution in an intermittent mandate to government; it designated the right of people to live their own lives.

Thomas Paine and the Rights of Man

Thomas Paine's pamphlet *Common Sense* (1776) and his "Crisis" papers (1776–83) were important influences on the American Revolution, while his *Rights of Man* (1791) was a defence of the French Revolution and of republican principles. All contributed to his reputation as one of the greatest political propagandists in history.

Travelling to Europe after the American Revolution, Paine became enraged by Burke's attack on the uprising of the French people in his *Reflections on the Revolution in France*. Although Paine admired Burke's stand in favour of the American Revolution, he rushed into print with his celebrated answer, *Rights of Man*. The book immediately created a sensation, and the work was quickly reprinted in the United States, where it was widely distributed. When Burke replied, Paine came back with *Rights of Man, Part II,* published in 1792.

What began as a defence of the French Revolution evolved into an analysis of the basic reasons for discontent in European society and a remedy for the evils of arbitrary government, poverty, illiteracy, unemployment, and war. Paine spoke out effectively in favour of republicanism as against monarchy and went on to outline a plan for popular education, relief of the poor, pensions for aged people, and public works for the unemployed, all to be financed by the levying of a progressive income tax.

The Rights of Women

During the Enlightenment women began to demand that the new reformist rhetoric about liberty, equality, and natural rights be applied to both sexes, and feminist voices finally coalesced into a coherent movement.

Initially, Enlightenment philosophers focused on the inequities of social class and caste to the exclusion of gender. Rousseau, for example, portrayed women as silly and frivolous creatures, born to be subordinate to men. Women, he claimed, have a natural vocation to be wives and mothers; they are to leave public affairs to men. He put forward the harmonious domestic family as a new cultural ideal and stigmatized ancien régime society, with its emphasis on fashion and its influential "public women", such as royal mistresses and the Salon hostesses who played a critical role in promoting the Enlightenment. Rousseau's insistence that mothers should breastfeed their children clashed with the realities of French life, where the employment of wetnurses was more common than in any other European country.

In addition, the Declaration of the Rights of Man and of the Citizen, which defined French citizenship after the revolution of 1789, pointedly failed to address the legal status of women. Female intellectuals of the Enlightenment were quick to point out this omission and the limited scope of reformist rhetoric. Olympe de Gouges, a noted playwright, published *Déclaration des droits de la femme et de la citoyenne* (1791; *Declaration of the Rights of Woman and of the [Female] Citizen*), declaring women to be not only man's equal but his partner.

The following year Mary Wollstonecraft's *A Vindication of the Rights of Woman* (1792), the seminal English-language feminist work, was published in England. Challenging the notion that women exist only to please men, she proposed that women and men be given equal opportunities in education, work, and politics. Women, she wrote, are as naturally rational as men. Wollstonecraft argued that the educational system of her time deliberately trained women to be frivolous and incapable. She posited that an educational system that allowed girls the same advantages as boys would result in women who would be not only exceptional wives and mothers but also capable workers in many professions. Other early feminists had made similar pleas for improved education for women, but Wollstonecraft's work was unique in suggesting that the betterment of women's status be effected through such political change as the radical reform of national educational systems. Such change, she concluded, would benefit all society.

In the United States, feminist activism took root in the late 18th century when female abolitionists sought to apply the concepts of freedom and equality to their own social and political situations. Their work brought them into contact with female abolitionists in England who were reaching the same conclusions.

The American Revolution

It was in the climate of the Enlightenment political philosophies described above, and amid the growing realization of individuals' rights as citizens, that the two great 18th-century revolutions took place. The American Revolution of 1775–83 followed more than a decade of growing estrangement between the British crown and a large and influential segment of its North American colonies. In a royal proclamation of 1763, for instance, a line was drawn marking the limit of settlement from the British colonies, beyond which Indian trade was to be conducted through British-appointed commissioners.

Various measures to raise revenues were also imposed: the Plantation Act of 1764; a Currency Act (1764); and, most notably, the Stamp Act (1765), which enforced a stamp duty on a wide variety of transactions. At a Congress in New York in the summer of 1765 the latter was denounced as a violation of the Englishman's right to be taxed only through elected representatives. Although the act was repealed, in 1767 the Declaratory Act was passed, giving Parliament the power to bind or legislate the colonies "in all cases whatsoever", and Charles Townshend, the new Chancellor of the Exchequer, imposed duties on a wide range of necessities, including lead, glass, paint, paper, and tea.

The colonists were outraged. In Pennsylvania the lawyer and legislator John Dickinson wrote a series of essays, appearing in 1767 and 1768 as *Letters from a Farmer in Pennsylvania*, that were widely reprinted and exerted great influence in forming a united colonial opposition. Dickinson agreed that Parliament had supreme power where the whole empire was concerned, but he denied that it had power over internal colonial affairs; he quietly implied that the basis of colonial loyalty lay in its utility among equals rather than in obedience owed to a superior. Gradually, a wide-ranging non-importation policy against British goods was brought into operation.

The core of the colonists' case was that, as British subjects, they were entitled to the same privileges as their fellow subjects in Britain. They could not constitutionally be taxed without their own consent; and, because they were unrepresented in the Parliament that voted the taxes, they had not given this consent. James Otis, in two long pamphlets, ceded all sovereign power to Parliament with this proviso. Others now began to question whether Parliament did have lawful power to legislate over the colonies. In the late 1760s, James Wilson's *Considerations on the Nature and Extent of the Legislative Authority of the British Parliament* articulated the view that Parliament's lawful sovereignty stopped at the shores of Britain. In 1770, in the face of the American policy of non-importation, the Townshend tariffs were withdrawn – all except the tax on tea. Then, in 1773, Lord North's administration gave the the East India Company a monopoly of distribution in the colonies through the Tea Act. Many colonists denounced the act as a plot to induce Americans to buy – and therefore pay the tax on – legally imported tea. Boston was not the only port to threaten to reject the casks of taxed tea, but its reply was the most dramatic. On December 16 1773, a party of Bostonians, disguised as Mohawk Indians, boarded the ships at anchor and dumped some £10,000-worth of tea into the harbour. The British response was to close the port of Boston; and, in the Massachusetts Government Act, Parliament for the first time altered a colonial charter, substituting an appointive council for the elective one.

It was this action that spurred the meeting of a Continental Congress in Philadelphia in September 1774. The Virginia delegation's instructions, drafted by Thomas Jefferson and later published as *A Summary View of the Rights of British America* (1774), insisted on the autonomy of colonial legislative power and set forth a highly individualistic view of the basis of American rights: that the American colonies and other members of the British Empire were distinct states united under the king and thus subject only to the king and not to Parliament.

The first important decision of the Congress was on voting procedure: the decision to vote by colony was made on practical grounds – neither wealth nor population could be satisfactorily ascertained – but it had important consequences. Individual colonies, no matter what their size, retained a degree of autonomy that translated immediately into the language and prerogatives of sovereignty. The Congress committed the colonies to a carefully phased plan of economic pressure intended to force the British government to redress all colonial grievances.

When the British general Thomas Gage sent a force from Boston to destroy American rebel military stores at Concord, Massachusetts, fighting broke out between militia and British troops at Lexington and Concord on April 19 1775. Although most colonial leaders still hoped for reconciliation with Britain, the news stirred the delegates to more radical action. Steps were taken to put the continent on a war footing, with the Congress raising an army and appointing committees to deal with domestic supply and foreign affairs. In August 1775 the king declared a state of rebellion; by the end of the year, all colonial trade was banned.

Then in January 1776 the publication of Thomas Paine's *Common Sense* pamphlet put independence on the agenda. The Congress recommended that colonies form their own governments and assigned a committee to draft a declaration of independence. Thomas Jefferson's document consisted of two parts. The preamble set the claims of the United States on a basis of natural rights, with a dedication to the principle of equality; the second was a long list of grievances against the crown – not Parliament now, since the argument was that Parliament had no lawful power in the colonies. On July 2 the Congress itself voted for independence; on July 4 1776 it adopted the Declaration. It stated:

> We hold these truths to be self-evident, that all men are created equal, that they are endowed by their Creator with certain inalienable Rights, that among these are Life, Liberty and the pursuit of Happiness. That, to secure these rights, Governments are instituted among Men, deriving their just powers from the consent of the governed.

The British government had now authorized their forces in America to treat with the Americans and assure them pardon should they submit. The Americans, however, refused this offer of peace. The American Revolutionary War was transformed from a civil conflict within the British Empire to an international war when the Americans were joined by France in 1778, Spain in 1779, and the Netherlands in 1780. On October 19 1781 Britain's General Cornwallis surrendered to Washington's army and a force under the French Count de Rochambeau at Yorktown.

Under the preliminary Anglo-American peace treaty of 1782 Britain recognized the independence of the United States. Most of the states established their own constitutions. Elite power provided a lever for one of the most significant transformations of the era, one that took place almost without being either noticed or intended. This was the acceptance of the principle of proportional representation as the determining rule of political action. It was made not only possible but attractive when the larger aggregations of population broadly coincided with the highest concentrations of property: great merchants and landowners from populous areas could continue to exert political ascendancy so long as they retained some sort of hold on the political process. The principle re-emerged to dominate the distribution of voters in the House of Representatives and in the Electoral College under the new federal Constitution.

The Articles of Confederation, a plan of government organization adopted and put into practice by Congress in 1777, although not officially ratified by all the states until 1781, had given Congress the right to make requisitions on the states proportionate to their ability to pay. The Articles reflected strong preconceptions of state sovereignty. The Philadelphia Convention, which met in May 1787, was officially called for by the old Congress solely to remedy defects in the Articles of Confederation. But the "Virginia Plan" instead boldly proposed to introduce a new, national government in place of the existing confederation.

The Constitution of the new nation which emerged after a summer of debate embodied a much stronger principle of separation of powers than was generally to be found in the state constitutions. The chief executive was to be a single figure (a composite executive was discussed) and was to be elected by an electoral college, meeting in the states. The principal control on the president was the threat of impeachment. The Virginia Plan's proposal that representation be proportional to population in both houses was severely modified by the retention of equal representation for each state in the Senate. After some contention, anti-slavery forces gave way to a compromise by which three-fifths of the slaves would be counted as population for purposes of representation (and direct taxation).

Contemporary political theory expected the legislature to be the most powerful branch of government. Thus, to balance the system, the executive was given a veto, and a judicial system with powers of review was established. It was also implicit in the structure that the new, federal judiciary would have power to veto any state laws that conflicted with either the Constitution or with federal statutes. The Congress was endowed with the basic powers of a modern – and sovereign – government. This was a republic, and the United States could confer no aristocratic titles of honour. The states retained their civil jurisdiction; but there was an emphatic shift of the political centre of gravity to the federal government, of which the most fundamental indication was the universal understanding that this government would act directly on citizens, as individuals.

The draft Constitution aroused widespread opposition. Anti-federalists were strong in states such as Virginia, New York, and Massachusetts, where the economy was relatively successful and many people saw little need for such extreme remedies. Many firm republicans detected oligarchy in the structure of the Senate, with its six-year terms. The absence of a bill of rights aroused deep fears of central power.

The Bill of Rights, steered through the first Congress by James Madison's diplomacy, mollified much of the latent opposition. These first 10 amendments, ratified in 1791, adopted into the Constitution the basic English common-law rights that Americans had fought for. But they did more.

Unlike Britain, the United States secured a guarantee of free-dom for the press and the right of (peaceable) assembly. Also unlike Britain, church and state were formally separated in a clause that seemed to set equal value on the non-establishment of religion and its free exercise.

It took the Americans more than a decade to create a suitable framework of government based on the principles of independence but the new Constitution opened the door to modern liberal democracy – democracy in which the liberty of the individual is paramount. "The consent of the governed" was agreed to be the key to governmental legitimacy, and in practice the phrase rapidly came to mean "the consent of the majority".

The principle of representation was embodied in the US Constitution (the first section of which was entirely devoted to the establishment of Congress, the American parliament); this implied that there was no necessary limit to the size of a successful republic. From Plato to Jean-Jacques Rousseau, theorists had agreed that democracies had to be small, because by definition all their citizens had to be able to give their consent in person. Now that notion had been discarded.

The French Revolution

When the National Assembly announced the basic principles of its new regime in the Declaration of the Rights of Man and of the Citizen in August 1789, its authors believed it to have universal significance. "In the new hemisphere, the brave inhabitants of Philadelphia have given the example of a people who re-established their liberty," conceded one deputy, but "France would give that example to the rest of the world." Its concept of natural rights meant that the Revolution would not be bound by history and tradition but could reshape the contours of society according to reason.

The Revolution exploded in France in the summer of 1789, after many decades of ideological ferment, political decline, and social unrest. Ideologically, thinkers of the Enlightenment urged that governments should promote the greatest good of all people, not the narrow interests of a particular elite. They were hostile to the political power of the Roman Catholic Church as well as to the tax exemptions and landed power of the aristocracy. In France, the monarchy's finances were severely pressed, efforts to reform the tax structure foundered against the opposition of the aristocracy, and various groups were demanding economic and social change. Aristocrats wanted new political rights against royal power. The middle class sought a political voice to match their commercial importance and a government more friendly to their interests. The peasant majority, pressed by population growth, sought access to the lands of the aristocracy and the church, an end to remaining manorial dues and services, and relief from taxation.

These various discontents came to a head when Louis XVI called the Estates-General in 1789 to consider new taxes. Reform leaders, joined by some aristocrats and clergy, insisted that the Third Estate, representing elements of the urban middle class, be granted double the membership of the church and aristocratic estates, and that the entire body of Estates-General vote as a unit – they insisted, in other words, on a new kind of parliament. The king yielded, and the new National Assembly began to plan a constitution. The electors of Paris, who had continued to meet after choosing their deputies to the Estates-General, ousted the royal officials of the city government, formed a revolutionary municipality, and organized a citizens' militia, or national guard, to patrol the streets. Similar municipal revolutions occurred in 26 of the 30 largest French cities.

Riots in the summer of 1789 included a symbolic attack on the Bastille, a royal prison, and a series of risings in the countryside that forced the repeal of the remnants of manorialism and a proclamation of equality under the laws. By any standard, the fall of the Bastille to the Parisian crowd was a spectacular symbolic event – a seemingly miraculous triumph of the people against the power of royal arms. Louis XVI capitulated. The Parisian insurrection of July 14 not only saved the National Assembly from dissolution but altered the course of the Revolution by giving it a far more active, popular, and violent dimension.

Peasant insurgency propelled the Assembly into decreeing "the abolition of feudalism" as well as the church tithe, venality of office, regional privilege, and fiscal privilege. By sweeping away the old web of privileges, the August 4 decree permitted the Assembly to construct a new regime. Since it would take months to draft a constitution, the Assembly on August 27 promulgated its basic principles in a Declaration of the Rights of Man and of the Citizen. It trumpeted religious freedom and liberty – proclaiming that "men are born and remain free and equal in rights" – and freedom of the press and assembly, while reaffirming property rights. A rallying point for the future, the declaration stood as the death certificate of the ancien régime.

From 1789 to 1791 the National Assembly acted as a constituent assembly, drafting a constitution for the new regime while also governing from day to day. The constitution established a limited monarchy, with a clear separation of powers in which the king was to name and dismiss his ministers. This liberal phase of the French Revolution was followed, between 1792 and 1794, by a more radical period. Economic conditions deteriorated, prompting new urban riots. Roman Catholic and other groups rose in opposition to the revolution, resulting in forceful suppression and a corresponding growing insistence on loyalty to revolutionary principles. Most prominent revolutionaries belonged to the Jacobin Club, from constitutional royalists such as the Comte de Mirabeau, the Marquis de Lafayette, and the Comte de Barnave to radicals such as Jacques-Pierre Brissot, Alexandre Sabès Pétion, and Maximilien Robespierre.

By 1791 the Assembly found itself caught in a cross fire between the machinations of counter-revolutionaries – émigrés, royalist newspapers, refractory clergy – and the denunciations of radicals. In April 1792 France went to war against a coalition of Austria, Prussia, and the émigrés. On August 10 1792, a huge crowd of armed Parisians stormed the royal palace after a fierce battle with the garrison. The Legislative Assembly then had no choice but to declare the king suspended. That night more than half the deputies themselves fled Paris, for the Legislative Assembly, too, had lost its mandate. Those who remained ordered the election by universal male suffrage of a National Convention. It would judge the king, draft a new republican constitution, and govern France during the emergency. On September 21 the National Convention convened, ending the vacuum of authority that had followed the August 10 insurrection. Its first major task was to decide the fate of the ex-king. He was executed on January 21 1793.

Led by its Committee of Public Safety, the Convention placated the popular movement with decisive actions. It proclaimed the need for terror against the Revolution's enemies, made economic crimes such as hoarding into capital offences, and decreed a system of price and wage controls known as the Maximum. The Law of Suspects empowered local revolutionary committees to arrest "those who by their conduct, relations or language spoken or written, have shown themselves partisans of tyranny or federalism and enemies of liberty". About 17,000 death sentences were handed down by the military commissions and revolutionary tribunals of the Terror.

Governmental centralization increased; the decimal system was introduced. Mass military conscription was organized for the first time in European history, with the argument that, now that the government belonged to the people, the people must serve it loyally. A new constitution proclaimed the universal suffrage of man, and reforms in education and other areas were widely discussed. This radical phase of the revolution brought increasing military success to revolutionary troops in effectively reorganized armies, which conquered parts of the Low Countries and Germany and carried revolutionary laws in their wake. The revolution was beginning to become a European phenomenon.

Jacobin rule was replaced by a more moderate consolidation after 1795, during which, however, military expansion continued in several directions, notably in parts of Italy. The needs of war, along with recurrent domestic unrest, prompted a final revolutionary regime change, in 1799, that brought General Napoleon Bonaparte to power. Napoleon's regime confirmed many revolutionary changes within France, although Napoleon was a dictator and maintained only a sham parliament and rigorously policed press and assembly. Equality under the law was for the most part enhanced through sweeping new law codes; hereditary privileges among adult males became a thing of the past. A strongly centralized government recruited bureaucrats according to their abilities. Religious freedom survived, despite some conciliations to Roman Catholic opinion. Freedom of internal trade and encouragements to technical innovation allied the state with commercial growth. Sales of church land were confirmed, and rural France emerged as a nation of strongly independent peasant proprietors.

Napoleon's conquests cemented the spread of French revolutionary legislation to much of western Europe. The old regime was dead in Belgium, western Germany, and northern Italy. Prussia and Russia introduced important political reforms as a means of strengthening the state to resist the Napoleonic war machine. Prussia expanded its school system and modified serfdom; it also began to recruit larger armies. Britain was less affected, protected by its powerful navy and an expanding industrial economy that ultimately helped wear Napoleon down; but, even in Britain, the French revolutionary example spurred a new wave of democratic agitation.

Enlightened Despotism

While in America and France constitutional change and reform came through revolution, the main source of enlightened reform in some European countries was the crown. A change in attitude was apparent in the decline of religious resentments and discriminations. Religious toleration, however, was not the only article of faith of the Enlightenment. Its vision of a happier future included the reformation of education, the abolition of poverty, the alleviation of sickness, and the elimination of injustice. While the hopes of the enlightened reformers of the 18th century far outstripped their accomplishments, the practical results of their efforts should not be underestimated.

According to the doctrines of benevolent despotism, however, the chief instrument for the improvement of society was not private philanthropy but government action. The state had the primary responsibility for preparing the way for the golden age that, in the opinion of many intellectuals, awaited humankind. The extent to which official policy conformed to rationalist theory depended, in central Europe as elsewhere, on the personality and ability of the ruler.

Both of the leading powers of the Holy Roman Empire followed the teachings of benevolent despotism, though with substantially different results. The emperor Joseph II, a well-meaning though doctrinaire reformer, attempted to initiate a revolution from above against the opposition of powerful forces that continued to cling to tradition. After his mother Maria Theresa's death in 1780, Joseph tried to finish her work of reform. The judiciary and the executive had already been separated at the top; Joseph extended this process to the lower administrative levels. In 1786 the Universal Code of Civil Law was issued. Under Maria Theresa the physician Gerard van Swieten had organized a public health service, and in Joseph's time the General Hospital in Vienna was considered one of the best equipped in Europe. The monarchy's finances were balanced. The reorganization of the army secured Joseph's position in Europe. He ordered the abolition of serfdom; by the Edict of Toleration he established religious equality before the law, and he granted freedom of the press. The emancipation of the Jews within a short time endowed cultural life with new vitality.

Joseph's conflict with the Roman Catholic Church, however, posed more difficult problems. He established national training colleges for priests and deprived the bishops of their authority and limited their communications with the pope. The power of the church was even more affected by the dissolution of more than 700 monasteries not engaged in useful activities such as teaching or hospital work. The 36,000 monks forced to leave their orders were given an annuity or money to return home; those so returning could continue as secular priests.

Joseph's passionate zeal to change everything and to force a new form of life on his subjects met with embittered resistance, chiefly in such strongly traditional countries as the Austrian Netherlands and Hungary. His uncompromising programme of innovation also alienated the landed aristocracy, whose support was essential for the effective operation of the government. The emperor encountered mounting unrest, which did not end until his death in 1790, and the subsequent abandonment of most of the reforms that he had promulgated.

Frederick II of Prussia was more successful as an enlightened autocrat, but only because he was more cautious. Under his leadership Prussia became one of the great states of Europe. He also emerged quickly as a leading exponent of the ideas of enlightened government. His insistence on the primacy of state over personal or dynastic interests and his religious toleration widely affected the dominant intellectual currents of the age. Even more than his younger contemporaries, Catherine II the Great of Russia and Joseph II, it was Frederick who, during the mid-18th century, established in the minds of educated Europeans a notion of what "enlightened despotism" should be.

In 1749 and 1764 he issued decrees limiting the obligations of the peasant to his lord, and in 1748 he ordered officers not to treat their men "like serfs"; but these were essentially efforts to prevent the plight of the peasant from becoming so desperate that he would be driven into flight and thus jeopardize the supply of recruits to the army. Frederick invited settlers to cultivate reclaimed lands, and he encouraged entrepreneurs to increase the industrial capacity of Prussia. His religious tolerance, however, was one of the things that helped to mark him in the eyes of contemporaries as a truly enlightened ruler. The abolition of judicial torture, one of his first acts as king, also showed his genuine belief in this aspect of enlightened reform. On an even more fundamental level, the General Education Regulations (General-Landschul-Reglement) of 1763 attempted to create a system of universal primary education throughout the Prussian monarchy. Lack of resources limited its practical effect, but it was the most ambitious effort of its kind hitherto seen anywhere in Europe.

Many of the truly successful innovations were in the judicial system, where the reforming efforts of Samuel von Cocceji resulted in all judges in higher and appellate courts being appointed only after they had passed a rigorous examination. Cocceji also inspired the establishment in 1750 of a new Superior Consistory to supervise church and educational affairs and began the process of legal codification that culminated after Frederick's death in the issue of the Prussian Common Law (Das Allgemeine Preussische Landrecht) of 1794, one of the most important 18th-century efforts of this kind, which defined the principles and practices of an absolute government and a corporative society. Yet Frederick was also convinced that the Prussian landed noblemen, the Junkers, were the backbone of the state, and he continued accordingly to uphold the alliance between crown and aristocracy on which his kingdom had been built.

The achievements of benevolent despotism among the minor states of the Holy Roman Empire varied considerably. Some princes employed their inherited authority in a serious effort to improve the lot of their subjects. Charles Frederick of Baden, for example, devoted himself to the improvement of education in his margravate, and he even abolished serfdom, though manorial obligations remained. Charles Augustus of Saxe-Weimar-Eisenach was a hardworking administrator of his small Thuringian principality, whose capital, Weimar, he transformed into the cultural centre of Germany. Charles

Eugene of Württemberg, on the other hand, led a life of profligacy and licentiousness in defiance of protests by the estates of the duchy.

Following the death of Charles XII of Sweden in 1718, his sister Ulrika Eleonora was elected, but she abdicated in 1720 in favour of her husband, Frederick of Hessen (who ruled until 1751). This period saw a transition from absolutism to a parliamentary form of government in Sweden. The real reason for the change was the complete failure of the policy of "greatness" connected with Carolingian absolutism. According to the constitutional laws of 1720–23, the power now rested with the estates. The estates met regularly in the Riksdag (parliament), which designated the council. There the king was accorded a double vote but had no right to make decisions. In the Riksdag, decision-making took place in the "Secret Committee", from which the peasants, or the fourth estate, were excluded.

A true parliamentary system gradually developed, which, although hampered by cumbersome procedures, is a notable parallel to the contemporary English system. The political changes that marked the period are especially significant because of their influence on the Swedish constitution. Despite the turmoil that prevailed, the period was notable for its social and cultural advances. Ideas about land reform were formulated; progress in science was encouraged; and the Swedish press was initiated.

Gustav III, who succeeded to the Swedish throne in 1771, was an intelligent and cultured advocate of the Enlightenment. The new king began his reign with futile efforts to mediate between the contending factions of the Riksdag. But in August 1772 he seized effective power of the government and established a new constitution which, replacing that of 1720, increased the crown's powers at the expense of the Riksdag.

In the following years Gustav III introduced a number of enlightened reforms: torture as an instrument of legal investigation was abolished; freedom of the press was granted; the poor law was amended; religious toleration was accorded; free trade was promoted; the navy was strengthened; and in 1777 a comprehensive currency reform was carried out. The Riksdag Gustav III convened in 1778 proved tractable, but his reforms eventually aroused dissatisfaction among the nobility. The Riksdag of 1786 rejected most of Gustav's reforming policies.

Catherine the Great, the German-born empress of Russia (1762–96), led her country into full participation in the political and cultural life of Europe, carrying on the work begun by Peter the Great, and with her ministers reorganized the administration and law of the Russian Empire. Since her early days in Russia she had dreamed of establishing a reign of order and justice, spreading education, creating a court to rival Versailles, and developing a national culture that would be more than an imitation of French models. Her attempts at reform, however, were less than successful.

A disciple of the English and French liberal philosophers, she saw very quickly that the reforms advocated by Montesquieu or Rousseau, which were difficult enough to put into practice in Europe, did not at all correspond to the realities of an anarchic and backward Russia. In 1767 she convened a commission composed of delegates from all the provinces and from all social classes (except the serfs) for the purpose of ascertaining the true wishes of her people and framing a constitution. The debates went on for months and came to nothing. Catherine's Instruction to the commission was a draft of a constitution and a code of laws. It was considered too liberal for publication in France and remained a dead letter in Russia.

However, Catherine, like all the crowned heads of Europe, felt seriously threatened by the French Revolution. The divine right of royalty and the aristocracy was being questioned, and Catherine, although a "friend of the Enlightenment", had no intention of relinquishing her own privileges: "I am an aristocrat, it is my profession." In 1790 the writer A.N. Radishchev, who attempted to publish a work openly critical of the abuses of serfdom, was tried, condemned to death, then pardoned and exiled. Ironically, the sentiments Radishchev expressed were very similar to Catherine's Instruction of 1767.

7

PHILOSOPHY, ETHICS, AND RELIGION

The Rationalist Tradition

Whereas the philosophy of the Enlightenment was primarily epistemological and empiricist – concerned with explaining the nature and origin of knowledge in experience – the philosophy of the early modern period had been metaphysical and rationalistic – concerned with understanding the whole of reality through the power of reason alone.

Sir Francis Bacon, a source of inspiration for generations of later philosophers, had conceived of philosophy as a new technique of reasoning that would re-establish natural science on a firm foundation. In the *Advancement of Learning* (1605), he had charted the map of knowledge: history, which depends on the human faculty of memory; poetry, which depends on imagination; and philosophy, which depends on reason. To reason, however, Bacon assigned a completely experiential function. Fifteen years later, in his *Novum Organum*, he wrote that "the true business of philosophy must be . . . to apply the understanding . . . to a fresh examination of particulars."

Bacon's hope for a new birth of science depended not only on vastly more numerous and varied experiments but also on the use of a new method – tables of presence, of absence, and of degree – to establish the true causes of phenomena (the subject of physics) and the true "forms" of things (the subject of metaphysics – the study of the nature of being).

His enduring place in the history of philosophy lies, however, in his single-minded advocacy of experience as the only source of valid knowledge and in his profound enthusiasm for the perfection of natural science.

Thomas Hobbes shared with Bacon a strong concern for philosophical method. He produced one of the most systematic philosophies of the early modern period – an almost completely consistent description of humankind, civil society, and nature according to the tenets of mechanistic materialism. Hobbes' account of what philosophy is and ought to be clearly distinguished between content and method. As method, philosophy is simply reasoning or calculating by the use of words as to the causes or effects of phenomena. When a person reasons from causes to effects, he reasons synthetically; when he reasons from effects to causes, he reasons analytically. Hobbes classified the fields that form the content of philosophy as: (1) physics, (2) moral philosophy, and (3) civil philosophy. Physics is the science of the motions and actions of physical bodies conceived in terms of cause and effect. Moral philosophy (or, more accurately, psychology) is the detailed study of "the passions and perturbations of the mind" – that is, how minds are "moved" by desire, aversion, appetite, fear, anger, and envy. And civil philosophy deals with the concerted actions of people in a commonwealth – how, in detail, the wayward wills of human beings can be constrained by power (i.e., force) to prevent civil disorder and maintain peace.

Hobbes skirted, rather than solved, the philosophical problems about consciousness that had been raised by his contemporary René Descartes. Descartes' philosophy was dualistic, making a complete split between mind and matter. A crucial figure in the history of philosophy, Descartes combined the influences of the past into a synthesis that was striking in its originality and yet congenial to the scientific temper of the age. In the minds of all later historians, he counts as the progenitor of the modern spirit of philosophy.

From the past there seeped into the Cartesian synthesis doctrines about God from St Anselm and St Thomas Aquinas, a theory of the will from St Augustine, a deep sympathy with the stoicism of the Romans, and a sceptical method taken indirectly from the Greek philosophers Pyrrho and Sextus Empiricus. Descartes was also a great mathematician and the author of many important physical and anatomical experiments; he profoundly respected the work of Galileo. Descartes espoused empiricism in the physiological researches described in the *Discours de la méthode* (1637; *Discourse on Method*), a mechanistic interpretation of the physical world and of human action in the *Principia Philosophiae* (1644; *Principles of Philosophy*) and *Les passions de l'âme* (1649; *The Passions of the Soul*), and a mathematical bias in *Regulae ad Directionem Ingenii* (1701; *Rules for the Direction of the Mind*) and the metaphysics of the *Meditationes de Prima Philosophia* (1642; *Meditations on First Philosophy*). But it is the mathematical theme that clearly predominates in his philosophy.

In his *Principles*, Descartes defined philosophy as "the study of wisdom" or "the perfect knowledge of all one can know". Its chief utility is "for the conduct of life" (morals), "the conservation of health" (medicine), and "the invention of all the arts" (mechanics). He expressed the relation of philosophy to practical endeavours in the famous metaphor of the "tree": the roots are metaphysics, the trunk is physics, and the branches are morals, medicine, and mechanics. For Descartes, therefore, the most important part of the tree was the trunk. In other words, Descartes busied himself with metaphysics only in order to provide a firm foundation for physics. Thus, the *Discourse on Method*, which provides a synoptic view of Cartesian philosophy, shows it to be a physics founded upon metaphysics.

Descartes' mathematical bias was reflected in his determination to ground natural science not in sensation and probability (as did Bacon) but in premises that could be known with absolute certainty. Thus his metaphysics in essence consisted of three principles:

1. To employ the procedure of complete and systematic doubt to eliminate every belief that does not pass the test of indubitability (scepticism).
2. To accept no idea as certain that is not clear, distinct, and free of contradiction (mathematicism).
3. To found all knowledge upon the bedrock certainty of self-consciousness, so that "I think, therefore I am" becomes the only innate idea unshakable by doubt (subjectivism).

From the indubitability of the self, Descartes inferred the existence of a perfect God; and, from the fact that a perfect being is incapable of falsification or deception, he concluded that the ideas about the physical world that God has implanted in human beings must be true. The achievement of certainty about the natural world was thus guaranteed by the perfection of God and by the "clear and distinct" ideas that are his gift.

Cartesian metaphysics is the fountainhead of rationalism in modern philosophy, for it suggests that the mathematical criteria of clarity, distinctness, and logical consistency are the ultimate test of meaningfulness and truth. This stance is profoundly anti-empirical. For Descartes the understanding is vastly superior to the senses, and only reason can ultimately decide what constitutes truth in science.

The tradition of continental rationalism was carried on by two philosophers of genius: Benedict de Spinoza in Holland and his younger contemporary Gottfried Wilhelm Leibniz in Germany. Whereas Bacon's philosophy had been a search for method in science and Descartes' basic aim had been the achievement of scientific certainty, Spinoza's speculative system was one of the most comprehensive of the early modern period. Spinoza, in common with Hobbes, had a mechanistic world view and a political philosophy that sought political stability in centralized power. He also introduced the concept of philosophy as a personal and moral quest for wisdom and the achievement of human perfection.

Spinoza's magnum opus, the *Ethics* (1677), borrowed much from Descartes: the goal of a rational understanding of principles, the terminology of "substance" and "clear and distinct ideas", and the expression of philosophical knowledge in a complete deductive system using the geometric model of the *Elements* of Euclid (*c.* 300 BC). Spinoza conceived of the universe pantheistically as a single infinite substance, which he called "God", with the dual attributes (or aspects) of thought and extension. Extension is differentiated into plural "modes", or particular things, and the world as a whole possesses the properties of a timeless logical system – a complex of completely determined causes and effects. For Spinoza, the wisdom that philosophy seeks is ultimately achieved when one perceives the universe in its wholeness through the "intellectual love of God", which merges the finite individual with eternal unity and provides the mind with the pure joy that is the final achievement of its search.

Leibniz was a mathematician (he and Sir Isaac Newton independently discovered infinitesimal calculus), a jurist (he codified the laws of Mainz), a diplomat, a historian to royalty, and a court librarian in a princely house. Yet he was also one of the most original philosophers of the early modern period. Leibniz conceived of logic as a mathematical calculus. He was the first to distinguish "truths of reason" from "truths of fact" and to contrast the necessary propositions of logic and mathematics, which hold in all "possible worlds", with the contingent propositions of science, which hold only in some possible worlds (including the actual world). He saw clearly that, as the first kind of proposition is governed by the principle of contradiction (a proposition and its negation cannot both be true), the second is governed by the principle of sufficient reason (nothing exists or is the case without a sufficient reason).

In metaphysics, Leibniz – in contrast to Descartes' dualism and Spinoza's monism – posited the existence of an infinite number of spiritual substances, which he called "monads", each different, each a percipient of the universe around it, and each mirroring that universe from its own point of view. However, the differences between Leibniz's philosophy and that of Descartes and Spinoza are less significant than their similarities, in particular their extreme rationalism. In the *Principes de la nature et de la grâce fondés en raison* (1714; *Principles of Nature and of Grace Founded in Reason*), Leibniz stated a maxim that could fairly represent the entire school: "True reasoning depends upon necessary or eternal truths, such as those of logic, numbers, geometry, which establish an indubitable connection of ideas and unfailing consequences."

Locke and Berkeley

Although they both lived and worked in the late 17th century, Sir Isaac Newton and John Locke were the true fathers of the Enlightenment. Newton was the last of the scientific geniuses of the age, and his great *Principia* – the *Philosophiae Naturalis Principia Mathematica* (1687; *Mathematical Principles of Natural Philosophy*) – was the first scientific synthesis based on the application of mathematics to nature in every detail. The basic idea of the authority and autonomy of reason was, at root, the consequence of Newton's work. Following the spectacular achievement of Newton, it is impossible to exaggerate the enormous enthusiasm which the conviction that reason had succeeded in conquering the natural world kindled in all of the major thinkers of the late 17th and 18th centuries, from Locke to Kant.

Locke's *An Essay Concerning Human Understanding* (1689) marked a decisively new direction for modern philosophizing because it proposed what amounts to a new criterion of truth. Locke's aim in his essay – "to inquire into the origin, certainty, and extent of human knowledge" – involved three tasks:

1. To discover the origin of human ideas.
2. To determine their certainty and evidential value.
3. To examine the claims of all knowledge that is less than certain.

What was crucial for Locke, however, was that the second task is dependent upon the first. Following Renaissance custom,

Locke defined an idea as a mental entity: "whatever is the object of the understanding when a man thinks". But whereas for Descartes and the entire rationalist school the certainty of ideas had been a function of their self-evidence – i.e., of their clarity and distinctness – for Locke their validity depended expressly on the mode and manner of their origin. Thus, an intrinsic criterion of truth and validity was replaced with a genetic one.

Locke's exhaustive survey of mental contents is useful, if elaborate. Although he distinguished between ideas of sensation and ideas of reflection, the thrust of his efforts and those of his empiricist followers was to reduce the latter to the former, to minimize the originative power of the mind in favour of its passive receptivity to the sensory impressions received from without. Locke's classification of ideas into "simple" and "complex" was an attempt to distinguish mental contents that are derived directly from one or more of the senses (such as blueness or solidity, which come from a single sense such as sight or touch; and figure, space, extension, rest, and motion, which are the product of several senses combined), from complicated and compounded ideas of universals (such as a triangle and gratitude), substances, and relations (such as identity, diversity, and cause and effect).

Locke's *Essay* attempted to produce the total world of human conceptual experience from a set of elementary sensory building blocks, moving always from sensation toward thought and from the simple to the complex. The basic outcome of his epistemology was therefore:

1. That the ultimate source of human ideas is sense experience.
2. That all mental operations are a combining and compounding of simple sensory materials into complex conceptual entities.

Locke's theory of knowledge was based upon a kind of sensory atomism, in which the mind is an agent of discovery rather than of creation, and ideas are "like" the objects they represent, which in turn are the sources of the sensations the mind receives. Locke's theory also made the important distinction between "primary qualities" (such as solidity, figure, extension, motion, and rest), which are real properties of physical objects, and "secondary qualities" (such as colour, taste, and smell), which are merely the effects of such real properties on the mind.

It was precisely this dualism of primary and secondary qualities that Locke's successor, George Berkeley, sought to overcome. Although Berkeley was a bishop in the Anglican Church who professed a desire to combat atheistic materialism, his importance for the theory of knowledge lies rather in the way in which he demonstrated that, in the end, primary qualities are reducible to secondary qualities. In his major work, *A Treatise Concerning the Principles of Human Knowledge* (1710), Berkeley asserted that nothing exists except ideas and spirits (minds or souls). He distinguished three kinds of ideas: those that come from sense experience correspond to Locke's simple ideas of perception; those that come from "attending to the passions and operations of the mind" correspond to Locke's ideas of reflection; and those that come from compounding, dividing, or otherwise representing ideas correspond to Locke's compound ideas. By "spirit" Berkeley meant "one simple, undivided, active being". The activity of spirits consists of both understanding and willing: understanding is spirit perceiving ideas, and will is spirit producing ideas.

Berkeley's empiricism led to a denial of abstract ideas because he believed that general notions are simply fictions of the mind. Science, he argued, can easily dispense with the concept of matter: nature is simply that which human beings perceive through their sense faculties. This means that sense experiences themselves can be considered "objects for the mind". Furthermore, matter, as philosophers conceive it, does not exist, and indeed it is contradictory. For matter is supposedly unsensed extension, figure, and motion; but since extension, figure, and motion are ideas, they must be sensed. A physical object, therefore, is simply a recurrent group of sense qualities. With this important reduction of substance to quality, Berkeley became the father of the epistemological position known as phenomenalism, which remained an important influence in British philosophy well into the 20th century.

Hume and the Science of Human Nature

The third, and in many ways the most important, of the British empiricists was the sceptic David Hume. Hume's philosophical intention was to reap, humanistically, the harvest sowed by Newtonian physics, to apply the method of natural science to human nature. Hume followed Locke and Berkeley in approaching the problem of knowledge from a psychological perspective. He too found the origin of knowledge in sense experience. But Hume's relentless analysis discovered as much contingency in mind as in the external world. All uniformity in perceptual experience, he held, comes from "an associating quality of the mind".

Hume recognized two kinds of perception: "impressions" and "ideas". Impressions are perceptions that the mind experiences with the "most force and violence", and ideas are the "faint images" of impressions. Hume considered this distinction so obvious that he demurred from explaining it at any length: as he indicated in a summary explication in *A Treatise of Human Nature* (1739–40), impressions are felt, and ideas are thought.

All perceptions, whether impressions or ideas, can be either simple or complex. Whereas simple perceptions are not subject to further separation or distinction, complex perceptions are. An apple, for instance, is complex, insofar as it consists of a combination of simple perceptions of a certain shape, colour, texture, and aroma. It is noteworthy that, according to Hume, for every simple impression there is a simple idea that corresponds to it and differs from it only in force and vivacity, and vice versa. Thus, corresponding to the impression of red is the idea of red. This correlation does not hold true in general for complex perceptions; complex ideas do not have a correlate in reality. There is no complex idea, for example, corresponding to the complex impression of an extensive vista of the city of Rome.

Because the formation of every simple idea is always preceded by the experience of a corresponding simple impression, and because the experience of every simple impression is always followed by the formation of a corresponding simple idea, it follows, according to Hume, that simple impressions are the causes of their corresponding simple ideas.

There are two kinds of impressions: those of sensation and those of reflection. Regarding the former, Hume says little more than that sensation "arises in the soul originally from unknown causes". Impressions of reflection arise from a complicated series of mental operations. First, one experiences impressions of heat or cold, thirst or hunger, pleasure or pain; second, one forms corresponding ideas of heat or cold, thirst or hunger, pleasure or pain; and third, one's reflection on these ideas produces impressions of "desire and aversion, hope and fear".

Some explanation is needed for the fact that people tend to think in regular and predictable patterns. Hume says that the production of thoughts in the mind is guided by three principles: resemblance, contiguity, and cause and effect. Thus, a person who thinks of one idea is likely to think of another idea that resembles it; his thought is likely to run from red to pink to white or from dog to wolf to coyote. Concerning contiguity, people are inclined to think of things that are next to each other in space and time. Finally and most importantly, people tend to create associations between ideas of things that are causally related.

Hume uses the principle of resemblance for another purpose: to explain the nature of general ideas. Hume holds that there are no abstract ideas, and he affirms that all ideas are particular. Some of them, however, function as general ideas – i.e., ideas that represent many objects of a certain kind – because they incline the mind to think of other ideas that they resemble.

According to Hume, the mind is capable of apprehending two kinds of proposition or truth: those expressing "relations of ideas" and those expressing "matters of fact". The former can be intuited – i.e., seen directly – or deduced from other propositions. That a is identical with a, that b resembles c, and that d is larger than e are examples of propositions that are intuited. Unlike propositions about relations of ideas, propositions about matters of fact are known only through experience. By far the most important of these propositions are those that express or presuppose causal relations – e.g., "Fire causes heat" and "A moving billiard ball communicates its motion to any stationary ball it strikes." But how is it possible to know through experience that one kind of object or event causes another? What kind of experience would justify such a claim?

In the *Treatise*, Hume observes that our idea of causation contains three components: contiguity (i.e., near proximity) of time and place, temporal priority of the cause, and a more mysterious component, which he calls "necessary connection". In other words, when we say that x is a cause of y, we mean that instances of x and instances of y are always near each other in time and space, that instances of x occur before instances of y, and that there is some connection between x's and y's that makes it necessary that an instance of y occurs if an instance of x does.

It is easy to explain the origin in experience of the first two components of the idea of causation. In our past experience, all events consisting of a moving billiard ball striking a stationary one were quickly followed by events consisting of the movement of the formerly stationary ball. In addition, the first sort of event always preceded the second, and never the reverse. But whence the third component of the idea of causation, whereby we think that the striking of the stationary ball somehow necessitates that it will move?

Hume offers a "sceptical solution" of the problem of the origin of our idea of necessary connection. According to him, it arises from the feeling of "determination" that is created in the mind when it experiences the first member of a pair of events that it is long accustomed to experiencing together. When the mind observes the moving billiard ball strike the stationary one, it is moved by force of habit and custom to form an idea of the movement of the stationary ball. Hume's solution, however, does not justify this logically. Our only evidence for this is our past experience of contiguity and temporal precedence. "All inferences from experience, therefore, are effects of custom, not of reasoning."

The causal principle upon which all knowledge rests represents no necessary connections between things, therefore, but is simply the result of their constant conjunction in human minds. Moreover, the mind itself, far from being an independent power, is simply "a bundle of perceptions" without unity or cohesive quality. Hume's denial of a necessary order of nature on the one hand and of a substantial or unified self on the other precipitated a philosophical crisis from which Enlightenment philosophy was not to be rescued until the work of Kant.

Materialism in the 18th Century

Although the school of British empiricism represented the mainstream of Enlightenment philosophy until the time of Kant, it was by no means the only type of philosophy that the 18th century produced. There were many cross-currents of intellectual and philosophical expression.

The profound influence of Locke spread to France, where it not only resulted in the sceptical empiricism of Voltaire but also united with mechanistic aspects of Cartesianism to produce an entire school of sensationalistic materialism. Descartes' theory of the physical world, and especially his doctrine that animals are unconscious automata, had a mechanistic aspect that was taken up by 18th-century materialists, such as Julien de La Mettrie, the French physician whose appropriately titled *L'Homme machine* (1747; English translation *Man a Machine,* 1750) applied Descartes' view about animals to human beings.

Baron d'Holbach, whose *Système de la nature* (1770; *The System of Nature*) expounded a deterministic type of materialism in the light of evidence from contemporary science – humans became machines devoid of free will, and religion was excoriated as harmful and untrue – also propounded a hedonistic ethics as well as an uncompromising atheism, which provoked a reply even from the Deist Voltaire.

Étienne Bonnot de Condillac gave systematic expression to the views of Locke. Like Locke, Condillac maintained an empirical sensationalism based on the principle that observations made by sense perception are the foundation of human knowledge. The ideas of the *Essai sur l'origine des connaissances humaines* (1746; *Essay on the Origin of Human Knowledge*), are close to those of Locke, though on certain points Condillac modified Locke's position. In his most significant work, the *Traité des sensations* (1754; *Treatise on the Sensations*), Condillac questioned Locke's doctrine that the senses provide intuitive knowledge. He doubted, for example, that the human eye makes naturally correct judgements about the shapes, sizes, positions, and distances of objects. Examining the knowledge gained by each sense separately, he concluded that all human knowledge is transformed sensation, to the exclusion of any other principle, such as Locke's additional principle of reflection.

Denis Diderot, the 18th-century encyclopaedist, supported a broadly materialist outlook by considerations drawn from physiology, embryology, and the study of heredity. This position even found its way into many of the articles of the great French *Encyclopédie*.

Kant and the Critique of Reason

The works of Immanuel Kant, the greatest philosopher of the modern period, mark the true culmination of the philosophy of the Enlightenment. Historically speaking, Kant's great contribution was to elucidate both the sensory and the a priori, or non-empirical, elements in knowledge and thus to bridge the gap between the extreme rationalism of Leibniz and the extreme empiricism of Hume. But in addition to the brilliant content of his philosophical doctrines, Kant was responsible for three crucial philosophical innovations: a new definition of philosophy; a new conception of philosophical method; and a new structural model for the writing of philosophy.

Kant conceived of reason as being at the very heart of the philosophical enterprise. Philosophy's sole task, in his view, is to determine what reason can and cannot do. Philosophy, he said, "is the science of the relation of all knowledge to the essential ends of human reason"; its true aim is both constructive ("to outline the system of all knowledge arising from pure reason") and critical ("to expose the illusions of a reason that forgets its limits"). But in order for philosophy to be "the science of the highest maxims of reason", the philosopher must be able to determine the source, the extent, and the validity of human knowledge and the ultimate limits of reason. And these tasks require a special philosophical method.

Sometimes Kant called this the "transcendental method", but more often the "critical method". His purpose was to reject the dogmatic assumptions of the rationalist school, and his wish was to return to the semi-sceptical position with which Descartes had begun before his dogmatic pretensions to certainty took hold. Kant's method was to conduct a critical examination of the powers of a priori reason – an inquiry into what reason can achieve when all experience is removed. His method was based on the assumption that objects must conform to human knowledge – or to the human apparatus of knowing – rather than that human knowledge must conform to objects. The question then became: What is the exact nature of this knowing apparatus?

Unlike Descartes, Kant could not question that knowledge exists. No one raised in the Enlightenment could doubt, for example, that mathematics and Newtonian physics were real. Kant's methodological question was rather: How is mathematical and physical knowledge possible? How must human knowledge be structured in order to make these sciences secure? The attempt to answer these questions was the task of Kant's great work *Kritik der reinen Vernunft* (1781; *Critique of Pure Reason*).

Kant's aim was to examine reason not merely in one of its domains but in each of its employments according to the threefold structure of the human mind that he had inherited from Wolff. Thus the critical examination of reason in thinking (science) is undertaken in the *Critique of Pure Reason*, that of reason in willing (ethics) in the *Kritik der praktischen Vernunft* (1788; *Critique of Practical Reason*), and that of reason in feeling (aesthetics) in the *Kritik der Urteilskraft* (1790; *Critique of Judgement*).

The *Critique of Pure Reason* is divided into two parts. The "Transcendental Doctrine of Elements" deals with the sources of human knowledge, whereas the "Transcendental Doctrine of Method" draws up a methodology for the use of "pure reason" and its a priori ideas. The simplest way of describing the contents of the *Critique* is to say that it is a treatise about metaphysics: it seeks to show the impossibility of one sort of metaphysics and to lay the foundations for another. Leibnizian metaphysics, the object of his attack, is criticized for assuming that the human mind can arrive, by pure thought, at truths about entities, which, by their very nature, can never be objects of experience, such as God, human freedom, and immortality. Kant maintained that the mind has no such power and that the vaunted metaphysics is thus a sham.

As Kant saw it, the problem of metaphysics, as indeed of any science, is to explain how, on the one hand, its principles can be necessary and universal and yet involve also a knowledge of the real and so provide the investigator with the possibility of more knowledge than is analytically contained in what he already knows – i.e., more than is implicit in the meaning of his judgements. To meet these two conditions, Kant maintained, knowledge must rest on judgements that are a priori, for it is only as they are separate from the contingencies of experience that they could be necessary and yet also synthetic – i.e., so that the predicate term contains something more than is analytically contained in the subject. Thus, for example, the proposition that all bodies are extended is not synthetic but analytic because the notion of extension is contained in the very notion of body; whereas the proposition that all bodies are heavy is synthetic because weight supposes, in addition to the notion of body, the notion of bodies in relation to one another. Hence, the basic problem, as Kant formulated it, is to determine "How [i.e., under what conditions] are synthetic a priori judgements possible?"

This problem arises, according to Kant, in three fields, viz., in mathematics, physics, and metaphysics; and the three main divisions of the first part of the *Critique* deal respectively with these. In the "Transcendental Aesthetic", Kant argued that mathematics necessarily deals with space and time and then claimed that these are both a priori forms of human sensibility that condition whatever is apprehended through the senses. In the "Transcendental Analytic", the most crucial as well as the most difficult part of the book, he maintained that physics is a priori and synthetic because in its ordering of experience it uses concepts of a special sort. These concepts – "categories", he called them – are not so much read out of experience as read into it and, hence, are a priori, or pure, as opposed to empirical. But they differ from empirical concepts in something more than their origin: their whole role in knowledge is different; for, whereas empirical concepts serve to correlate particular experiences and so to bring out in a detailed way how experience is ordered, the categories have the function of prescribing the general form that this detailed order must take. They belong, as it were, to the very framework of knowledge.

But although they are indispensable for objective knowledge, the sole knowledge that the categories can yield is of objects of possible experience; they yield valid and real knowledge only when they are ordering what is given through sense in space and time.

In the "Transcendental Dialectic" Kant turned to consideration of a priori synthetic judgements in metaphysics. Here, he claimed, the situation is just the reverse from what it was in mathematics and physics. Metaphysics cuts itself off from sense experience in attempting to go beyond it and, for this very reason, fails to attain a single true a priori synthetic judgement. To justify this claim, Kant analysed the use that metaphysics makes of the concept of the unconditioned. Reason, according to Kant, seeks for the unconditioned or absolute in three distinct spheres: (1) in philosophical psychology it seeks for an absolute subject of knowledge; (2) in the sphere of cosmology, it seeks for an absolute beginning of things in time, for an absolute limit to them in space, and for an absolute limit to their divisibility; and (3) in the sphere of theology, it seeks for an absolute condition for all things. In each case, Kant claimed to show that the attempt is doomed to failure by leading to an antinomy in which equally good reasons can be given for both the affirmative and the negative position. The metaphysical "sciences" of rational psychology, rational cosmology, and natural theology thus turn out to be without foundation.

Kant's attack upon metaphysics was held by many in his own day to bring both religion and morality down with it. Yet Kant not only proposed to put metaphysics "on the sure path of science", but was prepared to say that he "inevitably" believed in the existence of God and in a future life.

The *Critique of Practical Reason* is Kant's moral philosophy and the standard source book for his ethical doctrines. There are many points of similarity between Kant's ethics and his epistemology. Just as the distinction between sense and intelligence was fundamental for the former, so is that between the inclinations and moral reason for the latter. And just as the nature of the human cognitive situation was elucidated in the first *Critique* by reference to the hypothetical notion of an intuitive understanding, so is that of the human moral situation clarified by reference to the notion of a "holy will". For a will of this kind there would be no distinction between reason and inclination; a being possessed of a holy will would always act as it ought. It would not, however, have the concepts of duty and moral obligation, which enter only when reason and desire find themselves opposed. In the case of human beings, the opposition is continuous, for they are at the same time both flesh and spirit. Hence, the moral life is a continuing struggle in which morality appears to the potential delinquent in the form of a law that demands to be obeyed for its own sake – a law, however, the commands of which are not issued by some alien authority but represent the voice of reason, which the moral subject can recognize as his own.

In the "Dialectic", Kant took up again the ideas of God, freedom, and immortality. Dismissed in the first *Critique* as objects that humans can never know because they transcend sense experience, he now argued that they are essential postulates for the moral life. Although not reachable in metaphysics, they are absolutely essential for moral philosophy. Practical, like theoretical, reason was for Kant formal rather than material – a framework of formative principles rather than a content of actual rules. This is why he put such stress on his first formulation of what he called the categorical imperative: "Act only on that maxim through which you can at the same time will that it should become a universal law." Lacking any insight into the moral realm, humans can only ask themselves whether what they are proposing to do has the formal character of law – the character, namely, of being the same for all persons similarly circumstanced.

The *Critique of Judgement* is best regarded as a series of appendices to the other two *Critiques*. The work falls into two main parts, called respectively "Critique of Aesthetic Judgement" and "Critique of Teleological Judgement". In the first of these, Kant analysed the notion of "aesthetic purposiveness" in judgements that ascribe beauty to something. Such a judgement, according to him, unlike a mere expression of taste, lays claim to general validity; yet it cannot be said to be cognitive because it rests on feeling, not on argument. The explanation lies in the fact that, when a person contemplates an object and finds it beautiful, there is a certain harmony between his imagination and his understanding, of which he is aware from the immediate delight that he takes in the object. Imagination grasps the object and yet is not restricted to any definite concept; whereas a person imputes the delight that he feels to others because it springs from the free play of his cognitive faculties, which are the same in all human beings.

In the second part of the *Critique of Judgement*, Kant considered teleology in nature as it is posed by the existence in organic bodies of things of which the parts are reciprocally means and ends to each other. In dealing with these bodies, one cannot be content with merely mechanical principles. Yet if mechanism is abandoned and the notion of a purpose or end of nature is taken literally, this seems to imply that the things to which it applies must be the work of some supernatural designer; but this would mean a passing from the sensible to the suprasensible, a step proved in the first *Critique* to be impossible. Kant answered this objection by admitting that teleological language cannot be avoided in taking account of natural phenomena; but it must be understood as meaning only that organisms must be thought of "as if" they were the product of design – and that is by no means the same as saying that they are deliberately produced.

Problems of Ethical Philosophy

It was Thomas Hobbes who brought ethics into the modern era. He developed an ethical position based only on the facts of human nature and the circumstances in which humans live. The philosophical edifice he constructed stands on its own foundations; God merely crowns the apex.

Hobbes started with a severe view of human nature: all voluntary acts of human beings are aimed at pleasure or self-preservation. His definition of good is equally devoid of religious or metaphysical assumptions. A thing is good, according to him, if it is "the object of any man's appetite or desire". He insisted that the term must be used in relation to a person – nothing is simply good in itself, independently of any person who may desire it.

This unpromising picture of self-interested individuals who have no notion of good apart from their own desires served as the foundation of Hobbes' account of justice and morality in his masterpiece, *Leviathan; or, The Matter, Form, and Power of a Commonwealth, Ecclesiastical and Civil* (1651). Starting with the premise that humans are self-interested and that the world does not provide for all their needs, Hobbes argued that in the hypothetical state of nature, before the existence of civil society, there was competition between individuals for wealth, security, and glory. What would ensue in such a state is Hobbes' famous "war of all against all", in which there could be no industry, commerce, or civilization, and in which human life would be "solitary, poor, nasty, brutish, and short". The struggle would occur because each individual would rationally pursue his own interests, but the outcome would be in no one's interests.

How can this disastrous situation be avoided? Not by an appeal to morality or justice; in the state of nature these ideas have no meaning. Yet, everyone wishes to survive, and everyone can reason. Reason leads people to seek peace if it is attainable, but to continue to use all the means of war if it is not. Peace may be obtained only by means of a social contract, in which each person agrees to give up his right to attack others in return for the same concession from everyone else. And such a contract must be enforced. To do this everyone must hand over his powers to some other person or group of persons who will punish anyone who breaches the contract: the "sovereign" or Leviathan – who might be a monarch, an elected legislature, or almost any other form of political authority.

There was, of course, immediate opposition to Hobbes' views. The English theologian Ralph Cudworth believed that the distinction between good and evil does not lie in human desires but is something objective that can be known by reason, just like the truths of mathematics. Henry More, another leading member of the Cambridge Platonists, attempted to give effect to the comparison between mathematics and morality by formulating moral axioms that could be recognized as self-evidently true. In marked contrast to Hobbes, More included an "axiom of benevolence": "If it be good that one man should be supplied with the means of living well and happily, it is mathematically certain that it is doubly good that two should be so supplied, and so on." Here, More was attempting to build on something that Hobbes himself accepted – namely, the desire of each individual to be supplied with the means of living well. More, however, wanted to enlist reason to show how one could move beyond this narrow egoism to a universal benevolence.

Samuel Clarke, a theologian and philosopher best known for his role as Newton's acolyte in a wide-ranging dispute with Leibniz, the next major intuitionist, accepted More's axiom of benevolence in slightly different words. He was also responsible for a "principle of equity", which, though derived from the Golden Rule so widespread in ancient ethics, was formulated with a new precision: "Whatever I judge reasonable or unreasonable for another to do for me, that by the same judgement I declare reasonable or unreasonable that I in the like case should do for him." As for the means by which these moral truths are known, Clarke accepted Cudworth's and More's analogy with truths of mathematics and added the idea that what human reason discerns is a certain "fitness or unfitness" about the relationship between circumstances and actions. The right action in a given set of circumstances is the fitting one; the wrong action is unfitting. This is something known intuitively and is self-evident.

Such intuitionism faces a serious problem that has always been a barrier to its acceptance: how does the discerning of a moral truth provide one with a motive sufficient to override the desire for profit? Some used the divine sanction of an all-powerful God. Other thinkers, however, wanted to show that it is reasonable to do what is good independently of the threats of any external power, human or divine. This desire lay behind the development of the major alternative to intuitionism in 17th- and 18th-century British moral philosophy: moral sense theory. The debate between the intuitionists and the moral sense theorists aired for the first time what is still one of the central issues in moral philosophy: is morality based on reason or on feelings?

The Moral Sense School

The term moral sense was first used by the 3rd Earl of Shaftesbury, whose writings reflect the optimistic tone both of the school of thought he founded and of so much of the philosophy of the 18th-century Enlightenment. Shaftesbury believed that Hobbes had erred by presenting a one-sided picture of human nature. Selfishness is not the only natural passion. There are also natural feelings such as benevolence, generosity, sympathy, gratitude, and so on. These feelings give one an "affection for virtue" – what Shaftesbury called a moral sense – which creates a natural harmony between virtue and self-interest. Shaftesbury was, of course, realistic enough to acknowledge that there are also contrary desires and that not all people are virtuous all of the time. Virtue could, however, be recommended because – and here Shaftesbury drew upon a theme of Greek ethics – the pleasures of virtue are superior to the pleasures of vice.

Joseph Butler, a bishop of the Church of England, developed Shaftesbury's position in two ways. He strengthened the case for a harmony between morality and enlightened self-interest by claiming that happiness occurs as a by-product of the satisfaction of desires for things other than happiness itself. Those who aim directly at happiness do not find it; those whose goals lie elsewhere are more likely to achieve happiness as well. Butler was not doubting the reasonableness of pursuing one's own happiness as an ultimate aim. He held, however, that direct and simple egoism is a self-defeating strategy. Egoists will do better for themselves by adopting immediate goals other than their own interests and living their everyday lives in accordance with these more immediate goals.

Butler's second addition to Shaftesbury's account was the idea of conscience. This he conceived as a second natural guide to conduct, alongside enlightened self-interest. Butler believed that there is no inconsistency between the two; he admitted, however, that sceptics may doubt "the happy tendency of virtue", and for them conscience can serve as an authoritative guide.

Butler also argued for a broader empiricism, which for him centred on the significance of humans as moral agents and on a reasonableness that need not always conform to a mathematical paradigm. In a matter of great consequence, a person's action can be reasonable even though there may be little supporting evidence for his decision and though, indeed, the evidence may be very much against it. It may, thus, often be a moral duty to act in such problematical circumstances. This led to Butler's famous doctrine of probability – "probability is the very guide of life."

The moral sense school reached its fullest development in the works of the Scottish philosopher Francis Hutcheson and his countryman David Hume. Hutcheson was concerned with showing, against the intuitionists, that moral judgement cannot be based on reason and therefore must be a matter of whether an action is "amiable or disagreeable" to one's moral sense. Like Butler's notion of conscience, Hutcheson's moral sense does not find pleasing only, or even predominantly, those actions that are in one's own interest. On the contrary, Hutcheson conceived moral sense as based on a disinterested benevolence. This led him to state, as the ultimate criterion of the goodness of an action, a principle that was to serve as the basis for the utilitarian reformers: "That action is best which procures the greatest happiness for the greatest numbers."

Hume, like Hutcheson, held that reason cannot be the basis of morality. His chief ground for this conclusion was that morality is essentially practical: there is no point in judging something good if the judgement does not incline one to act accordingly. Reason alone, however, Hume regarded as "the slave of the passions". Reason can show people how best to achieve their ends, but it cannot determine what those ends should be; it is incapable of moving one to action except in accordance with some prior want or desire. Hence, reason cannot give rise to moral judgements. "'Tis not contrary to reason to choose my total ruin, to prevent the least uneasiness of an Indian or person wholly unknown to me," Hume stated. His point was simply that to have these preferences is to have certain desires or feelings; they are not matters of reason at all.

Hume's forceful presentation of this argument against a rational basis for morality would have been enough to earn him a place in the history of ethics, but it is by no means his only achievement in this field. In the *Treatise* he points, almost as an afterthought, to the fact that writers on morality regularly start by making various observations about human nature or about the existence of a God – all statements of fact about what is the case – and then suddenly switch to statements about what ought or ought not to be done. Hume says that he cannot conceive how this new relationship of "ought" can be deduced from the preceding statements that were related by "is", and he suggests that these authors should explain how this deduction is to be achieved. The point has since been called Hume's Law and taken as proof of the existence of a gulf between facts and values, or between "is" and "ought".

Hume's positive account of morality is in keeping with the moral sense school: "The hypothesis which we embrace is plain. It maintains that morality is determined by sentiment. It defines virtue to be whatever mental action or quality gives to a spectator the pleasing sentiment of approbation; and vice the contrary." In other words, Hume takes moral judgements to be based on a feeling. They do not reflect any objective state of the world.

Normative Ethics and Utilitarianism

After the moral sense school, the focus shifted to which actions are right and which are wrong, the province of normative ethics. The impetus to the discussion of normative ethics was provided by the challenge of utilitarianism. The essential principle of utilitarianism was, as mentioned earlier, put forth by Hutcheson. Curiously, it was further developed by the English theologian William Paley. He held that right and wrong are determined by the will of God, yet because he believed that God wills the happiness of his creatures, his normative ethics were utilitarian: whatever increases happiness is right; whatever diminishes it is wrong.

Notwithstanding these predecessors, Jeremy Bentham is properly considered the father of modern utilitarianism. It was he who made the utilitarian principle serve as the basis for a unified and comprehensive ethical system that applies, in theory at least, to every area of life. Never before had a complete, detailed system of ethics been so consistently constructed from a single fundamental ethical principle.

Bentham's ethics began with the proposition that nature has placed human beings under two masters: pleasure and pain. Anything that seems good must be either directly pleasurable or thought to be a means to pleasure or to the avoidance of pain. Conversely, anything that seems bad must be either directly painful or thought to be a means to pain or to the deprivation of pleasure. From this Bentham argued that the words right and wrong can be meaningful only if they are used in accordance with the utilitarian principle, so that whatever increases the net surplus of pleasure over pain is right and whatever decreases it is wrong.

Bentham then considered how one is to weigh the consequences of an action and thereby decide whether it is right or wrong. One must, he says, take account of the pleasures and pains of everyone affected by the action, and this is to be done on an equal basis: "Each to count for one, and none for more than one." One must also consider how certain or uncertain the pleasures and pains are, their intensity, how long they last, and whether they tend to give rise to further feelings of the same or of the opposite kind. Bentham did not allow for distinctions in the quality of pleasure or pain as such; he affirmed that "quantity of pleasure being equal, pushpin is as good as poetry." This led his opponents to characterize his philosophy as one fit for pigs. Yet Bentham never thought that the aim of utilitarianism was to explain or to justify ordinary moral views; it was, rather, to reform them.

Philosophy and Religion

Although philosophers of the modern period are usually thought to be purely secular thinkers, in fact nothing could be further from the truth. From the early 17th century until the middle of the 18th century, all the great philosophers incorporated substantial religious elements into their work. Blaise Pascal in the 17th century had propagated a religious doctrine, in his 18 *Lettres écrites par Louis de Montalte à un provincial*, better known as *Lettres Provinciales* (1657; *Provincial Letters*), and *Pensées* (1670; *Thoughts*), that taught the experience of God through the heart rather than through reason. In his *Meditations*, Descartes offered two distinct proofs of the existence of God and asserted that no one who does not have a rationally well-founded belief in God can have knowledge in the proper sense of the term. Spinoza began his *Ethics* with a proof of God's existence and then discussed at length its implications for understanding all reality. And Berkeley explained the apparent stability of the sensible world by appealing to God's constant thought of it.

Among the reasons modern philosophers are mistakenly thought to be primarily secular thinkers is that many of their epistemological principles, including some that were designed to defend religion, were later interpreted as subverting the rationality of religious belief. Hobbes, for instance, argued that the proposition that faith is rational belonged not to the intellect but to the will. The significance of religious propositions, in other words, lies not in what they say but in how they are used. To profess a religious proposition is not to assert a factual claim about the world, which may then be supported or refuted with reasons, but merely to give praise and honour to God and to obey the commands of lawful religious authorities.

In *An Essay Concerning Human Understanding*, Locke further eroded the intellectual status of religious propositions by making them subordinate to reason in several respects. First, reason can restrict the possible content of propositions allegedly revealed by God; in particular, no proposition of faith can be a contradiction. Furthermore, because no revelation can contain an idea not derived from sense experience, we should not believe St Paul when he speaks of experiencing things as "eye hath not seen, nor ear heard, nor hath it entered into the heart of man to conceive . . .".

Another respect in which reason takes precedence over faith is that knowledge based on immediate sense experience is always more certain than any alleged revelation. Rational proofs in mathematics and science also cannot be controverted by divine revelation. "Nothing that is contrary to, and inconsistent with, the clear and self-evident dictates of reason", says Locke, "has a right to be urged or assented to as a matter of faith."

According to Locke, faith shares a room with probable truths, which are propositions of which reason cannot be certain. There are two types of probable truth: that which concerns observable matters of fact, and that which goes "beyond the discovery of our sense". Religious propositions can belong to either category. Thus the propositions "Caesar crossed the Rubicon" and "Jesus walked on water" belong to the first category, because they make claims about events that would be observable if they occurred; while propositions like "Angels exist" belong to the second category, because they concern entities that by definition cannot be objects of sense experience. Although it might seem that Locke's mixing of religious and scientific claims helped to secure a place for the former, in fact it did not. For Locke also held that "reason must judge" whether or not something is a revelation, and more generally that "Reason must be our last judge and guide in everything."

For Descartes, both the rise of modern science and the rediscovery of ancient scepticism were important influences. The challenge of scepticism, as Descartes saw it, is vividly described in his *Meditations*. Descartes distinguished two sources of knowledge: intuition and deduction. Intuition is an unmediated mental "seeing", or direct apprehension. Descartes' intuition of his own thinking guarantees that his belief that he is thinking is true. Thus, Descartes attempted to prove to his own satisfaction that God, the primary cause of his material universe and the laws of nature, exists; that the standard for knowing something is having a "clear and distinct" idea of it; that mind is more easily known than body; that the essence of matter is extension; and, finally, that most of his former beliefs are true. Unfortunately for Descartes, few people were convinced by these arguments.

Many of Descartes' successors can be best understood by reference to him. Nicolas Malebranche, a French Cartesian philosopher, and the occasionalist philosophers were more radical than Descartes; they dispensed with any unity whatever in human beings and linked together mind and body by means of the constant correlation effected by God himself, claiming that mental events were merely "occasions" for God effecting material change. For Spinoza, the whole universe had not only Descartes' two attributes of mentality and materiality but an infinite number of attributes, and it could be alternatively named God or Nature. Each existent in the world could be pictured as a particular whirlpool in an infinitely deep sea made up of endless layers of particular fluids of which man knows only two – mentality and materiality. Leibniz viewed Descartes' minds as the only ultimate existents, so that even material things were colonies of souls. God was viewed as the supreme monad (the ultimate substance) that establishes co-herence and harmony among all other monads. What appears to human beings as the external world is, so to speak, the result of blurred vision on the part of those groups of monads that are human beings.

Berkeley, in his major work, *A Treatise Concerning the Principles of Human Knowledge* (1710), retained Locke's beliefs in the existence of mind, substance, and causation as an unseen force or power in objects. As we have seen, for Berkeley, nothing existed except ideas and spirits (minds or souls). Ostensibly physical objects like tables and chairs were really nothing more than collections of sensible ideas. This philosophy later inspired the clichéd question of whether a tree falling in an uninhabited forest makes a sound, though Ber-keley would never considered it in these terms. He sometimes says that a table in an unperceived room would be perceived if someone were there. But does it exist when it is not perceived?

Berkeley's answer is that, when no human is perceiving a table or other such object, God is; and it is God's thinking that keeps the otherwise unperceived object in existence. Berkeley's doctrine that things unperceived by human beings continue to exist in the thought of God was not novel. It was part of the traditional belief of Christian philosophers from Augustine through Aquinas and at least to Descartes that God not only creates all things but also keeps them in existence by thinking of them.

According to Kant, because human beings can experience the world only as a system that is bounded by space and time and completely determined by causal laws, it follows that they can have no theoretical (i.e., scientific) knowledge of anything that is inconsistent with such a realm or that by definition exists independently of it – this includes God, human freedom, and the immortality of the soul. Nevertheless, belief in these ideas is justified, because each is a necessary condition of our conceiving of ourselves as moral agents. Kant held that all human beings, in their awareness of and reverence for the categorical imperative, share in one religion; the pre-eminence of Christianity lies in the conspicuous way in which Jesus enshrined this moral ideal.

Deism and "Natural Religion"

Inevitably, during the Enlightenment the method of reason was applied to religion itself. The product of a search for a natural – rational – religion was Deism, which, although never an organized movement, conflicted with Christianity for two centuries, especially in England and France. The English Deists – who included Charles Blount, the 3rd Earl of Shaftesbury, Anthony Collins, Thomas Woolston, Matthew Tindal, Thomas Morgan, Thomas Chubb, and John Toland –

espoused what they termed "natural religion", a certain body of religious knowledge that is inborn in every person or that can be acquired through the rational examination of nature, as opposed to the religious knowledge acquired through either revelation or the teaching of any church.

For the Deist a very few religious truths sufficed, and they were truths felt to be manifest to all rational beings: the existence of one God, often conceived of as architect or builder, the existence of a system of rewards and punishments administered by that God, and the obligation of human beings to virtue and piety. The Deists who presented purely rationalist proofs for the existence of God, usually variations on the argument from the apparent design or order of the universe, were able to derive support from the vision of the lawful physical world that Newton had delineated. Although the Deists differed among themselves, they joined in attacking both the existing religious establishment and the wild manifestations of the dissenters. The Deist ideal was sober natural religion without the trappings of Catholicism and the High Church in England, and free from the passionate excesses of Protestant fanatics.

For many religious Deists the teachings of Christ were not essentially novel but were, in reality, as old as creation, a republication of primitive monotheism. Religious leaders had arisen among many peoples – Socrates, Buddha, Muhammad – and their mission had been to effect a restoration of the simple religious faith of early people. Some writers, while admitting the similarity of Christ's message to that of other religious teachers, tended to preserve the unique position of Christianity as a divine revelation. It was possible to believe even in prophetic revelation and still remain a Deist, for revelation could be considered as a natural historical occurrence consonant with the definition of the goodness of God. The more extreme Deists, of course, could not countenance this degree of divine intervention in human affairs.

Natural religion was sufficient and certain; the tenets of all positive religions contained extraneous, even impure elements. Deists accepted the moral teachings of the Bible without any commitment to the historical reality of the reports of miracles. Most Deist argumentation attacking the literal interpretation of Scripture as divine revelation leaned upon the findings of 17th-century biblical criticism. Woolston, who resorted to an allegorical interpretation of the whole of the New Testament, was an extremist even among the more audacious Deists. He formally joined the Deists with his book *The Moderator Between an Infidel and an Apostate* (1725).

In addition to questioning prophecies and the resurrection of Christ, Woolston insisted on an allegorical interpretation of biblical miracles. He applied his principles in particular in *A Discourse on Our Saviour's Miraculous Power of Healing* (1730). Tindal was perhaps the most moderate of the group. Toland was violent; his denial of all mystery in religion was supported by analogies among Christian, Judaic, and pagan esoteric religious practices, equally condemned as the machinations of priests. In 1696 he published his celebrated *Christianity Not Mysterious*, in which he tried to show that not all biblical doctrines require faith in order to be understood but are, rather, perfectly intelligible to human reason unaided by divine revelation. The book caused a public uproar, and proceedings were brought against him.

The Deists were particularly vehement against any manifestation of religious fanaticism and enthusiasm. In this respect Shaftesbury's *Letter Concerning Enthusiasm* (1708) was probably the crucial document in propagating their ideas. Revolted by the Puritan fanatics of the previous century and by the wild hysteria of a group of French exiles prophesying in London in

1707, Shaftesbury denounced all forms of religious extravagance as perversions of true religion. Any description of God that depicted his impending vengeance, vindictiveness, jealousy, and destructive cruelty was blasphemous. Because sound religion could find expression only among healthy men, the argument was common in Deist literature that the preaching of extreme asceticism, the practice of self-torture, and the violence of religious persecutions were all evidence of psychological illness and had nothing to do with authentic religious sentiment and conduct. The Deist God, ever gentle, loving, and benevolent, intended men to behave toward one another in the same kindly and tolerant fashion.

Ideas of this general character were voiced on the Continent at about the same period by such men as Pierre Bayle, even though he would have rejected the Deist identification. During the heyday of the French philosophes, the more daring thinkers – Voltaire among them – gloried in the name Deist and declared the kinship of their ideas with those of rationalist English ecclesiastics, who would have repudiated the relationship. The dividing line between Deism and atheism among the philosophes was often rather blurred, as is evidenced by *Le Rêve de d'Alembert* (written in 1769; *The Dream of d'Alembert*), which describes a discussion between the two "fathers" of the *Encyclopédie*: the Deist d'Alembert and the atheist Diderot. Diderot had drawn his inspiration from Shaftesbury, and thus in his early career he was committed to a more emotional Deism. Later in life, however, he shifted to the atheist materialist circle of the Baron d'Holbach.

English Deism was transmitted to Germany primarily through translations of Shaftesbury. In a commentary on Shaftesbury published in 1720, Leibniz accepted the Deist conception of God as an intelligent creator but refused the contention that a God who metes out punishments is evil.

H.S. Reimarus, author of many philosophical works, maintained in his *Apologie oder Schutzschrift für die vernünftigen Verehrer Gottes* (*Defence for the Rational Adorers of God*) that the human mind by itself without revelation was capable of reaching a perfect religion. Reimarus did not dare to publish the book during his lifetime, but it was published in 1774–8 by Gotthold Ephraim Lessing, one of the great seminal minds in German literature. According to Lessing, the common person, uninstructed and unreflecting, will not reach a perfect knowledge of natural religion; he will forget or ignore it. Thus, the several positive religions can help people achieve more complete awareness of the perfect religion than could ever be attained by any individual mind.

William Paley and the Argument from Design

Although the argument for a divine designer of the universe had been propounded by medieval thinkers, it was developed in great detail in 17th- and 18th-century Europe by writers such as Robert Boyle, John Ray, Samuel Clarke, and William Derham and at the beginning of the 19th century by William Paley. They asked: is not the eye as manifestly designed for seeing, and the ear for hearing, as a pen for writing or a clock for telling the time; and does not such design imply a designer? The belief that the universe is a coherent and efficiently functioning system likewise, in this view, indicates a divine intelligence behind it.

Robert Boyle strove to demonstrate ways in which science and religion were mutually supportive. For Boyle, studying nature as a product of God's handiwork was an inherently religious duty. He argued that this method of study would, in return, illuminate God's omnipresence and goodness, thereby enhancing a scientist's understanding of the divine. *The Chris-*

tian Virtuoso (1690) summarized these views and may be seen as a manifesto of Boyle's own life as the model of a Christian scientist. In 1691 Ray published *The Wisdom of God Manifested in the Works of the Creation*, which argued that the correlation of form and function in organic nature demonstrates the necessity of an omniscient creator. In 1704–5 Samuel Clarke, who became chaplain to the bishop of Norwich and to Queen Anne, gave two sets of lectures, published as *A Demonstration of the Being and Attributes of God* (1705) and *A Discourse Concerning the Unchangeable Obligations of Natural Religion* (1706). In the first he attempted to prove the existence of God by a method "as near to Mathematical, as the nature of such a Discourse would allow". In the second he argued that the principles of morality are as certain as the propositions of mathematics and thus can be known by reason unassisted by faith.

It was an English Anglican priest, the utilitarian philosopher William Paley, the author of influential works on Christianity, ethics, and science, who wrote the standard exposition in English theology of the teleological argument for the existence of God, also known as the argument from design. His book *Natural Theology* (1802) is a sustained argument explaining the apparent design of humans and their parts, as well as the design of all sorts of organisms, in themselves and in their relations to one another and to their environment. Paley's fundamental claim is that "there cannot be design without a designer; contrivance, without a contriver; order, without choice means suitable to an end, and executing their office in accomplishing that end, without the end ever having been contemplated."

Natural Theology conveys extensive and accurate biological knowledge in such detail and precision as was available at the time of its publication. After each meticulous description of a

biological object or process, Paley drew again and again the
same conclusion – only an omniscient and omnipotent deity
could account for these marvels and for the enormous diversity
of inventions that they entail. The strength of the argument
against chance derived, according to Paley, from a notion that
he named relation: "wherever this is observed in the works of
nature or of man, it appears to me to carry along with it
decisive evidence of understanding, intention, art . . . all
depending upon the motions within, all upon the system of
intermediate actions."

The argument of design had been criticized by Hume in his
Dialogues Concerning Natural Religion (posthumously published in 1779). While Hume conceded that the world constitutes a more or less smoothly functioning system he
suggested that this may have come about as a result of the
chance permutations of particles falling into a temporary or
permanent self-sustaining order, which thus has the appearance of design. A century later Charles Darwin's discovery that
the adaptations displayed by living organisms are the result of
natural selection within a changing environment made the idea
of order without design much more plausible.

8

KEY FIGURES: THINKERS, WRITERS, AND REVOLUTIONARIES

The people who formulated the ideas of the Enlightenment fall into three groups. There were the scientists and philosophers, men like Isaac Newton and René Descartes, who began to develop the key ideas that propelled the huge changes of the period. There were the writers, those like David Hume and Jean-Jacques Rousseau, who created the philosophies that shaped the modern world. Finally, there were the political leaders, those like Thomas Paine and Edmund Burke, who would turn their world upside down.

They inherited a Renaissance world, in which there had been a rebirth of the ideas of classicism. People had begun to think about the kind of world they wanted – its economics, its politics, its culture, its science, its religion. In the Enlightenment they recast that world with ideas that would turn it into something recognizably modern, ideas that still frame how we live today.

Francis Bacon (1561–1626)

Bacon was born in London, the younger son of the Lord Keeper of the Great Seal, Sir Nicholas Bacon, by his second marriage. From 1573 to 1575 Bacon was educated at Trinity College, Cambridge, but his weak constitution caused him to suffer ill health there. He then went to France as a member of the English ambassador's suite. He was recalled abruptly after the sudden death of his father, who left him relatively little money. Bacon remained financially embarrassed virtually until his death.

In 1576 Bacon had been admitted as an "ancient" (senior governor) of Gray's Inn. In 1579 he took up residence there and after becoming a barrister in 1582 progressed in time through the posts of reader (lecturer at the Inn), bencher (senior member of the Inn) and queen's (from 1603 king's) counsel extraordinary, to those of solicitor general and attorney general. However, this did not satisfy his political and philosophical ambitions.

Bacon occupied himself with the tract "Temporis Partus Maximus" ("The Greatest Part of Time") in 1582; it has not survived. In 1584 he sat as member of Parliament for Melcombe Regis in Dorset and subsequently represented Taunton, Liverpool, the County of Middlesex, Southampton, Ipswich, and the University of Cambridge. In 1589 a "Letter of Advice" to the queen and *An Advertisement Touching the Controversies of the Church of England* indicated his political interests. In 1593 he took a stand objecting to the government's intensified demand for subsidies to help meet the expenses of the war against Spain. Elizabeth I took offence, and Bacon was in disgrace during several critical years when there were chances for legal advancement.

Some time before July 1591, Bacon had become ac-

quainted with the Earl of Essex, a favourite of the queen, but
although he recommended Bacon for several offices, Bacon
failed to obtain them. By 1598 Essex's failure in an expedi-
tion against Spanish treasure ships made him harder to
control and he returned against orders. In June 1600 Bacon
found himself as the queen's learned counsel taking part in
the informal trial of his patron. He was freed, but after
Essex's abortive attempt of 1601 to seize the queen and force
her dismissal of his rivals, Bacon viewed Essex as a traitor
and drew up the official report on the affair. After Essex's
execution Bacon, in 1604, published the *Apologie in Certaine
Imputations Concerning the Late Earle of Essex* in defence of
his own actions.

Bacon was one of the 300 new knights dubbed in 1603. The
following year he was confirmed as learned counsel and sat in
the first Parliament of the new reign under James I. In the
autumn of 1605 he published his *Advancement of Learning*,
dedicated to the king, and in the following summer he married
Alice Barnham, the daughter of a London alderman. It was not
until June 1607 that his petitions and his vigorous though vain
efforts to persuade the Commons to accept the king's proposals for union with Scotland were at length rewarded with the
post of solicitor general.

In 1609 his *De Sapientia Veterum* (*The Wisdom of the
Ancients*), in which he expounded what he took to be the
hidden practical meaning embodied in ancient myths, came
out. It proved to be, next to the *Essays* (1601), his most
popular book in his own lifetime. In 1614 he seems to have
written *The New Atlantis*, his far-seeing scientific utopian
work, not printed until 1626.

After the death of James' chief minister, Robert Cecil, Earl of
Salisbury in 1612, Bacon renewed his efforts to gain influence
with the king, writing a number of remarkable papers of

advice upon affairs of state and, in particular, upon the relations between crown and Parliament. Bacon was made attorney general in 1613. He came increasingly into conflict with Coke, the champion of the common law and of the independence of the judges. Eventually Coke was dismissed for defying an order. Bacon was appointed lord keeper of the great seal in March 1617. The following year he was made lord chancellor and Baron Verulam, and in 1620–21 he was created Viscount St Albans.

Between 1608 and 1620 he prepared at least 12 draftings of his most celebrated work, the *Novum Organum*, and wrote several minor philosophical works. He won the attention of scholars abroad as the author of the *Novum Organum*, published in 1620, and the developer of the *Instauratio Magna* (*Great Instauration*), a comprehensive plan to reorganize the sciences and to restore man to that mastery over nature that he was conceived to have lost by the fall of Adam.

In 1618 Bacon fell foul of George Villiers when he tried to interfere in the marriage of the daughter of his old enemy, Coke, and the younger brother of Villiers. Then, in 1621, two charges of bribery were raised against him. Bacon admitted the receipt of gifts but denied that they had ever affected his judgement. Unable to defend himself by discriminating between the various charges or cross-examining witnesses, he settled for a penitent submission and resigned the seal of his office. The sentence was harsh, and included a fine of £40,000, imprisonment in the Tower of London, disablement from holding any state office, and exclusion from Parliament and the verge of court (an area of 12 miles' radius centred on where the sovereign is resident).

Bacon did not have to stay long in the Tower, but the ban from access to the library of Charles Cotton and from consultation with his physician he found more galling. He offered his literary powers to provide the king with a digest of the laws, a history of Great Britain, and biographies of Tudor monarchs. He prepared memorandums on usury and on the prospects of a war with Spain; he expressed views on educational reforms; he even returned, as if by habit, to draft papers of advice to the king or to Buckingham and composed speeches he was never to deliver.

Two out of a plan of six separate natural histories were composed – *Historia Ventorum* (*History of the Winds*) appeared in 1622 and *Historia Vitae et Mortis* (*History of Life and Death*) in the following year. Also in 1623 he published the *De Dignitate et Augmentis Scientiarum*, a Latin translation, with many additions, of the *Advancement of Learning*. He also corresponded with Italian thinkers and urged his works upon them. In 1625 a third and enlarged edition of his *Essayes* was published. It was not until January 20 1623, however, that he was admitted to kiss the king's hand; a full pardon never came. He died at the Earl of Arundel's house on April 9 1626.

René Descartes (1596–1650)

René Descartes was born in La Haye (now Descartes), France. In 1606 he was sent to the Jesuit college at La Flèche, where young men were trained for careers in military engineering, the judiciary, and government administration. In 1614 he went to Poitiers, where he took a law degree in 1616. In 1618 he went to Breda in the Netherlands, where he spent 15 months as an informal student of mathematics and military architecture in the peacetime army of the Protestant stadholder, Prince Maurice. In Breda, Descartes was encouraged in his studies of science and mathematics by the physicist Isaac Beeckman, for whom he wrote the *Compendium Musicae* (*Compendium of Music*; written 1618, published 1650), his first surviving work.

Descartes spent the period between 1619 and 1628 travelling in northern and southern Europe. While in Bohemia, he invented analytic geometry. He also devised a universal method of deductive reasoning, based on mathematics, that is applicable to all the sciences, which he later formulated in *Discours de la méthode* (1637; *Discourse on Method*) and *Regulae ad Directionem Ingenii* (*Rules for the Direction of the Mind*; written by 1628 but not published until 1701). Descartes also investigated reports of esoteric knowledge.

Descartes shared a number of Rosicrucian goals and habits. He lived alone and in seclusion, changed his residence often, practised medicine without charge, attempted to increase human longevity, and took an optimistic view of the capacity of science to improve the human condition. Despite these affinities, Descartes rejected the Rosicrucians' magical and mystical beliefs.

In 1622 Descartes moved to Paris. There he gambled, rode, fenced, and went to the court, concerts, and the theatre. Among his friends were the poets Jean-Louis Guez de Balzac and Théophile de Viau, the mathematician Claude Mydorge, and Father Marin Mersenne, a man of universal learning who became Descartes' main contact with the larger intellectual world. At a talk in 1628, Descartes denied the alchemist Chandoux's claim that probabilities are as good as certainties in science and demonstrated his own method for attaining certainty. Within weeks Descartes left for the Protestant Netherlands, where he felt he could enjoy greater liberty; he did not return to France for 16 years.

In 1629 Descartes wrote the first draft of his *Meditationes de Prima Philosophia* (*Meditations on First Philosophy*). The physician Henri Regius, who taught Descartes' views at the

University of Utrecht in 1639, involved Descartes in a fierce controversy with the Calvinist theologian Gisbertus Voetius that continued for the rest of Descartes' life. In his *Letter to Voetius* of 1648, Descartes made a plea for religious tolerance and the rights of human beings. In 1635 Descartes' daughter Francine was born to Helena Jans but she died of scarlet fever at the age of five.

Just as he was about to publish *Le monde* (1664; *The World*), in 1633, Descartes learned that the Italian astronomer Galileo had been condemned for publishing the view that the Earth revolves around the Sun. Because of this, Descartes suppressed *The World*, hoping that eventually the church would retract its condemnation. In 1637 he published *Discourse on Method*, one of the first important modern philosophical works not written in Latin. In 1641 he published the *Meditations on First Philosophy*. The inclusion of critical responses by several eminent thinkers as well as Descartes' replies constituted a landmark of cooperative discussion in philosophy and science at a time when dogmatism was the rule.

Descartes' general goal was to help human beings master and possess nature. He provided understanding of the trunk of the tree of knowledge in *The World* and in works on dioptrics, meteorology and geometry, and he established its metaphysical roots in the *Meditations*. He then spent the rest of his life working on the branches of mechanics, medicine, and morals. Descartes' *L'Homme, et un traité de la formation du foetus* (*Man, and a Treatise on the Formation of the Foetus*) was published in 1664. In 1644 Descartes published *Principia Philosophiae* (*Principles of Philosophy*), a compilation of his physics and metaphysics. In 1644, 1647, and 1648, Descartes returned to France for brief visits on financial business and to oversee the translation into French of the *Principles*, the

Meditations, and the *Objections and Replies*. In 1647 he also suggested to Blaise Pascal the famous experiment of taking a barometer up Mount Puy-de-Dôme to determine the influence of the weight of the air.

The translator Claude Clerselier's brother-in-law, Hector Pierre Chanut, who was a French resident in Sweden and later ambassador, helped to procure a pension for Descartes from Louis XIV, though it was never paid. Later, Chanut engineered an invitation for Descartes to the court of Queen Christina, one of the most important and powerful monarchs in Europe. Descartes went reluctantly, arriving early in October 1649. While delivering statutes for a Swedish Academy of Arts and Sciences to the queen on February 1 1650, he caught a chill, and soon developed pneumonia. He died on February 11.

Robert Boyle (1627–91)

Robert Boyle was born into one of the wealthiest families in Britain, the fourteenth child and seventh son of Richard Boyle, the 1st Earl of Cork, secretary of state for Ireland. After education at Eton College and a grand tour with his brother, Boyle returned to England in 1644, where he took up residence at his hereditary estate of Stalbridge in Dorset. Here he embarked upon a literary career and in 1649 he began investigating nature via scientific experimentation. From 1647 until the mid-1650s, Boyle remained in close contact with a group of natural philosophers and social reformers gathered around the intelligencer Samuel Hartlib, most notably George Starkey, who heightened Boyle's interest in experimental chemistry.

In 1654 Boyle was invited to Oxford, where he was exposed to the latest developments in natural philosophy and became associated with a group of notable natural philosophers and physicians, including John Wilkins, Christopher Wren, and John Locke, who formed the "Experimental Philosophy Club". Much of Boyle's best-known work dates from this period, including the construction of the air pump with Robert Hooke. Their resultant discoveries were published in Boyle's first scientific publication, *New Experiments Physico-Mechanicall, Touching the Spring of the Air and its Effects* (1660). One of their findings, published in 1662, later became known as "Boyle's law".

Boyle's work emphasized experiment and observation, and he advocated a mechanistic view of the universe. Among his influential publications were *The Sceptical Chymist* (1661), and the *Origine of Formes and Qualities* (1666). Boyle also maintained a lifelong pursuit of transmutational alchemy. He was a devout and pious Anglican who keenly championed his faith, and his conception of his own life and the role of a Christian scientist was summarized in *The Christian Virtuoso* (1690).

In 1668 Boyle left Oxford and took up residence with his sister Katherine Jones, Vicountess Ranelagh, in her house on Pall Mall in London. There he set up an active laboratory, and published at least one book nearly every year. Living in London also provided him the opportunity to participate actively in the Royal Society. He was offered the presidency of the Royal Society (in 1680) and the episcopacy but declined both. He died at age 64 after a short illness exacerbated by his grief over Katherine's death a week earlier. He left his papers to the Royal Society and a bequest for establishing a series of lectures in defence of Christianity. These lectures, now known as the Boyle Lectures, continue to this day.

Benedict de Spinoza (1632–77)

Spinoza's grandfather and father were Portuguese Jews who had found refuge in Amsterdam after Holland's successful revolt against Spain and the granting of religious freedom. Spinoza's mother died when Benedict was a child. and in 1654 Benedict's father died. His studies were mainly Jewish, but he was an independent thinker and soon incurred the disapproval of the synagogue authorities for his interpretations of Scripture. The Jewish authorities, after trying vainly to silence Spinoza with bribes and threats, excommunicated him in July 1656, and he was banished from Amsterdam for a short period by the civil authorities. He stayed with Franciscus van den Enden, a former Jesuit and ardent classical scholar, who had opened a school in Amsterdam. At the same time, Spinoza was becoming expert at making lenses, supporting himself partly by grinding and polishing lenses for spectacles, telescopes, and microscopes; he also worked as a tutor.

Spinoza was a scientific humanist who justified power solely by its usefulness. He desired toleration and intellectual liberty, believing state power had no intrinsic divine or metaphysical authority. A kind of reading and discussion circle for the study of religious and philosophical problems came into being under the guidance of Spinoza. In order to collect his thoughts, however, and reduce them to a system, he withdrew in 1660 to Rijnsburg, near Leiden. There he wrote *Korte Verhandeling van God, de Mensch en deszelfs Welstand* (written *c.* 1662; English translation *Spinoza's Short Treatise on God, Man, and His Well-Being,* 1910) and *Tractatus de Intellectus Emendatione* (*Treatise on the Correction of the Understanding*), both of which were ready by April 1662. He also completed the greater part of his geometrical version of Descartes' *Principia Philosophiae* and the first book of his *Ethics*. The former was published under the title *Renati des Cartes Principiorum Philosophiae Pars I et II, More Geometrico Demonstratae, per Benedictum de Spinoza* (1663), with an introduction explaining that Spinoza did not share the views expressed in the book. This was the only book published in Spinoza's lifetime with his name on the title page.

Spinoza became dissatisfied with the informal method of exposition that he had adopted previously and turned instead to the geometrical method in the manner of Euclid's *Elements*. His masterpiece, the *Ethica Ordine Geometrico Demonstrata* (*Ethics*), was set out in this manner. Spinoza, like his contemporaries, held that definitions are not arbitrary but that there is a sense in which they may be correct or incorrect. In his unfinished *Tractatus de Intellectus Emendatione* (1670; *On the Improvement of the Understanding*), he held that a sound definition should make clear the possibility or the necessity of the existence of the object defined.

In May 1670 Spinoza moved to The Hague, where he remained until his death. When the *Ethics* was completed in 1675, Spinoza had to abandon the idea of publishing it, though manuscript copies were circulated among his close friends. Spinoza concentrated his attention on political problems and began his *Tractatus Politicus* (*Political Treatise*), which he did not live to finish. He died in 1677.

John Locke (1632–1704)

John Locke was reared in Pensford, six miles south of Bristol. In 1652 he entered Christ Church, Oxford. He interested himself in studies outside the traditional programme, particularly experimental science and medicine. He graduated in 1656, gaining an MA two years later, around which time he was elected a student (the equivalent of fellow) of Christ Church. In 1660, he was appointed tutor in his college.

In 1661 Locke inherited a portion of his father's estate, which ensured a modest annual income. His studentship would eventually be subject to termination unless he took holy orders, which he declined to do. Not wishing to make teaching his permanent vocation, he taught undergraduates for four years only. He served as secretary to a diplomatic mission to Brandenburg in 1665, and on his return was immediately offered, but refused, another diplomatic post. His chief interests at the time were natural science and the study of the underlying principles of moral, social, and political life. To remedy the narrowness of his education, he read contemporary philosophy. He also collaborated with Robert Boyle, who was a close friend, and Thomas Sydenham, an eminent medical scientist.

It was as a physician that Locke first came to the notice of the statesman Lord Ashley (later to become the 1st Earl of Shaftesbury). Introduced in 1666, the following year he joined Ashley's household in London as family physician and adviser on his general affairs. Ashley stood firmly for a constitutional monarchy, for a Protestant succession, for civil liberty, for toleration in religion, for the rule of Parliament, and for the economic expansion of Britain. Since these were already aims to which Locke had dedicated himself, there existed from the first a perfect understanding between them. Ashley entrusted Locke with negotiating his son's marriage with the daughter of the Earl of Rutland; he also made him secretary of the group that he had formed to increase trade with America. Locke helped to draft a constitution for the new colony of Carolina, a document that extended freedom of worship to all colonists, denying admission only to atheists.

During the following decades, Locke continued to pursue philosophical and scientific problems. In 1668 he became a fellow of the newly formed (1663) Royal Society. Groups of friends met in his rooms, and it was at one such meeting that Locke set out his view of human knowledge in two drafts (1671), the beginnings of the thinking that 19 years later would blossom into his famous *Essay*. In these London years, too, Locke encountered representatives of Cambridge Platonism, a school of Christian humanists. Their tolerance, emphasis on practical conduct, and rejection of materialism were features that he found most attractive. This school was closely related in spirit to another school that influenced Locke at this time, that of latitudinarianism.

In 1672 Ashley was raised to the peerage as the 1st Earl of Shaftesbury and at the end of that year was appointed lord high chancellor of England. Though he soon lost favour and was dismissed, while in office he established the Council of Trade and Plantations, of which Locke was secretary for two years. Locke, who suffered greatly from asthma, found the London air and his heavy duties unhealthy, and in 1675 returned to Oxford. Six months later he departed for France, where he stayed for four years (1675–9), spending most of his time in Paris and Montpellier. In France during the 1670s, Locke made contacts that deeply influenced his view of metaphysics and epistemology, particularly with the Gassendist school and its leader, François Bernier.

Upon Locke's return to England, he found the country torn by dissension. For a year Shaftesbury, one of the many who wished to bar James the Duke of York (later James II) as a Roman Catholic from the succession, had been imprisoned in the Tower, but, by the time Locke returned, he was back in favour once more as lord president of the Privy Council. When he failed, however, to reconcile the interests of the king and Parliament, he was dismissed; in 1681 he was arrested, tried, and finally acquitted by a London jury. A year later he fled to

Holland, where in 1683 he died. Locke, who was now being closely watched, crossed to Holland in September 1683.

While his sojourn in Holland was happier than he had expected it to be, at home, Locke was deprived of his studentship at Christ Church and named on a list sent to the Hague as one of 84 traitors wanted by the English government. He remained abroad for more than five years, until James II was overthrown, and William of Orange was invited by Protestants to seize the throne. Locke, in February 1689, crossed in the party that accompanied the Princess of Orange, now to be crowned Queen Mary II of England. He refused ambassadorial posts but accepted a membership in the Commission of Appeals. But the London air again bothered him, and in 1691 he retired to Oates, the house of his friends Sir Francis and Lady Masham in Essex, and subsequently made only occasional visits to London.

In these last years of his life, he was the intellectual leader of the Whigs and the younger generation turned to him constantly for guidance. In "the glorious, bloodless revolution", the main aims for which Shaftesbury and Locke had fought were achieved: England became a constitutional monarchy; advances were made in securing the liberty of subjects in the law courts; and in achieving greater religious toleration and freedom of thought and expression. Locke himself drafted the arguments that saw the restrictive Act for the Regulation of Printing abolished in 1695 and the freedom of the press secured.

The main task of this last period of his life, however, was the publication of his works: The *Epistola de Tolerantia* (1689; *A Letter Concerning Toleration*), *Two Treatises of Government* (1690), and *An Essay Concerning Human Understanding*, which was not published until December 1689. Locke's last years were spent in the peaceful retreat of Oates. Locke's letters to Edward Clarke from Holland, advising him on the best upbringing for his son formed the basis of his influential *Some Thoughts Concerning Education* (1693). In 1695 he published a dignified plea for a less dogmatic Christianity in *The Reasonableness of Christianity*. John Locke was buried in the parish church of High Laver.

Sir Isaac Newton (1642–1727)

Isaac Newton was born in Woolsthorpe, the only son of a local yeoman, who had died three months before, and of Hannah Ayscough. Within two years his mother married a second time and her husband left young Isaac with his grandmother. For nine years Isaac was effectively separated from his mother, and his pronounced psychotic tendencies have been ascribed to this traumatic event. After his mother was widowed a second time, she determined that her first-born son should manage her now considerable property. Newton could not bring himself to concentrate on rural affairs, however, and he was sent back to the grammar school in Grantham to prepare for the university. By June 1661, he was ready to matriculate at Trinity College, Cambridge. Some time during his undergraduate career, he discovered the works of the French philosopher René Descartes and the other mechanical philosophers.

Beginning in 1664 Newton wrote the *Quaestiones* in his notebook, revealing that he had by then discovered the new conception of nature that provided the framework of the scientific revolution. He had also read Henry More, the Cambridge Platonist, and was thereby introduced to another intellectual world, the magical hermetic tradition, which sought to explain natural phenomena in terms of alchemical and magical concepts. Newton had also begun his mathematical studies. He discovered the binomial theorem, and he developed the calculus, a more powerful form of analysis that employs infinitesimal considerations in finding the slopes of curves and areas under curves. By 1669 Newton was ready to write a tract summarizing his progress, *De Analysi per Aequationes Numeri Terminorum Infinitas* (*On Analysis by Infinite Series*), which circulated in manuscript through a limited circle and made his name known. During the next two years he revised it as *De Methodis Serierum et Fluxionum* (*On the Methods of Series and Fluxions*). The word fluxions, Newton's private rubric, indicates that the calculus had been born. He had become the leading mathematician in Europe.

Newton received his bachelor's degree in April 1665, but that year the plague closed the university, and for most of the following two years he was forced to stay at his home. He was elected to a fellowship in Trinity College in 1667, after the university reopened. Two years later he was recommended for the chair of mathematics. For this he had to deliver an annual course of lectures. He chose the work he had done in optics.

His theory of colours, like his later work, was first transmitted to the world through a paper to the Royal Society of London. This first led him into disagreement with Robert Hooke, one of the leaders of the Royal Society, a dispute that would continue on and off for the rest of his life. Newton was unable rationally to confront criticism, and less than a year after submitting the paper, he was so unsettled by the discussion that he withdrew into virtual isolation. In 1675, during a visit to London, however, Newton thought he heard Hooke accept his theory and was emboldened to bring forth a second paper, identical to most of Book II as it later appeared in the *Opticks*. This demonstrated for the first time the existence of periodic optical phenomena.

In 1704 Newton combined a revision of his optical lectures with the paper of 1675 and a small amount of additional material in his *Opticks*. A second piece which Newton had sent with the paper of 1675 provoked new controversy. Entitled *An Hypothesis Explaining the Properties of Light*, it was in fact a general system of nature. Hooke apparently claimed that Newton had stolen its content from him, and Newton boiled over again, though the issue was quickly controlled by an exchange of formal, excessively polite letters. Newton was also engaged in another exchange on his theory of colours with a circle of English Jesuits in Liège, and their contention that his experiments were mistaken lashed him into a fury. In 1678, the correspondence provoked a complete nervous breakdown and for six years he withdrew from intellectual commerce except when others initiated a correspondence, which he always broke off as quickly as possible.

During his time of isolation, Newton immersed himself in alchemy and his conception of nature underwent a decisive change. His *Hypothesis of Light* of 1675, with its universal ether, had been a standard mechanical system of nature. In about 1679, Newton abandoned this thesis and began to ascribe the phenomena to attractions and repulsions between particles of matter. Late in 1679 another application for the idea was suggested in a letter from Hooke, who mentioned his analysis of planetary motion. From Newton's work on this, the crucial propositions on which the law of universal gravitation would ultimately rest would eventually emerge.

In 1684, Newton sent a short tract entitled *De Motu* (*On Motion*) to the astronomer Edmond Halley, who had visited him. In two and a half years, this grew into *Philosophiae Naturalis Principia Mathematica* (*Mathematical Principles of Natural Philosophy*), containing the laws of motion of visible bodies. When the Royal Society received the completed manuscript of Book I in 1686, Hooke again raised the cry of plagiarism, a charge that cannot be sustained in any meaningful sense. Hooke would have been satisfied with a generous acknowledgement; Newton, instead, went through his manuscript and eliminated nearly every reference to Hooke.

The *Principia* immediately raised Newton to international prominence. Newton found satisfaction in the role of patron to young scientists. His friendship with Fatio de Duillier, a Swiss-born mathematician resident in London who shared Newton's interests, was the most profound experience of his adult life. He broadened his circle and tasted London life. When Newton, a fervent if unorthodox Protestant, helped to lead the resistance of Cambridge to James II's attempt to Catholicize it, he made the acquaintance of a broader group, including John Locke. Fatio suggested that he find a position in London, and in 1696, he was appointed warden of the mint. Although he did not resign his Cambridge appointments until 1701, he moved to London and henceforth centred his life there.

In 1693, the termination of his relationship with Fatio precipitated a crisis. Samuel Pepys and John Locke, both personal friends of Newton, received wild, accusatory letters. Both men were alarmed for Newton's sanity; and, in fact, Newton had suffered at least his second nervous breakdown. The crisis passed, and Newton recovered his stability. Only briefly did he ever return to sustained scientific work, however. In his later years, he devoted much time to religion and theology. In 1703 he was elected president of the Royal Society. In 1705 Queen Anne knighted him, the first occasion on which a scientist was so honoured.

Newton's rule of the Royal Society brought him into confrontations with John Flamsteed, the Astronomer Royal, and Gottfried Wilhelm Leibniz, the German philosopher and mathematician. In the 1690s, as he worked on the lunar theory, Newton tried to force the publication of Flamsteed's catalogue of stars. Flamsteed's observations, the fruit of a lifetime of work, were, in effect, seized despite his protests and prepared for the press by his mortal enemy, Edmond Halley. Flamsteed by court order had the printed catalogue returned to him before it was generally distributed. Newton sought his revenge by systematically eliminating references to Flamsteed's help in later editions of the *Principia*.

Newton's conflict with Leibniz had them both making charges of plagiarism over the origination of calculus. While it is established that Newton developed the calculus before Leibniz seriously pursued mathematics, it is also agreed that Leibniz later arrived at the calculus independently. However, because Newton had only hinted in the *Principia* at his method, not publishing it until he appended two papers to the *Opticks* in 1704, Leibniz's paper of 1684 first made the calculus a matter of public knowledge. Newton appointed an "impartial" committee to investigate the issue, secretly wrote the report officially published by the society, and reviewed it anonymously in the *Philosophical Transactions*. The battle with Leibniz dominated the final 25 years of Newton's life.

Until nearly the end, Newton presided at the Royal Society and supervised the mint. During his last years, his niece, Catherine Barton Conduitt, and her husband lived with him.

Charles-Louis de Secondat, Baron de La Brède et de Montesquieu (1689–1755)

Baron de Montesquieu was educated at the Collège de Juilly, which provided a sound education on enlightened and modern lines. Charles-Louis left Juilly in 1705, continued his studies at the faculty of law at the University of Bordeaux, graduated and became an advocate in 1708. In 1715 he married Jeanne de

Lartigue, a wealthy Protestant, who brought him a respectable dowry of 100,000 livres and in due course presented him with two daughters and a son, Jean-Baptiste. In 1716 his uncle, Jean-Baptiste, Baron de Montesquieu, died and left to his nephew his estates, with the barony of Montesquieu, near Agen, and the office of deputy president in the Parlement of Bordeaux. The young Montesquieu, at 27, was now socially and financially secure.

In 1721 he published his *Lettres persanes* (English translation *Persian Letters*, 1722), in which he gave a brilliant satirical portrait of French and particularly Parisian civilization, supposedly seen through the eyes of two Persian travellers. The work's anonymity was soon penetrated, and Montesquieu became famous. Montesquieu now sought to reinforce his literary achievement with social success. Going to Paris in 1722, he was assisted in entering court circles by the Duke of Berwick, and made the acquaintance of the English politician Viscount Bolingbroke, whose political views were later to be reflected in Montesquieu's analysis of the English constitution. In Paris his interest in the routine activities of the Parlement in Bordeaux, however, had dwindled. His office was marketable, and in 1726 he sold it, a move that served both to re-establish his fortunes, and enabled him to enter the French Academy.

He embarked on a grand tour, ending it in the company of the statesman and wit Lord Chesterfield in England, where he remained until the spring of 1731. Here he was presented at court and received by the Prince of Wales, at whose request he later made an anthology of French songs. He was elected a Fellow of the Royal Society, attended parliamentary debates, read the political journals of the day, became a Freemason and bought extensively for his library. His stay in England was one of the most formative periods of his life.

On his return to France he decided to devote himself to literature. Apart from a tiny but controversial treatise on *La monarchie universelle* (*The Universal Monarchy*), printed in 1734 but at once withdrawn (so that only his own copy is extant), he was occupied with an essay on the English constitution and with his *Considérations sur les causes de la grandeur des Romains et de leur décadence* (1734; *Considerations on the Causes of the Grandeur and Decadence of the Romans*). After the publication of the *Considerations*, he embarked on a major work on law and politics, which appeared in November 1748 under the title *De l'esprit des lois, ou du rapport que les lois doivent avoir avec la constitution de chaque gouvernement, les moeurs, le climat, la religion, le commerce, etc.* (*The Spirit of the Laws*, 1750).

After the book was published, praise came to Montesquieu. The philosophers of the Enlightenment accepted him as one of their own, as indeed he was. The work was controversial, however, and a variety of denunciatory articles and pamphlets appeared. Notwithstanding the favourable disposition of the pope, the work was placed on the Index of Forbidden Books in 1751. This, though it dismayed Montesquieu, was but a momentary setback. He had already published his *Défense de l'esprit des lois* (1750; *Defence of the Spirit of the Laws*).

It was to be expected that the editors of the *Encyclopédie* should wish to have his collaboration, and d'Alembert asked him to write on democracy and despotism. Montesquieu declined, saying that he had already had his say on those themes but would like to write on taste. The resultant *Essai sur le goût* (*Essay on Taste*), first drafted about 25 years earlier, was his last work.

Thomas Hobbes (1588–1679)

Hobbes' father, a vicar, abandoned his three children to the care of his brother, a well-to-do glover in Malmesbury. At 15, Hobbes went to Magdalen Hall in Oxford, where he devoted most of his time to books of travel and the study of maps. Upon his graduation in 1608, he became a private tutor to William Cavendish, afterward 2nd Earl of Devonshire. In 1610 Hobbes visited France and Italy with his pupil. On returning home he decided to make himself a classical scholar. The chief fruit of Hobbes' classical studies was his translation of Thucydides, published in 1629. The same year Hobbes went abroad again, as travelling companion to the son of Sir Gervase Clifton.

The turning point in his intellectual history occurred at about this time, when, in Euclid's *Elements*, he traced the proofs back through proposition after proposition and was thus demonstratively convinced of their truth. In 1630 Hobbes was recalled from Paris to teach the young Earl of Devonshire, William Cavendish, son of his late patron. He began to investigate the diversity of motion, laying out his ideas in his first known philosophical work, *A Short Tract on First Principles*.

During a third trip abroad, this time with the younger Cavendish, Hobbes' interest in science and philosophy was stimulated by his contact with the leaders of the new thought in Europe. He was able to discuss his ideas in Paris with the circle of Marin Mersenne and, in 1636, with Galileo. He then planned a philosophical trilogy: *De Corpore* (1655; *Concerning the Body*) was to show that physical phenomena are explicable in terms of motion; *De Homine* (1658; *Concerning Man*) was to show what specific bodily motions are involved in human cognition and appetition; and *De Cive* (1642;

Concerning Citizenship) was to deduce from what had already been established the proper organization of men in society.

In 1637 Hobbes returned to England to find the country in the political ferment that preceded the Civil War, and he decided because of this threat to publish the last part of his planned philosophy first. *The Elements of Law, Natural and Politic* – Part I on man and Part II on citizenship – was circulated in manuscript in 1640. It contained most of the political and psychological doctrines for which Hobbes is famous and which reappeared in *De Cive* and *Leviathan*.

When strife became acute in 1640, Hobbes feared for his safety and retired to Paris. He was soon in contact with later fugitives from England. He rejoined the Mersenne circle, wrote "objections" to the *Meditationes* and the *Dioptrique* of René Descartes, and in 1642 published *De Cive*. Hobbes spent the next four years working on optics and on *De Corpore*. In 1646 the young Prince of Wales, later to become Charles II, sought refuge in Paris, and Hobbes accepted an invitation to instruct him in mathematics.

He turned once more to political theory. In 1647 he published a second, augmented edition of *De Cive* and in 1651 an English version. In 1650 the manuscript of *The Elements of Law* was published in two parts, as *Human Nature* and *De Corpore Politico* (*Of the Body Politic*). Hobbes' masterpiece *Leviathan; or, The Matter, Form, and Power of a Commonwealth, Ecclesiastical and Civil* was published in 1651.

Though Hobbes was now 63 years of age, he was to retain his vigour for another quarter of a century. Hobbes had made enemies at Oxford by the publication of *Leviathan*, and he now came under attack for the philosophies published in *De Corpore*, which was published at last in 1655. Hobbes had been so impressed by Galileo's achievements in mechanics that he sought to explain all phenomena and, indeed, sense itself in terms of the motion of bodies. Further disagreements raged over his onslaught on the newfangled methods of mathematical analysis in *Dialogus Physicus, sive de Natura Aeris* (1661; *Dialogue on Physics, or on the Nature of Air*) and his *De Principiis et Ratiocinatione Geometrarum* (1666), which was designed to humble the professors of geometry by showing that their works contained much uncertainty and error. *Quadratura Circuli, Cubatio Sphaerae, Duplicatio Cubi* (1669; *The Squaring of the Circle, The Cubing of the Sphere, The Doubling of the Cube*) gave Hobbes' solutions to these famous problems – solutions promptly refuted by the mathematician John Wallis. In 1678 appeared his last piece of all, *Decameron Physiologicum* (*Ten Questions of Physiology*), a new set of dialogues on physiological questions.

After the Restoration in 1660, Hobbes enjoyed a new prominence. Though his presence at court scandalized the bishops and the chancellor, the king relished his wit. He even granted Hobbes a pension of £100 a year and had his portrait hung in the royal closet. It was not until 1666, when the House of Commons prepared a bill against atheism and profaneness, that Hobbes felt seriously endangered, for the committee to which the bill was referred was instructed to investigate *Leviathan*. Hobbes, then verging upon 80, burned such of his papers as he thought might compromise him and set himself to inquire into the state of the law of heresy.

The results of his investigations appeared in three short dialogues and in a tract entitled *An Historical Narration Concerning Heresy and the Punishment Thereof* (1680), in which he maintained that since the abolition of the high court of commission there was no court of heresy to which he was amenable and that, in any case, nothing was to be declared heresy but what was at variance with the Nicene Creed.

Although Parliament dropped the bill on atheism, Hobbes could never afterward get permission to print anything on subjects relating to human conduct, the king apparently having made it the price of his protection that no fresh provocation should be offered to popular sentiment.

In his last years Hobbes amused himself by returning to the classical studies of his youth. His autobiography in Latin verse with its playful humour, occasional pathos, and sublime self-complacency was brought forth at the age of 84. In 1675 he produced a translation of the *Odyssey* in rugged English rhymes, and as late as four months before his death, he was promising his publisher "somewhat to print in English".

Anthony Ashley Cooper, 3rd Earl of Shaftesbury (1671–1713)

Shaftesbury's early education was directed by John Locke, and he attended Winchester College. He entered Parliament in 1695 and, succeeding as 3rd Earl of Shaftesbury in 1699, attended Parliament regularly in the House of Lords for the remainder of William III's reign. He pursued an independent policy in the House of Lords as well as in the House of Commons. In July 1702 he retired from public life.

Shaftesbury's philosophy owed something to the Cambridge Platonists, who had stressed the existence in man of a natural moral sense. Shaftesbury advanced this concept against both the orthodox Christian doctrine of the fall and against the premise that the state of nature was a state of unavoidable warfare. Shaftesbury's neoplatonism, his contention that what man sees of beauty or truth is only a shadow of absolute beauty or truth, dominated his attitude to religion and to the arts.

During his lifetime his fame as a writer was comparatively slight, for he published little before 1711; in that year appeared his *Characteristicks of Men, Manners, Opinions, Times,* in which his chief works were assembled. The effect of this book was immediate and was felt on the European continent as well as in England; indeed, English Deism was transmitted to Germany almost entirely through translations of his writings.

Voltaire (François-Marie Arouet) (1694–1778)

Voltaire attended the Jesuit college of Louis-le-Grand in Paris, where he learned to love literature, the theatre, and social life. After leaving, he was employed as secretary at the French embassy in The Hague, where he became infatuated with the daughter of an adventurer. Fearing scandal, the French ambassador sent him back to Paris. Despite his father's wishes, he wanted to devote himself wholly to literature, and he frequented the Temple, then the centre of free-thinking society. After the death of Louis XIV, under the morally relaxed Regency, Voltaire became the wit of Parisian society. But when he dared to mock the dissolute regent, the Duc d'Orléans, he was banished from Paris and then imprisoned in the Bastille for nearly a year (1717).

Behind his cheerful facade, he was fundamentally serious and set himself to learn the accepted literary forms. In 1718, after the success of *Oedipe*, the first of his tragedies, he was acclaimed as the successor of the great classical dramatist Jean Racine and thenceforward adopted the name of Voltaire. He worked at an epic poem whose hero was Henry IV, in which his contemporaries saw the ideal of tolerance that inspired the poem. These literary triumphs earned him a pension from the regent and the warm approval of the young queen, Marie. He thus began his career of court poet.

In the Salons he professed an aggressive Deism, which scandalized the devout. As the result of a quarrel with the

Chevalier de Rohan, he was beaten, taken to the Bastille, and then conducted to Calais on May 5 1726, from where he set out for London. In England he met such English men of letters as Pope, Swift, and Congreve. He admired the liberalism of English institutions, and was convinced that it was because of their personal liberty that the English, notably Sir Isaac Newton and John Locke, were in the forefront of scientific thought. He returned to France at the end of 1728 or the beginning of 1729 and decided to present England as a model to his compatriots in the *Lettres philosophiques* or *Lettres sur les Anglais* (1734; *Philosophical Letters* or *Letters on England*).

Scandal followed publication of this work and a warrant of arrest was issued in May of 1734. Voltaire took refuge in the château of Mme du Châtelet at Cirey in Champagne. She was passionately drawn to the sciences and metaphysics and a laboratory of the physical sciences was installed. After *Adélaïde du Guesclin* (1734), a play about a national tragedy, Voltaire brought *Alzire* to the stage in 1736 with great success. In his *Éléments de la philosophie de Newton* (1738; *Elements of the Philosophy of Newton*), he popularized those discoveries of English science.

Because of a lawsuit, he followed Mme du Châtelet to Brussels in May 1739, and thereafter they were constantly on the move between Belgium, Cirey, and Paris. Voltaire corresponded with the Crown Prince of Prussia, and when the prince acceded to the throne as Frederick II (the Great), he visited him. When the War of the Austrian Succession broke out, Voltaire was sent to Berlin (1742–3) on a secret mission to rally the King of Prussia – who was proving himself a faithless ally – to the assistance of the French army. Such services brought him into favour again at Versailles and he was appointed historiographer, gentleman of the king's chamber, and academician. He amassed a vast fortune through the manipulations of Joseph Pâris Duverney, the financier in charge of military supplies.

At this time he wrote his first *contes* (stories). *Micromégas* (1752) measures the littleness of man in the cosmic scale; *Vision de Babouc* (1748) and *Memnon* (1749) dispute the philosophic optimism of Gottfried Wilhelm Leibniz and Alexander Pope. In 1748 at Commercy, where he had joined the court of Stanislaw (the former king of Poland), he detected the love affair of Mme du Châtelet and the poet Saint-Lambert. The next year she died in childbirth. The failure of some of his later plays aggravated his sense of defeat. He yielded to the invitation of Frederick II and set out for Berlin on June 28 1750. At first he was enchanted by his sojourn but he became involved in a lawsuit with a moneylender and quarrels with prominent noblemen, and left Prussia in 1753. At length he found asylum at Geneva, where he purchased a house called Les Délices, at the same time securing winter quarters at Lausanne. He now completed his two major historical studies, *Le Siècle de Louis XIV* (1751; *The Age of Louis XIV*), a book on the century of Louis XIV, and *Essai sur les moeurs* (first complete edition, 1756), which traced the course of world history since the end of the Roman Empire.

At Geneva, he had at first been welcomed and honoured as the champion of tolerance. But soon he made those around him feel uneasy. His presentation of plays was stopped, and his improper mock-heroic poem "La Pucelle" (1755) was printed by booksellers in spite of his protests. In 1758 he wrote what was to be his most famous work, *Candide*.

In 1758 Voltaire bought Ferney together with Tourney in France, on the Swiss border. By crossing the frontier he could thus safeguard himself against police incursion from either country. At Ferney, Voltaire developed a modern estate, renovated the church and meddled in Genevan politics, taking the side of the workers (or *natifs*, those without civil rights), and installing a stocking factory and watchworks on his estate in order to help them. In 1777 he received a popular acclamation from the people of Ferney. In 1815 the Congress of Vienna halted the annexation of Ferney to Switzerland in his honour.

His main interest at this time was his opposition to *l'infâme*, a word he used to designate the church, especially when it was identified with intolerance. He multiplied his personal attacks, directing *Le sentiment des citoyens* (1764) against Rousseau. He constructed a personal *Encyclopédie*, the *Dictionnaire philosophique* (1764), enlarged after 1770 by *Questions sur l'Encyclopédie*. Among the mass of writings of this period are *Le blanc et le noir* (*The White and the Black*), *Princesse de Babylone*, a panorama of European philosophies in the fairyland style of *The Thousand and One Nights*; and *Le taureau blanc*. Again and again Voltaire returned to his chosen themes: the establishment of religious tolerance; the growth of material prosperity; respect for the rights of man by the abolition of torture and useless punishments.

Tancrède proved to be Voltaire's last triumph. It was the theatre that brought him back to Paris in 1778, to direct the rehearsals of *Irène*. On March 30 he went to the French Academy amid acclamations, and, when *Irène* was played before a delirious audience, he was crowned in his box. His health was profoundly impaired by all this excitement and on May 30 he died. His remains were transferred to the Panthéon during the Revolution in July 1791.

David Hume (1711–76)

Hume was the younger son of Joseph Hume, the modestly circumstanced laird, or lord, of Ninewells, a small estate about

nine miles distant from Berwick-upon-Tweed. He entered
Edinburgh University when he was about 12 years old and
left it at 14 or 15, as was then usual. Pressed a little later to
study law (in the family tradition on both sides), he found it
distasteful and instead read voraciously in the wider sphere of
letters. Because of the intensity and excitement of his intellectual discovery, he had a nervous breakdown in 1729, from
which it took him a few years to recover.

In 1734, after trying his hand in a merchant's office in
Bristol, he came to the turning point of his life and retired to
France for three years. Most of this time Hume spent at La
Flèche on the Loire, studying and writing *A Treatise of Human
Nature*, his attempt to formulate a full-fledged philosophical
system. Returning to England in 1737, he set about publishing
the *Treatise*. The poor reception of this, his first and very
ambitious work, depressed him; but his next venture, *Essays,
Moral and Political* (1741–2), won some success. Perhaps
encouraged by this, he became a candidate for the chair of
moral philosophy at Edinburgh in 1744. Objectors alleged
heresy and even atheism, pointing to the *Treatise* as evidence.
Unsuccessful, Hume left the city, where he had been living
since 1740, and began a period of wandering on the
Continent.

During his years of wandering some fruits of his studies
appeared: a further *Three Essays, Moral and Political* (1748)
and *Philosophical Essays Concerning Human Understanding*
(1748), better known as *An Enquiry Concerning Human
Understanding*, the title Hume gave to it in a revision of
1758. The *Enquiry Concerning the Principles of Morals*
(1751) was a rewriting of Book III of the *Treatise*. It was in
these works that Hume expressed his mature thought.

Following the publication of these works, Hume spent
several years (1751–63) in Edinburgh, with two breaks in

London. In 1752 Hume was made keeper of the Advocates' Library at Edinburgh and turned to historical writing. His *History of England*, extending from Caesar's invasion to 1688, came out between 1754 and 1762, preceded by *Political Discourses* (1752). These brought him fame, abroad as well as at home. He also wrote *Four Dissertations* (1757), which he regarded as a trifle, although it included a rewriting of Book II of the *Treatise* (completing his purged restatement of this work) and a brilliant study of "the natural history of religion".

The most colourful episode of his life ensued: in 1763 he left England to become secretary to the British embassy in Paris under the Earl of Hertford. For four months in 1765 he acted as chargé d'affaires at the embassy. When he returned to London at the beginning of 1766 (to become, a year later, under-secretary of state), he brought Jean-Jacques Rousseau, the Swiss philosopher connected with the *Encyclopédie* of Diderot and d'Alembert, with him and found him a refuge from persecution in a country house at Wootton in Staffordshire.

In 1769, somewhat tired of public life and of England too, he again established a residence in his beloved Edinburgh. He issued five further editions of his *History of England* between 1762 and 1773 as well as eight editions of his collected writings (omitting the *Treatise*, *History*, and ephemera) under the title *Essays and Treatises* between 1753 and 1772, besides preparing the final edition of this collection, which appeared posthumously (1777), and *Dialogues Concerning Natural Religion*, held back under pressure from friends and not published until 1779. His curiously detached autobiography, *The Life of David Hume, Esquire, Written by Himself* (1777; the title is his own), is dated April 18 1776. He died in his Edinburgh house after a long illness and was buried on Calton Hill.

Jean-Jacques Rousseau (1712–78)

Rousseau's mother died in childbirth and he was brought up by his father. His father got into trouble with the civil authorities and had to leave Geneva to avoid imprisonment. Thus Rousseau lived for six years as a poor relation in his mother's family, until he, too, at the age of 16, fled from Geneva to live the life of an adventurer and a Roman Catholic convert in the kingdoms of Sardinia and France.

Rousseau was fortunate in finding in the province of Savoy a benefactress named the Baronne de Warens, who provided him with a refuge in her home and employed him as her steward. She also furthered his education to such a degree that the boy who had arrived on her doorstep as a stammering apprentice who had never been to school developed into a philosopher, a man of letters, and a musician.

Rousseau reached Paris when he was 30 and met Denis Diderot. The two soon became immensely successful as the centre of a group of intellectuals who gathered round the great French *Encyclopédie*. At this time Rousseau wrote music as well as prose, and one of his operas, *Le devin du village* (1752; *The Cunning-Man*), attracted so much admiration from the king and the court that he might have enjoyed an easy life as a fashionable composer. Then, at the age of 37 Rousseau had what he called an "illumination" while walking to Vincennes to visit Diderot, when it came to him in a "terrible flash" that modern progress had corrupted instead of improved men. He went on to write his first important work, a prize essay for the Academy of Dijon entitled *Discours sur les sciences et les arts* (1750; *A Discourse on the Sciences and the Arts*), in which he argues that the history of man's life on earth has been a history of decay. Throughout his life he kept returning to the thought that man is good by nature but has been corrupted by society and civilization.

In 1752 Rousseau became involved in a dispute over the performance of *opera buffa*, the new Italian opera – which he was against in contrast to many of the Encyclopédists – and decided to devote his energies henceforth to literature and philosophy. He began to look back at some of the austere principles that he had learned as a child. He had by then acquired a mistress, an illiterate laundry maid named Thérèse Levasseur. To the surprise of his friends, he took her with him to Geneva, presenting her as a nurse. Although her presence caused some murmurings, Rousseau was readmitted easily to the Calvinist communion of his youth, his literary fame having made him very welcome to a city that prided itself as much on its culture as on its morals.

Rousseau had by this time completed a second *Discourse* in response to a question set by the Academy of Dijon: "What is the origin of the inequality among men and is it justified by natural law?" In response to this challenge he produced a masterpiece of speculative anthropology, his *Discours sur l'origine et les fondements de l'inégalité parmi les hommes* (1755; *Discourse on the Origin and Basis of Inequality Among Men*). The argument follows on from that of his first *Discourse* by developing the proposition that natural man is good and then tracing the successive stages by which man has descended from primitive innocence to corrupt sophistication. Having written the *Discourse* to explain how men had lost their liberty in the past, he went on to write another book, *Du contrat social ou princpes du droit politique* (1762; *The Social Contract; or Principles of Political Right*), to suggest how they might recover their liberty in the future.

In 1754 Rousseau had returned to Paris and the company of his friends around the *Encyclopédie*. But he became increasingly ill at ease in such worldly society and began to quarrel with his fellow philosophes. By the time his *Lettre à d'Alem-*

bert sur les spectacles (1758; *Letter to Monsieur d'Alembert on the Theatre*) appeared in print, defending the Calvinist orthodoxy of Geneva, which had been criticized in d'Alembert's article on the city for the *Encyclopédie*, Rousseau had already left Paris to pursue a life closer to nature on the country estate of his friend Mme d'Épinay near Montmorency. When the hospitality of Mme d'Épinay proved to entail much the same social round as that of Paris, Rousseau retreated to a nearby cottage, under the protection of the Maréchal de Luxembourg. But even this highly placed friend could not save him in 1762 when his treatise on education, *Émile*, was published and scandalized the pious Jansenists of the French Parlements. Described by the author as a treatise on education, *Émile* is not about schooling but about the upbringing of a rich man's son by a tutor who is given unlimited authority over him. At the same time the book sets out to explore the possibilities of an education for republican citizenship. In Paris, as in Geneva, they ordered the book to be burned and the author arrested; all the Maréchal de Luxembourg could do was to provide a carriage for Rousseau to escape from France. Rousseau spent the rest of his life as a fugitive.

The years at Montmorency had been the most productive of his literary career; besides *The Social Contract* and *Émile, Julie; ou la nouvelle Héloïse* (1761; *Julie; or The New Eloise*) came out within 12 months, all three works of seminal importance. *The New Eloise* was clearly inspired by Rousseau's own curious relationship – at once passionate and platonic – with Sophie d'Houdetot, a noblewoman who lived near him at Montmorency. In *La profession de foi du vicaire savoyard* (1765; *The Profession of Faith of a Savoyard Vicar*) Rousseau sets out what may fairly be regarded as his own religious views. Rousseau could never entertain doubts about God's existence or about the immortality of the soul. He also attached great importance to conscience, opposing this both to the bloodless categories of rationalistic ethics and to the cold tablets of biblical authority.

This minimal creed put Rousseau at odds with the orthodox adherents of the churches and with the openly atheistic philosophes of Paris, so that he felt himself increasingly isolated, tormented, and pursued. He reacted to the suppression of *The Social Contract* in Geneva by indicting the regime of that city-state in a pamphlet entitled *Lettres écrites de la montagne* (1764; *Letters Written from the Mountain*) in which Geneva was depicted as a republic that had been taken over by "25 despots". After that Rousseau temporarily found refuge in England, after the Scottish philosopher David Hume took him there and secured the offer of a pension from King George III; but once in England, various symptoms of paranoia began to manifest themselves in Rousseau, and he returned to France incognito. Believing that Thérèse was the only person he could rely on, he finally married her in 1768, when he was 56 years old.

In the remaining 10 years of his life Rousseau produced primarily autobiographical writings, mostly intended to justify himself against the accusations of his adversaries. The most important was his *Confessions*. He also wrote *Rousseau juge de Jean-Jacques* (1780; *Rousseau, Judge of Jean-Jacques*) to reply to specific charges by his enemies and *Les rêveries du promeneur solitaire* (1782; *Reveries of the Solitary Walker*). In his last years, he was once again afforded refuge on the estates of great French noblemen, first the Prince de Conti and then the Marquis de Girardin, in whose park at Ermenonville he died.

Denis Diderot (1713–84)

Diderot was the son of a widely respected master cutler. He was tonsured in 1726, though he did not in fact enter the church. Awarded the degree of master of arts in the University of Paris in 1732, he then studied law as an articled clerk in the office of Clément de Ris. He dropped an early ambition to enter the theatre and, instead, taught for a living, led a penurious existence as a publisher's hack, and wrote sermons for missionaries. He frequented the coffee houses, particularly the Régence and the Procope, where he met the philosopher Jean-Jacques Rousseau in 1741 and established a friendship with him that was to last for 15 years, until it was broken by a quarrel.

In 1741 he met Antoinette Champion, daughter of a linen draper, and in 1743 he married her – secretly, because of his father's disapproval. In order to earn a living, Diderot undertook translation work and in 1745 published a free translation of the *Inquiry Concerning Virtue* by the 3rd Earl of Shaftesbury, whose fame and influence he spread in France. Diderot's own *Pensées philosophiques* (1746; *Philosophic Thoughts*), an original work with new and explosive anti-Christian ideas, contains many passages directly translated from or inspired by Shaftesbury. The proceeds of this publication, as of his allegedly indecent novel *Les bijoux indiscrets* (1748; *The Indiscreet Jewels*), were used to meet the demands of his mistress, Madeleine de Puisieux, with whom he broke a few years later. In 1755 he met Sophie Volland, with whom he formed an attachment that was to last more than 20 years.

In 1745 the publisher André Le Breton approached Diderot with a view to bringing out a French translation of Ephraim Chambers' *Cyclopaedia*. Diderot undertook the task with the distinguished mathematician Jean le Rond d'Alembert as co-editor but soon profoundly changed the nature of the publication, broadening its scope and turning it into an important organ of radical and revolutionary opinion.

In 1749 Diderot published the *Lettre sur les aveugles* (*An*

Essay on Blindness), remarkable for its proposal to teach the blind to read through the sense of touch. This daring exposition of the doctrine of materialist atheism, with its emphasis on human dependence on sense impression, led to Diderot's arrest and incarceration in the prison of Vincennes for three months. Diderot's work on the *Encyclopédie*, however, was not interrupted for long, and in 1750 he outlined his programme for it in a *Prospectus*, which d'Alembert expanded into the momentous *Discours préliminaire* (1751). The history of the *Encyclopédie*, from the publication of the first volume in 1751 to the distribution of the final volumes of plates in 1772, was checkered with delays, criticisms and problems with censorship.

While editing the *Encyclopédie*, Diderot managed to compose most of his own important works as well. In 1751 he published his *Lettre sur les sourds et muets* (*Letter on the Deaf and Dumb*), which studies the function of language and deals with points of aesthetics, and in 1754 he published the *Pensées sur l'interprétation de la nature* (*Thoughts on the Interpretation of Nature*), an influential short treatise on the new experimental methods in science. Among his philosophical works, special mention may be made of *L'Entretien entre d'Alembert et Diderot* (written 1769, published 1830; *Conversation Between d'Alembert and Diderot*), *Le rêve de d'Alembert* (written 1769, published 1830; *D'Alembert's Dream*), and the *Eléments de physiologie* (1774–80; *Elements of Physiology*). In these works Diderot developed his materialist philosophy and arrived at startling intuitive insights into biology and chemistry. He also wrote four works of prose fiction. Diderot's plays make tedious reading today, but his theories on drama, expounded in *Entretiens sur le fils naturel* (1757; *Discussion on the Illegitimate Son*) and *Discours sur la poésie dramatique* (*Discourse on Dramatic Poetry*), were to exercise a determining influence on the German dramatist

Gotthold Lessing. His analysis of art, artists, and the technique of painting, and his *Essai sur la peinture* (written 1765, published 1796; *Essay on Painting*) have won him post-humous fame.

The completion of the *Encyclopédie* in 1772 left Diderot without a source of income. To relieve him of financial worry, Catherine the Great first bought his library through an agent in Paris, requesting him to retain the books until she required them, and then appointed him librarian on an annual salary for the duration of his life. He wrote for her the *Plan d'une université pour le gouvernement de Russie* (*Plan of a University for the Government of Russia*). He stayed five months, long enough to become disillusioned with enlightened despot-ism as a solution to social ills.

In 1774 Diderot, now old and ill, worked on a refutation of Helvétius' work *De l'homme* (1772; *On Man*), which was an amplification of the destroyed *De l'esprit* (*On the Spirit*). He wrote *Entretien d'un philosophe avec la Maréchale* (*Conversation with the Maréchale*) and published in 1778 *Essai sur les règnes de Claude et de Néron* (*Essay on the Reigns of Claudius and Nero*). Usually known as *Essai sur la vie de Sénèque* (*Essay on the Life of Seneca*), the work may be regarded as an apologia for that Roman satirist and philosopher. The death of Sophie Volland in February 1784 was a great grief to him; he survived her by a few months, dying of coronary thrombosis in the house in the rue de Richelieu that Catherine the Great had put at his disposal.

Adam Smith (1723–90)

Adam Smith was the son by second marriage of Adam Smith, comptroller of customs at Kirkcaldy, and Margaret Douglas, daughter of a substantial landowner. At the age of 14, in 1737,

Smith entered the University of Glasgow, already remarkable as a centre of the Scottish Enlightenment. There he was deeply influenced by Francis Hutcheson, professor of moral philoso-phy, from whose economic and philosophical views he was later to diverge but whose magnetic character seems to have been a main shaping force in Smith's development. Graduating in 1740, Smith won a scholarship and travelled on horseback to Oxford, where he stayed at Balliol College. His years there were spent largely in self-education, from which Smith obtained a firm grasp of both classical and contemporary philosophy.

Returning to his home after an absence of six years, Smith cast about for suitable employment. The connections of his mother's family, together with the support of Lord Henry Kames, resulted in an opportunity to give a series of public lectures in Edinburgh. In 1751, at the age of 27, he was appointed professor of logic at Glasgow, from which post he transferred in 1752 to the more remunerative professorship of moral philosophy.

Smith then entered upon a period of extraordinary creativity, combined with a social and intellectual life that he afterward described as "by far the happiest, and most honourable period of my life". He was made dean of faculty in 1758. Among his wide circle of acquaintances were not only members of the aristocracy, many connected with the government, but also a range of intellectual and scientific figures that included Joseph Black, a pioneer in the field of chemistry; James Watt, later of steam-engine fame; Robert Foulis, a distinguished printer and publisher and subsequent founder of the first British Academy of Design; and, not least, the philosopher David Hume, a lifelong friend whom Smith had met in Edinburgh. Smith was also introduced during these years to the company of the great merchants who were carrying on the colonial trade that had opened to Scotland following its union with England in 1707. One of them, Andrew Cochrane, had been a provost of Glasgow and had founded the famous Political Economy Club. From Cochrane and his fellow merchants Smith undoubtedly acquired the detailed information concerning trade and business that was to give such a sense of the real world to *The Wealth of Nations*.

In 1759 Smith published his first work, *The Theory of Moral Sentiments*. Didactic, exhortative, and analytic by turns, it lays the psychological foundation on which *An Inquiry Into the Nature and Causes of the Wealth of Nations* was later to be built. The *Theory* quickly brought Smith wide esteem and in particular attracted the attention of Charles Townshend, later chancellor of the Exchequer responsible for the measures of taxation that ultimately provoked the American Revolution, who was searching for a tutor for his stepson and ward, the young Duke of Buccleuch. Smith resigned his Glasgow post in 1763 and set off for France the next year as the tutor of the young duke.

They stayed mainly in Toulouse, where Smith began working on a book (eventually to be *The Wealth of Nations*), but had a two-month sojourn in Geneva, where he met Voltaire, for whom he had the profoundest respect. They then went to Paris, where Hume, then secretary to the British embassy, introduced Smith to the great literary Salons of the French Enlightenment. The stay in Paris was cut short when the younger brother of the Duke of Buccleuch, who had joined them in Toulouse, took ill and perished.

Smith worked in London until the spring of 1767 with Lord Townshend, a period during which he was elected a fellow of the Royal Society. Late that year he returned to Kirkcaldy, where the next six years were spent dictating and reworking *The Wealth of Nations*, followed by another stay of three years in London, where the work was finally completed and published in 1776.

The Wealth of Nations was received with admiration by Smith's wide circle of friends and admirers, although it was by no means an immediate popular success. The work finished, Smith went into semi-retirement. The final years of his life passed quietly, with several revisions of both major books but with no further publications. He died at the age of 67.

Immanuel Kant (1724–1804)

Kant lived in the remote province where he was born for his entire life. At the age of eight he entered a Pietist school and in 1740 he enrolled in the University of Königsberg as a theological student. Here Kant began reading the work of Newton and, in 1744, started his first book, dealing with a problem concerning kinetic forces. After the death of his father in 1746, he left the university and found employment as a family tutor. In 1755, aided by the kindness of a friend, he was able to complete his degree at the university and take up the position of *Privatdozent*, or lecturer, a position he held for 15 years.

He taught mathematics and physics initially, and soon also moral philosophy and logic, but he was never to lose his interest in scientific developments. That it was more than an amateur interest is shown by his publication within the next few years of several scientific works. The three dissertations he wrote exemplify his interests: *De Igne* (*On Fire*), in which he argued that bodies operate on one another through the medium of a uniformly diffused elastic and subtle matter that is the underlying substance of both heat and light; *Monodologia Physica* (1756), which contrasted the Newtonian methods of thinking with those employed in the philosophy then prevailing in German universities; and

Principiorum Primorum Cognitionis Metaphysicae Nova Dilucidato (1755), on the first principles of metaphysics.

During the 1760s he became increasingly critical of Leibnizianism. According to one of his students, Kant was then attacking Leibniz, Wolff, and Baumgarten, was a declared follower of Newton, and expressed great admiration for the moral philosophy of the Romanticist Jean-Jacques Rousseau. His principal work of this period was *Untersuchung über die Deutlichkeit der Grundsätze der natürlichen Theologie und der Moral* (1764; *An Inquiry into the Distinctness of the Fundamental Principles of Natural Theology and Morals*). In this work he attacked the claim of Leibnizian philosophy that philosophy should model itself on mathematics and aim at constructing a chain of demonstrated truths based on self-evident premises. Besides attacking the methods of the Leibnizians, he also began criticizing their leading ideas. Some indication of Kant's own possible alternative to the Leibnizian position can be gathered from his curious *Träume eines Geistersehers erläutert durch Träume der Metaphysik* (1766; *Dreams of a Spirit-Seer, Illustrated by Dreams of Metaphysics*). This work is an examination of the whole notion of a world of spirits, in the context of an inquiry into the spiritualist claims of Emanuel Swedenborg, a scientist and biblical scholar.

Finally, in 1770 Kant was appointed to the chair of logic and metaphysics, a position in which he remained active until a few years before his death. The *Inaugural Dissertation* of 1770 that he delivered on assuming his new position already contained many of the important elements of his mature philosophy. After the *Dissertation*, Kant published virtually nothing for 11 years. Then in the next next nine years he wrote the great *Critiques* which brought a revolution in philosophical thought and established the new direction in which it was to go in the years to come. In 1781 came the *Kritik der reinen Vernunft* (*Critique of Pure Reason*), in 1788 the *Kritik der praktischen Vernunft* (*Critique of Practical Reason*) and in 1790 the *Kritik der Urteilskraft* (*Critique of Judgement*).

The critical philosophy was soon being taught in every important German-speaking university, and young men flocked to Königsberg as a shrine of philosophy. From 1790 his health began to decline seriously. The writings that he then completed consist partly of an elaboration of subjects not previously treated in any detail, and partly of replies to criticisms and the clarification of misunderstandings. With the publication in 1793 of his work *Die Religion innerhalb der Grenzen der blossen Vernunft* (*Religion within the Boundary of Pure Reason*), Kant became involved in a dispute with Prussian authorities on the right to express religious opinions. He returned to the forbidden subject in his last major essay, *Der Streit der Fakultäten* (1798; *The Conflict of the Faculties*). After a gradual decline Kant died in Königsberg on February 12 1804.

Edward Gibbon (1737–94)

Gibbon's grandfather, Edward, had made a considerable fortune and his father, also Edward, was able to live an easy-going life in society and Parliament. This allowed Edward, too, to have independent means throughout his life. It was on visits to country houses with his father where he had the run of libraries filled with old folios that he early discovered his "proper food", history. By his fourteenth year he had already covered the main fields of his subsequent masterpiece, applying his mind as well to difficult problems of chronology.

He was entered at Magdalen College, Oxford, on April 3

1752, about three weeks before his fifteenth birthday. The authorities there failed to look after him or to note his absences from the college. Left to himself, Gibbon turned to theology and read himself into the Roman Catholic faith, into which he was received on June 8 1753. His father, outraged because under the existing laws his son had disqualified himself for all public service and office, acted swiftly, and Edward was dispatched to Lausanne and lodged with a Calvinist minister, the Rev. Daniel Pavillard. There, he mastered the bulk of classical Latin literature and studied mathematics and logic. He also became perfectly conversant with the language and literature of France, which exercised a permanent influence on him. These studies made him not only a man of considerable learning but a stylist for life. He was publicly readmitted to the Protestant communion at Christmas 1754.

He began his first work, written in French, *Essai sur l'étude de la littérature* (1761; English translation *An Essay on the Study of Literature*, 1764). In the latter part of his exile Gibbon entered more freely into Lausanne society. He attended Voltaire's parties. He formed an enduring friendship with a young Swiss, Georges Deyverdun, and also fell in love with and rashly plighted himself to Suzanne Curchod, a pastor's daughter of great charm and intelligence. In 1758 his father called Gibbon home shortly before his twenty-first birthday and settled an annuity of £300 on him. However, he found that his father and his stepmother were implacably opposed to his engagement, and he was compelled to break it off. He never again thought seriously of marriage.

From 1760 until the end of 1762, his studies were seriously interrupted by his service on home defence duties with the Hampshire militia. In January 1763, Gibbon left England and spent some time in Paris, making the acquaintance of several philosophes, Denis Diderot and Jean le Rond d'Alembert among others. In 1764 he went to Rome, where he made an exhaustive study of the antiquities and, on October 15 1764, while musing amid the ruins of the Capitol, was inspired to write of the decline and fall of the city.

At home, the next five years were the least satisfactory in Gibbon's life. He was dependent on his father and although aged nearly 30 had achieved little in life. He and Deyverdun published two volumes of *Mémoires littéraires de la Grande Bretagne* (1768–9). In 1770 he sought to attract some attention by publishing *Critical Observations on the Sixth Book of the Aeneid*. In 1770 his father died, and in 1772 Gibbon established himself in Bentinck Street, London, and concentrated on his Roman history. At the same time he entered fully into social life. In 1775 he was elected to the Club, the brilliant circle that the painter Sir Joshua Reynolds had formed round the writer and lexicographer Dr Samuel Johnson. In the previous year he had entered Parliament and was an assiduous, though silent, supporter of Lord North.

The first quarto volume of *The History of the Decline and Fall of the Roman Empire* was published in February 1776, immediately scoring a success that was resounding, if somewhat scandalous because of the last two chapters in which he dealt with great irony with the rise of Christianity. He was assailed by many pamphleteers and subjected to much ridicule. For the most part he ignored his critics. Only to those who had accused him of falsifying his evidence did he make a devastating reply in *A Vindication of Some Passages in the Fifteenth and Sixteenth Chapters of the Decline and Fall of the Roman Empire* (1779).

In the same year he obtained a valuable sinecure as a commissioner of trade and plantations. Shortly after that he composed *Mémoire justificatif* (1779; a French and English version, 1780), a masterly state paper in reply to continental criticism of the British government's policy in America. In 1781 he published the second and third volumes of his history, bringing the narrative down to the end of the empire in the West. In 1782, however, Lord North's government fell, and soon Gibbon's commission was abolished. To economize he left England and joined Deyverdun in a house at Lausanne. There he quietly completed his history in three more volumes, writing the last lines of it on June 27 1787. He soon returned to England with the manuscript, and these volumes were published on his fifty-first birthday, May 8 1788. The completion of this great work was acclaimed on all sides.

Returning to Lausanne, Gibbon turned mainly to writing his memoirs. His happiness was broken first by Deyverdun's death in 1789, quickly followed by the outbreak of the French Revolution and the subsequent apprehension of an invasion of Switzerland. He had now become very fat and his health was declining. In 1793 he suddenly returned to England on hearing of the death of Lady Sheffield, the wife of his long-standing friend Lord Sheffield whom he had met at Lausanne. The journey aggravated his ailments, and he died in a house in St James' Street, London.

John Wilkes (1725–97)

Wilkes was the second son of Israel Wilkes, a successful malt distiller. He was educated at an academy at Hertford and afterward privately tutored. His marriage on May 23 1747 to Mary Meade, heiress of the manor of Aylesbury, brought him a comfortable fortune and an assured status among the gentry of Buckinghamshire. Profligate by nature, Wilkes became a

member of the "Medmenham Monks", members of the so-
called Hell-Fire Club.

In 1754, at the suggestion of Earl Temple, Wilkes stood
unsuccessfully for election to Parliament for Berwick-upon-
Tweed. In 1757, after an election campaign said to have cost
him £7,000, much of it in bribes to voters, he was returned to
Parliament for Aylesbury. Recklessly overspending, and ever
deeper in debt, he hoped to retrieve his fortunes by political
advancement.

In 1762, as author of a political newspaper, the *North
Briton,* Wilkes began to give support to Earl Temple's campaign against the ministry of Lord Bute, partly provoking
Bute's decision to retire. Wilkes was now encouraged to
publish "No. 45" of the *North Briton,* attacking ministerial
statements in the King's Speech, which Wilkes described as
false. Wilkes was arrested but later released on the grounds
that the arrest had been a breach of parliamentary privilege.
However, when the government secured from Wilkes' private
press the proof sheets of "Essay on Woman", an obscene
parody on Alexander Pope's "Essay on Man", which Wilkes
had commenced, but not completed, printing, it was declared a
libel and a breach of privilege. At the same time the Commons,
on a government motion, declared "No. 45" a seditious libel.

During the Christmas vacation Wilkes, recovering from a
wound sustained in a duel provoked by exchanges in the
House, stole off to Paris to visit his daughter and decided
not to return to face prosecution. On January 20 1764, the
ministers carried the motion for his expulsion from the Commons. In February he was tried in absentia and found guilty of
publishing a seditious libel ("No. 45") and an obscene and
impious libel (the "Essay"). Sentence was deferred pending his
return, and in due course he was pronounced an outlaw for
impeding royal justice.

For the next four years Wilkes pursued a profligate career on the Continent, chiefly in Paris, vainly hoping that a change of ministry would bring in friends who would secure him relief and advancement. Early in 1768 he returned to London, determined to stand as an opponent of the government in the name of public liberty. The ministers, perhaps unwisely, failed to arrange his immediate arrest. Though defeated in London, he was elected for Middlesex. At the end of April he gave himself up to the authorities, and early in June his outlawry was reversed on a technical point. Then, waiving his privilege as a member of Parliament, he submitted to sentences totalling two years in jail and fines of £1,000 on the two charges on which he had been convicted in 1764.

Having made this gesture he wanted a pardon and restitution. In the following months he attempted to reopen the whole question of his conviction by a petition to the Commons complaining of illegality in the proceedings against him. The ministers once more secured his expulsion from the Commons on February 3 1769. The popularity in the metropolis of his stand against the government ensured his re-election for Middlesex on three subsequent occasions, until the House declared his defeated opponent, Henry Luttrell, the duly elected member and Wilkes was finally expelled.

In 1769 the Society for the Defence of the Bill of Rights was set up by supporters of Wilkes, to further his cause and to settle his debts. Though excluded from Parliament he determined to follow his ambitions and his vendetta with the ministers in the City of London, becoming an alderman in 1769, sheriff in 1771, and lord mayor in 1774. Re-elected for Middlesex in 1774, after pledging himself to the radical programme, he spoke on a number of occasions against the American Revolutionary War and once (1776) in support of parliamentary reform. In 1780, during the Gordon Riots against Roman

Catholics, he took firm action to put down the rioters, from whom a few years before he had been glad to receive support. In Middlesex he remained popular, being re-elected on his radical platform in 1780 and in 1784. In 1782 the expunging from the Commons journals of the resolution of 1769 against him vindicated his defence of the rights of parliamentary electors. After 1784 the issues that had made him popular were cold, and his fire was spent. He died in London in 1797.

Edmund Burke (1729–97)

Burke, the son of a solicitor, entered Trinity College, Dublin, in 1744 and moved to London in 1750 to begin his studies at the Middle Temple. There follows an obscure period in which Burke lost interest in his legal studies, was estranged from his father, and spent some time wandering about England and France. In 1756 he published anonymously *A Vindication of Natural Society: A View of the Miseries and Evils Arising to Mankind*, a satirical imitation of the style of Viscount Bolingbroke that was aimed at both the destructive criticism of revealed religion and the contemporary vogue for a "return to Nature".

A contribution to aesthetic theory, *A Philosophical Enquiry into the Origin of Our Ideas of the Sublime and Beautiful*, which appeared in 1757, gave him some reputation in England. In agreement with the publisher Robert Dodsley, Burke initiated *The Annual Register* as a yearly survey of world affairs; the first volume appeared in 1758 under his (unacknowledged) editorship, and he retained this connection for about 30 years. In 1757 Burke married Jane Nugent. From this period also date his numerous literary and artistic friendships, including those with Dr Samuel Johnson, Oliver Goldsmith, Sir Joshua Reynolds, and David Garrick.

After an unsuccessful first venture into politics, Burke was appointed secretary in 1765 to the Marquess of Rockingham, leader of one of the Whig groups, and he entered the House of Commons that year. Burke remained Rockingham's secretary until the latter's death in 1782. Burke took an active part in the domestic constitutional controversy of George III's reign when the king was seeking to reassert a more active role for the crown without infringing on the limitations of the royal prerogative set by the revolution settlement of 1689. Burke's chief comment on this issue is his pamphlet *Thoughts on the Cause of the Present Discontents* (1770).

In 1774 Burke was elected a member of Parliament for Bristol. He held this seat for six years. For the rest of his parliamentary career he was member for Malton, a pocket borough of Lord Rockingham's. It was at Bristol that Burke made the well-known statement on the role of the member of Parliament: the elected member should be a representative, not a mere delegate pledged to obey undeviatingly the wishes of his constituents.

Burke gave only qualified support to movements for parliamentary reform; his main concern was the curtailment of the crown's powers. He made a practical attempt to reduce this influence as one of the leaders of the movement that pressed for parliamentary control of royal patronage and expenditure. He was also connected with an act regulating the civil list.

A second great issue that confronted Burke in 1765 was the quarrel with the American colonies. Burke's best-known statements on this issue are two parliamentary speeches, "On American Taxation" (1774) and "On Moving his Resolutions for Conciliation with the Colonies" (1775), as well as "A Letter to . . . the Sheriffs of Bristol, on the Affairs of America" (1777). Authority, he argued, must be exercised with respect for the temper of those subject to it, if there was not to be collision of power and opinion. Burke made a wide historical survey of the growth of the colonies and of their present economic problems. In the place of narrow legalism he called for a more pragmatic policy on Britain's part that would admit the claims of circumstance, utility, and moral principle in addition to those of precedent.

Burke was also concerned with other imperial issues. On Ireland, he consistently advocated relaxation of the economic and penal regulations, and steps toward legislative independence. He also devoted many years to the problems of India. Burke in the 1760s and 1770s opposed interference by the English government in the East India Company's affairs as a violation of chartered rights. As the most active member of a select committee appointed in 1781 to investigate the administration of justice in India, Burke drafted the East India Bill of 1783, which proposed that India be governed by a board of independent commissioners in London. After the defeat of the bill, Burke's indignation came to centre on Warren Hastings, governor-general of Bengal from 1772 to 1785. It was at Burke's instigation that Hastings was impeached in 1787.

After the outbreak of the French Revolution in 1789, Burke, after a brief suspension of judgement, was both hostile to it and alarmed by favourable English reaction. He was provoked into writing his *Reflections on the Revolution in France* (1790). Burke's deeply-felt antagonism to the new movement propelled him to the plane of general political thought; it provoked a host of English replies, of which the best known is Thomas Paine's *Rights of Man* (1791–2).

In 1794, at the conclusion of Hastings' impeachment, Burke retired from Parliament. His last years were clouded by the death of his only son, on whom his political ambitions had come to centre. He continued to write, defending himself from his critics, deploring the condition of Ireland, and opposing any recognition of the French government (notably in "Three Letters Addressed to a Member of the Present Parliament on the Proposals for Peace, with the Regicide Directory of France" [1796–7]).

Thomas Paine (1737–1809)

Paine was born of a Quaker father and an Anglican mother. His formal education was meagre, and at 13 he began work with his father as a corset maker and then tried various other occupations unsuccessfully, finally becoming an officer of the excise. Paine's life in England was marked by repeated failures. He had two brief marriages. He was dismissed from the excise office after he published a strong argument in 1772 for a raise in pay as the only way to end corruption in the service. Just when his situation appeared hopeless, he met Benjamin Franklin in London, who advised him to seek his fortune in America and gave him letters of introduction.

Paine arrived in Philadelphia on November 30 1774. His first regular employment was helping to edit the *Pennsylvania Magazine*. In addition Paine published numerous articles and some poetry, anonymously or under pseudonyms. One such article was "African Slavery in America", a scathing denunciation of the African slave trade, which he signed "Justice and Humanity".

Paine had arrived in America when the conflict between the colonists and England was reaching its height. After blood was spilled at the Battle of Lexington and Concord on April 19 1775, Paine argued that the cause of America should not be just a revolt against taxation but a demand for independence. He put this idea into *Common Sense*, which came off the press on January 10 1776. The 50-page pamphlet sold more than 500,000 copies within a few months. More than any other single publication, *Common Sense* paved the way for the Declaration of Independence, unanimously ratified July 4 1776.

During the war that followed, Paine served as volunteer aide-de-camp to General Nathanael Greene. His great contribution to the patriot cause was the 16 "Crisis" papers issued between 1776 and 1783, each one signed "Common Sense". "The American Crisis. Number I", published on December 19 1776, opened with the inflammatory words: "These are the times that try men's souls," and Washington ordered it read to all the troops at Valley Forge.

In 1777 Congress appointed Paine secretary to the Committee for Foreign Affairs. He held the post until early in 1779, when he became involved in a controversy with Silas Deane, a member of the Continental Congress, whom Paine accused of seeking to profit personally from French aid to the United States. But in revealing Deane's machinations, Paine was forced to quote from secret documents to which he had access as secretary of the Committee for Foreign Affairs. As a result he was forced to resign his post.

Paine's desperate need of employment was relieved when he was appointed clerk of the General Assembly of Pennsylvania on November 2 1779. In this capacity he had frequent opportunity to observe that American troops were at the end of their patience because of lack of pay and scarcity of supplies. Paine took $500 from his salary and started a subscription for the relief of the soldiers. In 1781, pursuing the same goal, he accompanied John Laurens to France. The money, clothing, and ammunition they brought back with them were important to the final success of the Revolution. Paine also appealed to the separate states to cooperate for the well-being of the entire nation. In "Public Good" (1780) he included a call for a national convention to establish a strong central government under "a continental constitution".

At the end of the American Revolution, Paine again found himself poverty-stricken. His patriotic writings had sold by the hundreds of thousands, but he had refused to accept any profits in order that cheap editions might be widely circulated. In a petition to Congress endorsed by Washington, he pleaded for financial assistance. It was buried by Paine's opponents in Congress, but Pennsylvania gave him £500 and New York a farm in New Rochelle. Here Paine devoted his time to inventions, concentrating on an iron bridge without piers and a smokeless candle.

In April 1787 Paine left for Europe to promote his plan to build a single-arch bridge across the wide Schuylkill River near Philadelphia. But he was soon diverted and in December 1789 he published anonymously a warning against the attempt of Prime Minister William Pitt to involve England in a war with France over Holland, reminding the British people that war had "but one thing certain and that is increase of taxes". But it was the French Revolution that now filled Paine's thoughts. Enraged by Edmund Burke's attack on the uprising of the French people in his *Reflections on the Revolution in France*, he rushed into print with his celebrated answer, *Rights of Man* (1791). The book immediately created a sensation. At least eight editions were published in 1791, and the work was quickly reprinted in America, where it was widely distributed by the Jeffersonian societies. When Burke replied, Paine came back with *Rights of Man, Part II*, published in February 1792.

To the ruling class Paine's proposals spelled "bloody revolution", and the government ordered the book banned and the publisher jailed. Paine himself was indicted for treason, and an order went out for his arrest. But he was en route to France, having been elected to a seat in the National Convention, before the order for his arrest could be delivered. Paine was tried in absentia, found guilty of seditious libel, and declared an outlaw, and *Rights of Man* was ordered permanently suppressed.

In France Paine hailed the abolition of the monarchy but deplored the terror against the royalists and fought unsuccessfully to save the life of King Louis XVI, favouring banishment rather than execution. He was to pay for his efforts to save the king's life when the radicals under Robespierre took power. Paine was imprisoned from December 28 1793, to November 4 1794, when, with the fall of Robespierre, he was released and, though seriously ill, readmitted to the National Convention.

While in prison, the first part of Paine's *Age of Reason* was published (1794), and it was followed by Part II after his release (1796). The publication of his last great pamphlet, "Agrarian Justice" (1797), with its attack on inequalities in property ownership, added to his many enemies in establishment circles. Paine remained in France until September 1 1802, when he sailed for the United States. He quickly discovered that his services to the country had been all but forgotten and that he was widely regarded only as the world's greatest infidel. Despite his poverty and his physical condition, worsened by occasional drunkenness, Paine continued his attacks on privilege and religious superstitions. He died in New York City in 1809 and was buried in New Rochelle.

Thomas Jefferson (1743–1826)

Jefferson's father, Peter Jefferson, was a self-educated surveyor, while his mother, Jane Randolph Jefferson, was descended from one of the most prominent families in Virginia. In 1760, Jefferson entered the College of William and Mary in Williamsburg. He read law with Wythe, the leading legal scholar in Virginia, from 1762 to 1767, then left Williamsburg to practice.

In 1768 he made two important decisions: first, to build his own home, eventually named Monticello and, second, to stand as a candidate for the House of Burgesses. He entered the Virginia legislature just as opposition to the taxation policies of the British Parliament was coalescing and his support for resolutions opposing Parliament's authority over the colonies was resolute.

In 1772 he married Martha Wayles Skelton, an attractive and delicate young widow whose dowry more than doubled his holdings in land and slaves. In 1774 he wrote *A Summary View of the Rights of British America*, which was quickly published, and catapulted him into visibility as an early advocate of American independence. His reputation thus enhanced, the Virginia legislature appointed him a delegate to the Second Continental Congress in the spring of 1775.

Jefferson's inveterate shyness prevented him from playing a significant role in the debates within the Congress. His chief role was as a draftsman of resolutions. In that capacity, on June 11 1776, he was appointed to a five-person committee, to draft a formal statement of the reasons why a break with Great Britain was justified; this became the Declaration of Independence. Jefferson returned to Virginia in October 1776 and immediately launched an extensive project for the reform of the state's legal code to bring it in line with the principles of the American Revolution. He sought and secured the abolition of primogeniture, entail, and remnants of feudalism that discouraged a broad distribution of property; he proposed a comprehensive plan of educational reform designed to assure access at the lowest level for all citizens and state support at the higher levels for the most talented; and he advocated a law prohibiting any religious establishment and requiring complete separation of church and state. The last two proposals were bitterly contested. Taken together, these legal reforms capture the essence of Jefferson's political philosophy.

At the end of what was probably the most creative phase of his public career, personal misfortune struck. Elected governor of Virginia in 1779, he was caught off-guard by a surprise British invasion in 1780 against which the state was defenceless. His flight from approaching British troops was described in the local press, somewhat unfairly, as a cowardly act of abdication. Then, in September 1782, his wife died after a difficult delivery in May of their third daughter. These two disasters caused him to vow that he would never again desert his family for his country.

Jefferson agreed, albeit reluctantly, to serve as a delegate to the Continental Congress in December 1782, where his major contribution was to set forth the principle that territories in the West should not be treated as colonies but rather should enter the Union with status equal to the original states once certain conditions were met. Then, in 1784, he agreed to replace Franklin as American minister to France. During his five-year sojourn in Paris, his only significant achievement was the negotiation of a $400,000 loan from Dutch bankers that allowed the American government to consolidate its European debts. It was also during this period that he became briefly infatuated with Maria Cosway, who was married to a prominent English miniaturist. Then, in 1788, he initiated a sexual liaison with his attractive young mulatto slave Sally Hemings. He departed France late in 1789, just at the onset of mob violence.

Even before his departure from France, Jefferson had overseen the publication of *Notes on the State of Virginia*. *Notes* contained an extensive discussion of slavery, a strong assertion that it violated the principles on which the American Revolution was based, and the most explicit assessment that Jefferson ever wrote of what he believed were the biological differences between blacks and whites. Despite this, Jefferson owned, on average, about 200 slaves at any point in time. To protect himself from facing the reality of his problematic status as plantation master, he constructed a paternalistic self-image as a benevolent father caring for what he called "my family".

Jefferson returned to the United States in 1789 to serve as the first secretary of state under President George Washington. His major concern about the new Constitution was the absence of any bill of rights. During his tenure as secretary of state (1790–93), foreign policy was his chief responsibility. While all parties embraced some version of the neutrality doctrine, the specific choices posed by the ongoing competition for supremacy in Europe between England and France produced a bitter conflict. Jefferson favoured a pro-French version of neutrality, arguing that the Franco-American treaty of 1778 obliged the United States to honour past French support during the war for independence, and that the French Revolution embodied the "spirit of '76" on European soil. This remained his unwavering position throughout the decade.

Jefferson's position on domestic policy during the 1790s was a variation on the same ideological dichotomy. Jefferson came to regard the consolidation of power at the federal level as a diabolical plot to subvert the true meaning of the American Revolution. As Jefferson saw it, the entire Federalist commitment to an energetic central government with broad powers over the domestic economy replicated the arbitrary policies of Parliament and George III, which the American Revolution had supposedly repudiated as monarchical and aristocratic practices, incompatible with the principles of republicanism. By the middle years of the decade two distinctive political camps had emerged, calling themselves Federalists and Republicans (later Democratic-Republicans). An embryonic version of the party structure was congealing, and Jefferson, assisted and advised by Madison, established the rudiments of the first opposition party in American politics under the Republican banner.

In 1796 he ran for the presidency against Adams. The highly combustible political culture of the early republic reached a crescendo in the election of 1800; Jefferson was elected on the thirty-sixth ballot. The major message of Jefferson's inaugural address was conciliatory. Its most famous line ("We are all republicans – we are all federalists") suggested that the scatological party battles of the previous decade must cease. He described his election as a recovery of the original intentions of the American Revolution. In Jefferson's truly distinctive and original formulation, the coherence of the American republic did not require the mechanisms of a powerful state to survive or flourish.

In 1804 Jefferson was easily re-elected. Initially, at least, his policies as president reflected his desire for decentralization. The major achievement of his first term defied his own principles. In 1803 Napoleon decided to consolidate his resources for a new round of the conflict with England by selling the vast Louisiana region, and although it violated Jefferson's constitutional scruples, he reasoned that the opportunity to double the national domain was too good to miss. His major disappointment also had its origins in Europe with the resumption of the Napoleonic Wars, which resulted in naval blockades in the Atlantic and Caribbean that severely curtailed American trade and pressured the US government to take sides in the conflict. Jefferson's response was the Embargo Act (1807), which essentially closed American ports to all foreign imports and American exports. By the time he left office in March 1809, Jefferson was a tired and beaten man.

During the last 17 years of his life Jefferson maintained a crowded and active schedule. Monticello became a veritable hotel during these years, on occasion housing 50 guests. The lack of privacy caused Jefferson to build a separate house on his Bedford estate about 90 miles (140 km) from Monticello, where he periodically fled for seclusion. He died on July 4 1826.

Maximilien de Robespierre (1758–94)

Robespierre was the son of a lawyer in Arras. In 1769 he was awarded a scholarship to the famous college of Louis-le-Grand in Paris, where he distinguished himself in philosophy and law. He received a law degree in 1781 and became a lawyer at Arras, where he set up house with his sister Charlotte. He was appointed a judge at the Salle Épiscopale, a court with jurisdiction over the provostship of the diocese. His private practice provided him with a comfortable income.

He was admitted to the Arras Academy in 1783 and soon became its chancellor and later its president. By 1788 Robespierre was already well known for his altruism. As a lawyer representing poor people, he had alarmed the privileged classes by his protests in his *Mémoire pour le Sieur Dupond* (*Report for Lord Dupond*) against royal absolutism and arbitrary justice. When the summoning of the Estates-General was announced, he issued an appeal entitled *À la nation artésienne sur la nécessité de réformer les Etats d'Artois* (*To the People of Artois on the Necessity of Reforming the Estates of Artois*). In March 1789 the citizens of Arras chose him as one of their representatives, and the Third Estate (the commons) of the bailiwick elected him fifth of the eight deputies from Artois. Thus he began his political career at the age of 30.

Robespierre was kept out of the committees and from the presidency of the National Assembly; only once, in June 1790, was he elected secretary of the National Assembly. In April he had presided over the Jacobins, a political club promoting the ideas of the French Revolution. In October he was appointed a judge of the Versailles tribunal.

Robespierre nevertheless decided to devote himself fully to his work in the National Assembly, where the constitution was being drawn up. Grounded in ancient history and the works of the French philosophers of the Enlightenment, he welcomed the Declaration of the Rights of Man and of the Citizen, which formed the preamble of the French constitution of September 3 1791, and he insisted that all laws should conform to it. He fought for universal suffrage, for unrestricted admission to the national guard, to public offices, and to the commissioned ranks of the army, and for the right to petition. He opposed the royal veto, the abuses of ministerial power, and religious and racial discrimination. He defended actors, Jews, and black slaves and supported the reunion of Avignon, formerly a papal possession, with France in September 1791. In May he had successfully proposed that all new deputies be elected to the next legislature so that, as a new body, it would better express the people's will.

His passionate fight for liberty won him more enemies, who called him a dangerous individual – and worse. After the flight of Louis XVI (June 20–21 1791), for which Robespierre vainly demanded his trial, the slanders against the Revolutionary deputy became twice as violent. He hastened the vote on the constitution so as to attract "as many of the democratic party as possible". Martial law was proclaimed, and at the Champ-de-Mars the national guard opened fire on a group demanding the abdication of the king. Robespierre, his life threatened, went to live with the family of the cabinetmaker Maurice Duplay. He managed to keep the Jacobin Club alive after all of its moderate members had joined a rival club. When the

National Assembly dissolved itself, the people of Paris organized a triumphal procession for Robespierre.

Although he had excluded himself and his colleagues from
the new Legislative Assembly, Robespierre continued to be
politically active, giving up the lucrative post of public pro-
secutor of Paris, to which he had been elected in June 1791.
Henceforth, he spoke only at the Jacobin Club, until August
1792. When Brissot's supporters stirred up opinion against
him, Robespierre founded a newspaper, *Le défenseur de la
constitution* (*Defence of the Constitution*), which strengthened
his hand, and attacked Lafayette.

The reverses suffered by the French army after France had
declared war on Austria and Prussia had been foreseen by
Robespierre, and, when invasion threatened, the people rallied
to him. When the insurrection broke out on August 10 1792,
Robespierre took no part in the attack on the Tuileries Palace,
but his *section* Les Piques nominated him to the insurrectional
Commune. He exonerated the mob, and on September 5 the
people of Paris elected him to head the delegation to the
National Convention.

The Girondins – who favoured political but not social
democracy and who controlled the government and the civil
service – accused Robespierre of dictatorship from the first
sessions of the National Convention. At the king's trial, which
began in December 1792, Robespierre called for death. His
new journal, *Les lettres à ses commettants* (*Letters to his
Constituents*), kept the provinces informed. The king's execution did not, however, resolve the struggle between the Girondins and the Montagnards, the deputies of the extreme left.
A kind of "popular front" was formed between the Parisian
sansculottes, the poor, ultraleft republicans, and the Montagnards. On May 26 1793, Robespierre called on the people
"to rise in insurrection". Five days later he supported a decree

of the National Convention indicting the Girondin leaders and Dumouriez's accomplices. On June 2 the decree was passed against 29 of them.

After the fall of the Girondins, the Montagnards were left to deal with the country's desperate position. In his diary, Robespierre noted that what was needed was "une volonté une" ("one single will"), and this dictatorial power was to characterize the Revolutionary government. Its essential organs had been created, and he set himself to make them work. On July 27 1793, Robespierre took his place on the Committee of Public Safety, which had first been set up in April. He strove to prevent division among the revolutionaries by relying on the Jacobin societies and the vigilance committees. Henceforward his actions were to be inseparable from those of the government as a whole. As president of the Jacobin Club and then of the National Convention, he denounced the schemes of the Parisian radicals known as the Enragés, who were using the food shortage to stir up the Paris *sections*. Robespierre answered the demonstrators on September 5 by promising maximum prices for all foodstuffs and a Revolutionary militia for use in the interior against counter-revolutionaries and grain hoarders.

In order to bring about a mass conscription, economic dictatorship, and total war, he asked to intensify the Reign of Terror. But he objected to pointless executions, protecting those deputies who had protested the arrest of the Girondins and of the king's sister. Those who wanted to halt the Reign of Terror and the war attacked the policies of the Committee of Public Safety with increasing violence.

A Deist in the style of Rousseau, Robespierre disapproved of the anti-Christian movement and the "masquerades" of the cult of reason. In a report to the National Convention in May, he affirmed the existence of God and the immortality of the soul and strove to rally the revolutionaries around a civic religion and the cult of the Supreme Being. The National Convention elected him president, on 16 Prairial (June 4), by a vote of 216 out of 220. In this capacity he led the festival of the Supreme Being ("Etre suprême") in the Tuileries Gardens on 20 Prairial (June 8), which was to provide his enemies with another weapon against him.

After the law of 22 Prairial (June 10) reorganizing the Revolutionary Tribunal, which had been formed in March 1793 to condemn all enemies of the regime, opposition to Robespierre grew; it was led by those *représentants en mission* whom he had threatened. His influence was challenged in the Committee of Public Safety itself, and the Committee of General Security – which felt slighted by the General Police Bureau directed by Robespierre, Georges Couthon, and Louis de Saint-Just – became even more hostile. In the cafes he was accused of being a moderate.

Unremitting work and frequent speeches had undermined Robespierre's health, and he became irritable and distant. Embittered by the slanders and by the accusations of dictatorship being spread both by the royalists and by his colleagues, the Montagnards, he stayed away from the National Convention and then, after 10 Messidor (June 28), from the Committee of Public Safety, confining his denunciations of counter-revolutionary intrigues to the Jacobin Club. At the same time, he began to lose the support of the people. From his partial retirement Robespierre followed the unleashing of the Great Terror in the summer of 1794 and the progress of opposition.

Attempting to regain his hold on public opinion, Robespierre reappeared at the Committee of Public Safety on 5 Thermidor (July 23) and then, on 8 Thermidor (July 26), at the National Convention, to which he turned as his judge. His last speech was at first received with applause, then with disquiet, and finally the parliamentary majority turned against him. Despite his successful reception that evening at the Jacobin Club, Robespierre's adversaries succeeded the next day in preventing him from speaking before the Convention, which indicted him together with his brother, Augustin, and three of his associates. Robespierre was taken to the Luxembourg prison, but the warden refused to jail him. Declared an outlaw by the National Convention, Robespierre severely wounded himself by a pistol shot in the jaw at the Hôtel de Ville, throwing his friends into confusion. The soldiers of the National Convention attacked the Hôtel de Ville and easily seized Robespierre and his followers. In the evening of 10 Thermidor (July 28), the first 22 of those condemned, including Robespierre, were guillotined before a cheering mob on the Place de la Révolution (now the Place de la Concorde).

The Jacobin Club (1789–94)

The Jacobins originated as the Club Breton at Versailles, where the deputies from Brittany to the Estates-General (later the National Assembly) of 1789 met with deputies from other parts of France to concert their action. The group was reconstituted, probably in December 1789, after the National Assembly moved to Paris, under the name of Society of the Friends of the Constitution, but it was commonly called the Jacobin Club. Its purpose was to protect the gains of the Revolution against a possible aristocratic reaction. The club soon admitted non-deputies – usually prosperous bourgeois and men of letters – and acquired affiliates throughout France. By July 1790 there were about 1,200 members in the Parisian club and 152 affiliate clubs.

In July 1791 the Jacobin Club split over a petition calling for the removal of Louis XVI after his unsuccessful attempt to flee

France; many of the moderate deputies left to join the rival club of the Feuillants. Maximilien Robespierre was one of the few deputies who remained, and he assumed a position of prominence in the club.

After the overthrow of the monarchy, in August 1792 (in which the Jacobin Club, still reluctant to declare itself republican, did not have a direct role), the club entered a new phase as one of the major groups directing the Revolution. With the proclamation of the republic in September, the club changed its name to Society of the Jacobins, Friends of Liberty and Equality. It acquired a democratic character with the admission of the leftist Montagnard deputies in the National Convention (the new legislature) and also a more popular one as it responded to the demands of the Parisian working and artisan class. Through the early phase of the Convention, the club was a meeting place for the Montagnards, and it agitated for the execution of the king (January 1793) and for the overthrow of the moderate Girondins (June 1793).

With the establishment of the Revolutionary dictatorship, beginning in the summer of 1793, the local Jacobin clubs became instruments of the Reign of Terror. (In 1793 there were probably 5,000 to 8,000 clubs throughout France, with a nominal membership of 500,000.) The clubs, as part of the administrative machinery of government, had certain duties: they raised supplies for the army and policed local markets. As centres of public virtue, the clubs watched over people whose opinions were suspect, led the dechristianizing movement, and organized Revolutionary festivals.

The Parisian club was increasingly associated with Robespierre, who dominated the Revolutionary government through his position on the Committee of Public Safety. It supported Robespierre in his attacks on the enemies of the Revolution and helped him resist the growing demands of the discontented workers for a controlled economy. After the fall of Robespierre on 9 Thermidor, year II (July 27 1794), the Parisian club, now a symbol of dictatorship and terror, was temporarily closed. It reopened as a centre of opposition to the Thermidorian government, but it was permanently closed on 21 Brumaire, year III (November 11 1794). The Club du Panthéon in 1795 and Club du Manège of 1799 briefly revived the Jacobin spirit, while some local clubs lasted until the year VIII (1799–1800) despite their having been officially banned.

Mary Wollstonecraft (1759–97)

The daughter of a farmer, Wollstonecraft taught school and worked as a governess, experiences that inspired her views in *Thoughts on the Education of Daughters* (1787). In 1788 she began working as a translator for the London publisher James Johnson, who published several of her works, including the novel *Mary: A Fiction* (1788). Her mature work on woman's place in society is *A Vindication of the Rights of Woman* (1792), which calls for women and men to be educated equally.

In 1792 Wollstonecraft left England to observe the French Revolution in Paris, where she lived with an American, Captain Gilbert Imlay. In the spring of 1794 she gave birth to a daughter, Fanny. The following year, distraught over the breakdown of her relationship with Imlay, she attempted suicide. Wollstonecraft returned to London to work again for Johnson and joined the influential radical group that gathered at his home and that included William Godwin, Thomas Paine, Thomas Holcroft, William Blake, and, after 1793, William Wordsworth. In 1796 she began a liaison with Godwin, and on March 29 1797, Mary being pregnant, they were married. The marriage was happy but brief; Mary Wollstonecraft Godwin died 11 days after the birth of her second daughter, Mary.

The publication of *Vindication* caused considerable controversy but failed to bring about any immediate reforms. From the 1840s, however, members of the incipient American and European women's movements resurrected some of the book's principles.

KEY TEXTS: EXTRACTS
AND FURTHER READING

Extracts

René Descartes, *Discourse on Method* (1637)

from Part II

Among the branches of philosophy, I had, at an earlier
period, given some attention to logic, and among those of
the mathematics to geometrical analysis and algebra, – three
arts or sciences which ought, as I conceived, to contribute
something to my design. But, on examination, I found that,
as for logic, its syllogisms and the majority of its other
precepts are of avail – rather in the communication of what
we already know, or even as the art of Lully, in speaking
without judgement of things of which we are ignorant, than
in the investigation of the unknown; and although this
science contains indeed a number of correct and very excellent precepts, there are, nevertheless, so many others, and
these either injurious or superfluous, mingled with the former, that it is almost quite as difficult to effect a severance of

the true from the false as it is to extract a Diana or a Minerva from a rough block of marble.

Then as to the analysis of the ancients and the algebra of the moderns, besides that they embrace only matters highly abstract, and, to appearance, of no use, the former is so exclusively restricted to the consideration of figures, that it can exercise the understanding only on condition of greatly fatiguing the imagination; and, in the latter, there is so complete a subjection to certain rules and formulas, that there results an art full of confusion and obscurity calculated to embarrass, instead of a science fitted to cultivate the mind.

By these considerations I was induced to seek some other method which would comprise the advantages of the three and be exempt from their defects. And as a multitude of laws often only hampers justice, so that a state is best governed when, with few laws, these are rigidly administered; in like manner, instead of the great number of precepts of which logic is composed, I believed that the four following would prove perfectly sufficient for me, provided I took the firm and unwavering resolution never in a single instance to fail in observing them.

The first was never to accept anything for true which I did not clearly know to be such; that is to say, carefully to avoid precipitancy and prejudice, and to comprise nothing more in my judgement than what was presented to my mind so clearly and distinctly as to exclude all ground of doubt.

The second, to divide each of the difficulties under examination into as many parts as possible, and as might be necessary for its adequate solution.

The third, to conduct my thoughts in such order that, by commencing with objects the simplest and easiest to know, I might ascend by little and little, and, as it were, step by step, to the knowledge of the more complex; assigning in thought a certain order even to those objects which in their own nature do not stand in a relation of antecedence and sequence.

And the last, in every case to make enumerations so complete, and reviews so general, that I might be assured that nothing was omitted.

John Locke, *Two Treatises on Government* (1690)

from Second Treatise, Chapter XVIII, "Of Tyranny"
Sec. 199 . . . Tyranny is the exercise of power beyond right, which no body can have a right to. And this is making use of the power any one has in his hands, not for the good of those who are under it, but for his own private separate advantage. When the governor, however entitled, makes not the law, but his will, the rule; and his commands and actions are not directed to the preservation of the properties of his people, but the satisfaction of his own ambition, revenge, covetousness, or any other irregular passion . . .

Sec. 202. Wherever law ends, tyranny begins, if the law be transgressed to another's harm; and whosoever in authority exceeds the power given him by the law, and makes use of the force he has under his command, to compass that upon the subject, which the law allows not, ceases in that to be a magistrate; and, acting without authority, may be opposed, as any other man, who by force invades the right of another.

This is acknowledged in subordinate magistrates. He that hath authority to seize my person in the street, may be opposed as a thief and a robber, if he endeavours to break into my house to execute a writ, notwithstanding that I know he has such a warrant, and such a legal authority, as will empower him to arrest me abroad. And why this should not hold in the highest, as well as in the most inferior magistrate, I would gladly be informed. Is it reasonable, that the eldest brother, because he has the greatest part of his father's estate, should thereby have a right to take away any of his younger brother's portions? Or that a rich man, who possessed a whole country, should from thence have a right to seize, when he pleased, the cottage and garden of his poor neighbour?

The being rightfully possessed of great power and riches, exceedingly beyond the greatest part of the sons of Adam, is so far from being an excuse, much less a reason, for rapine and oppression, which the endamaging another without authority is, that it is a great aggravation of it: for the exceeding the bounds of authority is no more a right in a great, than in a petty officer; no more justifiable in a king than a constable; but is so much the worse in him, in that he has more trust put in him, has already a much greater share than the rest of his brethren, and is supposed, from the advantages of his education, employment, and counsellors, to be more knowing in the measures of right and wrong.

Sec. 203. May the commands then of a prince be opposed? May he be resisted as often as any one shall find himself aggrieved, and but imagine he has not right done him? This will unhinge and overturn all polities, and, instead of government and order, leave nothing but anarchy and confusion.

Sec. 204. To this I answer, that force is to be opposed to nothing, but to unjust and unlawful force; whoever makes any opposition in any other case, draws on himself a just condemnation both from God and man.

Joseph Addison, "Pleasures of Imagination", *Spectator* No. 411, June 21 1712

Our sight is the most perfect and most delightful of all our senses. It fills the mind with the largest variety of ideas, converses with its objects at the greatest distance, and continues the longest in action without being tired or satiated with its proper enjoyments. The sense of feeling can indeed give us a notion of extension, shape, and all other ideas that enter at the eye, except colours; but at the same time it is very much straitened and confined in its operations, to the number, bulk, and distance of its particular objects. Our sight seems designed to supply all these defects, and may be considered as a more delicate and diffusive kind of touch, that spreads itself over an infinite multitude of bodies, comprehends the largest figures, and brings into our reach some of the most remote parts of the universe.

It is this sense which furnishes the imagination with its ideas; so that by the pleasures of the imagination, or fancy (which I shall use promiscuously), I here mean such as arise from visible objects, either when we have them actually in our view, or when we call up their ideas into our minds by paintings, statues, descriptions, or any the like occasion. We cannot, indeed, have a single image in the fancy that did not make its first entrance through the sight; but we have the power of retaining, altering, and compounding those images, which we have once received, into all the varieties of picture and vision that are most agreeable to the imagination; for by this faculty a man in a dungeon is capable of entertaining himself with scenes and landscapes more beautiful than any that can be found in the whole compass of nature.

There are few words in the English language which are employed in a more loose and uncircumscribed sense than those of the fancy and the imagination. I therefore thought it necessary to fix and determine the notion of these two words, as I intend to make use of them in the thread of my following speculations, that the reader may conceive rightly what is the subject which I proceed upon. I must therefore desire him to remember, that by the pleasures of the imagination, I mean only such pleasures as arise originally from sight, and that I divide these pleasures into two kinds my design being first of all to discourse of those primary pleasures of the imagination, which entirely proceed from such objects as are before our eyes; and in the next place to speak of those secondary pleasures of the imagination which flow from the ideas of visible objects, when the objects are not actually before the eye, but are called up into our memories, or formed into agreeable visions of things that are either absent or fictitious.

The pleasures of the imagination, taken in their full extent, are not so gross as those of sense, nor so refined as those of the understanding. The last are, indeed, more preferable, because they are founded on some new knowledge or improvement in the mind of man; yet it must be confessed, that those of the imagination are as great and as transporting as the other. A beautiful prospect delights the soul, as much as a demonstration; and a description in Homer has charmed more readers than a chapter in Aristotle. Besides, the pleasures of the imagination have this advantage above those of the understanding, that they are more obvious, and more easy to be acquired. It is but opening the eye, and the scene enters. The colours paint themselves on the fancy, with very little attention of thought or application of mind in the beholder. We are struck, we know not how, with the symmetry of anything we see, and immediately assent to the beauty of an object, without inquiring into the particular causes and occasions of it.

A man of polite imagination is let into a great many pleasures, that the vulgar are not capable of receiving. He can converse with a picture, and find an agreeable companion in a statue. He meets with a secret refreshment in a description, and often feels a greater satisfaction in the prospect of fields and meadows, than another does in the possession. It gives him, indeed, a kind of property in everything he sees, and makes the most rude, uncultivated parts of nature administer to his pleasures: so that he looks upon the world, as it were in another light, and discovers in it a multitude of charms, that conceal themselves from the generality of mankind.

There are, indeed, but very few who know how to be idle and innocent, or have a relish of any pleasures that are not criminal: every diversion they take is at the expense of some one virtue or another, and their very first step out of business is into vice or folly. A man should endeavour, therefore, to make the sphere of his innocent pleasures as wide as possible, that he may retire into them with safety, and find in them such a satisfaction as a wise man would not blush to take. Of this nature are those of the imagination, which do not require such a bent of thought as is necessary to our more serious employments, nor, at the same time, suffer the mind to sink into that negligence and remissness, which are apt to accompany our more sensual delights, but, like a gentle exercise to the faculties, awaken them from sloth and idleness, without putting them upon any labour or difficulty.

We might here add, that the pleasures of the fancy are more conducive to health, than those of the understanding, which are worked out by dint of thinking, and attended with too violent a labour of the brain. Delightful scenes, whether in nature, painting, or poetry, have a kindly influence on the body, as well as the mind, and not only serve to clear and brighten the imagination, but are able to disperse grief and melancholy, and to set the animal spirits in pleasing and agreeable motions. For this reason Sir Francis Bacon, in his

Essay upon Health, has not thought it improper to prescribe to his reader a poem or a prospect, where he particularly dissuades him from knotty and subtle disquisitions, and advises him to pursue studies that fill the mind with splendid and illustrious objects, as histories, fables, and contemplations of nature.

Voltaire, *Letters on England* (1734)

Chapter VIII, "On Mr Locke"

Perhaps no man ever had a more judicious or more methodical genius, or was a more acute logician than Mr Locke, and yet he was not deeply skilled in the mathematics. This great man could never subject himself to the tedious fatigue of calculations, nor to the dry pursuit of mathematical truths, which do not at first present any sensible objects to the mind; and no one has given better proofs than he, that it is possible for a man to have a geometrical head without the assistance of geometry. Before his time, several great philosophers had declared, in the most positive terms, what the soul of man is; but as these absolutely knew nothing about it, they might very well be allowed to differ entirely in opinion from one another . . .

Such a multitude of reasoners having written the romance of the soul, a sage at last arose, who gave, with an air of the greatest modesty, the history of it. Mr Locke has displayed the human soul in the same manner as an excellent anatomist explains the springs of the human body. He everywhere takes the light of physics for his guide. He sometimes presumes to speak affirmatively, but then he presumes also to doubt.

Instead of concluding at once what we know not, he examines gradually what we would know. He takes an infant at the instant of his birth; he traces, step by step, the progress of his understanding; examines what things he has in common with beasts, and what he possesses above them. Above all, he consults himself: the being conscious that he himself thinks.

"I shall leave," says he, "to those who know more of this matter than myself, the examining whether the soul exists before or after the organisation of our bodies. But I confess that it is my lot to be animated with one of those heavy souls which do not think always; and I am even so unhappy as not to conceive that it is more necessary the soul should think perpetually than that bodies should be for ever in motion."

With regard to myself, I shall boast that I have the honour to be as stupid in this particular as Mr Locke. No one shall ever make me believe that I think always: and I am as little inclined as he could be to fancy that some weeks after I was conceived I was a very learned soul; knowing at that time a thousand things which I forgot at my birth; and possessing when in the womb (though to no manner of purpose) knowledge which I lost the instant I had occasion for it; and which I have never since been able to recover perfectly.

Mr Locke, after having destroyed innate ideas; after having fully renounced the vanity of believing that we think always; after having laid down, from the most solid principles, that ideas enter the mind through the senses; having examined our simple and complex ideas; having traced the human mind through its several operations; having shown that all the languages in the world are imperfect, and the great abuse that is made of words every moment, he at last comes to consider the extent or rather the narrow limits of human knowledge.

It was in this chapter he presumed to advance, but very modestly, the following words: "We shall, perhaps, never be capable of knowing whether a being, purely material, thinks or not." This sage assertion was, by more divines than one, looked upon as a scandalous declaration that the soul is material and mortal. Some Englishmen, devout after their way, sounded an alarm. The superstitious are the same in society as cowards in an army; they themselves are seized with a panic fear, and communicate it to others.

It was loudly exclaimed that Mr Locke intended to destroy religion; nevertheless, religion had nothing to do in the affair, it being a question purely philosophical, altogether independent of faith and revelation. Mr Locke's opponents needed but to examine, calmly and impartially, whether the declaring that matter can think, implies a contradiction; and whether God is able to communicate thought to matter. But divines are too apt to begin their declarations with saying that God is offended when people differ from them in opinion; in which they too much resemble the bad poets, who used to declare publicly that Boileau spake irreverently of Louis XIV, because he ridiculed their stupid productions . . .

If I might presume to give my opinion on so delicate a subject after Mr Locke, I would say, that men have long disputed on the nature and the immortality of the soul. With regard to its immortality, it is impossible to give a demonstration of it, since its nature is still the subject of controversy; which, however, must be thoroughly understood before a person can be able to determine whether it be immortal or not. Human reason is so little able, merely by its own strength, to demonstrate the immortality of the soul, that it was absolutely necessary religion should reveal it to us.

It is of advantage to society in general, that mankind should believe the soul to be immortal; faith commands us to do this; nothing more is required, and the matter is cleared up at once. But it is otherwise with respect to its nature; it is of little importance to religion, which only requires the soul to be virtuous, whatever substance it may be made of. It is a clock which is given us to regulate, but the artist has not told us of what materials the spring of this clock is composed.

I am a body, and, I think, that's all I know of the matter. Shall I ascribe to an unknown cause, what I can so easily impute to the only second cause I am acquainted with? Here all the school philosophers interrupt me with their arguments, and declare that there is only extension and solidity in bodies, and that there they can have nothing but motion and figure. Now motion, figure, extension and solidity cannot form a thought, and consequently the soul cannot be matter. All this so often repeated mighty series of reasoning, amounts to no more than this: I am absolutely ignorant what matter is; I guess, but imperfectly, some properties of it; now I absolutely cannot tell whether these properties may be joined to thought. As I therefore know nothing, I maintain positively that matter cannot think. In this manner do the schools reason.

Mr Locke addressed these gentlemen in the candid, sincere manner following: At least confess yourselves to be as ignorant as I. Neither your imaginations nor mine are able to comprehend in what manner a body is susceptible of ideas; and do you conceive better in what manner a substance, of what kind soever, is susceptible of them? As you cannot comprehend either matter or spirit, why will you presume to assert anything?

Jean-Jacques Rousseau, *The Social Contract; or Principles of Political Right* (1762)

Book I, Chapter I

Man is born free; and everywhere he is in chains. One thinks himself the master of others, and still remains a greater slave than they. How did this change come about? I do not know. What can make it legitimate? That question I think I can answer.

If I took into account only force, and the effects derived from it, I should say: "As long as a people is compelled to obey, and obeys, it does well; as soon as it can shake off the yoke, and shakes it off, it does still better; for, regaining its liberty by the same right as took it away, either it is justified in resuming it, or there was no justification for those who took it away." But the social order is a sacred right which is the basis of all other rights. Nevertheless, this right does not come from nature, and must therefore be founded on conventions . . .

I suppose men to have reached the point at which the obstacles in the way of their preservation in the state of nature show their power of resistance to be greater than the resources at the disposal of each individual for his maintenance in that state. That primitive condition can then subsist no longer; and the human race would perish unless it changed its manner of existence.

But, as men cannot engender new forces, but only unite and direct existing ones, they have no other means of preserving themselves than the formation, by aggregation, of a sum of forces great enough to overcome the resistance. These they have to bring into play by means of a single motive power, and cause to act in concert.

This sum of forces can arise only where several persons come together: but, as the force and liberty of each man are the chief instruments of his self-preservation, how can he pledge them without harming his own interests, and neglecting the care he owes to himself? This difficulty, in its bearing on my present subject, may be stated in the following terms:

"The problem is to find a form of association which will defend and protect with the whole common force the person and goods of each associate, and in which each, while uniting himself with all, may still obey himself alone, and remain as free as before."

This is the fundamental problem of which the Social Contract provides the solution.

The clauses of this contract are so determined by the nature of the act that the slightest modification would make them vain and ineffective; so that, although they have perhaps never been formally set forth, they are everywhere the same and everywhere tacitly admitted and recognized, until, on the violation of the social compact, each regains his original rights and resumes his natural liberty, while losing the conventional liberty in favour of which he renounced it.

These clauses, properly understood, may be reduced to one – the total alienation of each associate, together with all his rights, to the whole community; for, in the first place, as each gives himself absolutely, the conditions are the same for all; and, this being so, no one has any interest in making them burdensome to others.

The Instructions of Catherine II to the Legislative Commission of 1767

The Instructions to the Commissioners for Composing a New Code of Laws
Chapter XIX
439. Of the Composition of the Laws.

447. Every subject, according to the order and Place to which he belongs, is to be inserted separately in the Code of Laws – for instance, under judicial, military, commercial, civil, or the police, city or country affairs, etc. etc.

448. Each law ought to be written in so clear a style as to be perfectly intelligible to everyone, and, at the same time, with great conciseness. For this reason explanations or interpretations are undoubtedly to be added (as occasion shall require) to enable judges to perceive more readily the force as well as use of the law . . .

449. But the utmost care and caution is to be observed in adding these explanations and interpretations, because they may sometimes rather darken than clear up the case; of which there are many instances [in the existing laws].

450. When exceptions, limitations, and modifications are not absolutely necessary in a law, in that case it is better not to insert them; for such particular details generally produce still more details.

451. If the Legislator desires to give his reason for making any particular law, that reason ought to be good and worthy of the law . . .

452. Laws ought not to be filled with subtle distinctions, to demonstrate the brilliance of the Legislator; they are made for people of moderate capacities as well as for those of genius. They are not a logical art, but the simple and plain reasoning of a father who takes care of his children and family.

453. Real candour and sincerity ought to be displayed in every part of the laws; and as they are made for the punishment of crimes, they ought consequently to include in themselves the greatest virtue and benevolence.

454. The style of the laws ought to be simple and concise: a plain direct expression will always be better understood than a studied one.

455. When the style of laws is tumid and inflated, they are looked upon only as a work of vanity and ostentation . . .

511. A Monarchy is destroyed when a Sovereign imagines that he displays his power more by changing the order of things than by adhering to it, and when he is more fond of his own imaginations than of his will, from which the laws proceed and have proceeded.

512. It is true there are cases where Power ought and can exert its full influence without any danger to the State. But there are cases also where it ought to act according to the limits prescribed by itself.

513. The supreme art of governing a State consists in the precise knowledge of that degree of power, whether great or small, which ought to be exerted according to the different exigencies of affairs. For in a Monarchy the prosperity of the State depends, in part, on a mild and condescending government.

514. In the best constructed machines, Art employs the least moment, force, and fewest wheels possible. This rule holds equally good in the administration of government; the most simple expedients are often the very best, and the most intricate the very worst.

515. There is a certain facility in this method of governing: It is better for the Sovereign to encourage, and for the Laws to threaten . . .

519. It is certain that a high opinion of the glory and power of the Sovereign would increase the strength of his administration; but a good opinion of his love of justice will increase it at least as much.

520. All this will never please those flatterers who are daily instilling this pernicious maxim into all the sovereigns on Earth, that Their people are created for them only. But We think, and esteem it Our glory to declare, that "We are created for Our people." And for this reason, We are obliged to speak of things just as they ought to be. For God forbid that after this legislation is finished any nation on Earth should be more just and, consequently, should flourish more than Russia. Otherwise, the intention of Our laws would be totally frustrated; an unhappiness which I do not wish to survive.

521. All the examples and customs of different nations which are introduced in this work [the Instructions] ought to produce no other effect than to cooperate in the choice of those means which may render the people of Russia, humanly speaking, the most happy in themselves of any people upon the Earth.

Adam Smith, *An Inquiry into the Nature and Causes of the Wealth of Nations* (1776)

Chapter 1, "Of the Division of Labour"

The greatest improvements in the productive powers of labour, and the greater part of the skill, dexterity, and judgement, with which it is anywhere directed, or applied, seem to have been the effects of the division of labour. The effects of the division of labour, in the general business of society, will be more easily understood, by considering in what manner it operates in some particular manufactures. It is commonly supposed to be carried furthest in some very trifling ones; not perhaps that it really is carried further in them than in others of more importance: but in those trifling manufactures which are destined to supply the small wants of but a small number of people, the whole number of workmen must necessarily be small; and those employed in every different branch of the work can often be collected into the same workhouse, and placed at once under the view of the spectator.

In those great manufactures, on the contrary, which are destined to supply the great wants of the great body of the people, every different branch of the work employs so great a number of workmen, that it is impossible to collect them all into the same workhouse. We can seldom see more, at one time, than those employed in one single branch. Though in such manufactures, therefore, the work may really be divided into a much greater number of parts, than in those of a more trifling nature, the division is not near so obvious, and has accordingly been much less observed.

To take an example, therefore, from a very trifling manufacture, but one in which the division of labour has been very often taken notice of, the trade of a pin-maker: a workman not educated to this business (which the division of labour has rendered a distinct trade), nor acquainted with the use of the machinery employed in it (to the invention of which the same division of labour has probably given occasion), could scarce, perhaps, with his utmost industry, make one pin in a day, and certainly could not make twenty. But in the way in which this business is now carried on, not only the whole work is a peculiar trade, but it is divided into a number of branches, of which the greater part are likewise peculiar trades. One man draws out the wire; another straights it; a third cuts it; a fourth points it; a fifth grinds it at the top for receiving the head; to make the head requires two or three distinct operations; to put it on is a peculiar business; to whiten the pins is another; it is even a trade by itself to put them into the paper; and the important business of making a pin is, in this manner, divided into about eighteen distinct operations, which, in some manufactories, are all performed by distinct hands, though in others the same man will sometimes perform two or three of them.

I have seen a small manufactory of this kind, where ten men only were employed, and where some of them consequently performed two or three distinct operations. But though they were very poor, and therefore but indifferently accommodated with the necessary machinery, they could, when they exerted themselves, make among them about twelve pounds of pins in a day. There are in a pound upwards of four thousand pins of a middling size. Those ten persons, therefore, could make among them upwards of forty-eight thousand pins in a day. Each person, therefore, making a tenth part of forty-eight thousand pins, might be considered as making four thousand eight hundred pins in a day. But if they had all wrought separately and independently, and without any of them having been educated to this peculiar business, they certainly could not each of them have made twenty, perhaps not one pin in a day; that is, certainly, not the two hundred and fortieth, perhaps not the four thousand eight hundredth, part of what they are at present capable of performing, in consequence of a proper division and combination of their different operations.

In every other art and manufacture, the effects of the division of labour are similar to what they are in this very trifling one, though, in many of them, the labour can neither be so much subdivided, nor reduced to so great a simplicity of operation. The division of labour, however, so far as it can be introduced, occasions, in every art, a proportionable increase of the productive powers of labour. The separation of different trades and employments from one another, seems to have taken place in consequence of this advantage.

Declaration of Independence (1776)

In Congress, July 4 1776

When in the Course of human events, it becomes necessary for one people to dissolve the political bands which have connected them with another, and to assume among the powers of the earth, the separate and equal station to which the Laws of Nature and of Nature's God entitle them, a decent respect to the opinions of mankind requires that they should declare the causes which impel them to the separation. We hold these truths to be self-evident, that all men are created equal, that they are endowed by their Creator with certain unalienable Rights, that among these are Life, Liberty and the pursuit of Happiness. That to secure these rights, Governments are instituted among Men, deriving their just powers from the consent of the governed, That whenever any Form of Government becomes destructive of these ends, it is the Right of the People to alter or to abolish it, and to institute new Government, laying its foundation on such principles and organizing its powers in such form, as to them shall seem most likely to effect their Safety and Happiness.

Prudence, indeed, will dictate that Governments long established should not be changed for light and transient causes; and accordingly all experience hath shown, that mankind are more disposed to suffer, while evils are sufferable, than to right themselves by abolishing the forms to which they are accustomed. But when a long train of abuses and usurpations, pursuing invariably the same Object evinces a design to reduce them under absolute Despotism, it is their right, it is their duty, to throw off such Government, and to provide new Guards for their future security. Such has been the patient sufferance of these Colonies; and such is now the necessity which constrains them to alter their former Systems of Government. The history of the present King of Great Britain is a history of repeated injuries and usurpations, all having in direct object the establishment of an absolute Tyranny over these States.

To prove this, let Facts be submitted to a candid world. He has refused his Assent to Laws, the most wholesome and necessary for the public good. He has forbidden his Governors to pass Laws of immediate and pressing importance, unless suspended in their operation till his Assent should be obtained; and when so suspended, he has utterly neglected to attend to them. He has refused to pass other Laws for the accommodation of large districts of people, unless those people would relinquish the right of Representation in the Legislature, a right inestimable to them and formidable to tyrants only. He has called together legislative bodies at places unusual, uncomfortable, and distant from the depository of their public Records, for the sole purpose of fatiguing them into compliance with his measures. He has dissolved Representative Houses repeatedly, for opposing with manly firmness his invasions on the rights of the people. He has refused for a long time, after such dissolutions, to cause others to be elected; whereby the Legislative powers, incapable of Annihilation, have returned to the People at large for their exercise; the State remaining in the mean time exposed to all the dangers of invasion from without, and convulsions within. He has endeavoured to prevent the population of these States; for that purpose obstructing the Laws for Naturalization of Foreigners; refusing to pass others to encourage their migration hither, and raising the conditions of new Appropriations of Lands. He has obstructed the Administration of Justice, by refusing his Assent to Laws for establishing Judiciary powers. He has made judges dependent on his Will alone, for the tenure of their offices, and the amount and payment of their salaries. He has erected a multitude of New Offices, and sent hither swarms of Officers to harrass our people, and eat out their substance. He has kept among us, in times of peace, Standing Armies, without the Consent of our legislatures. He has affected to render the Military independent of and superior to the Civil power. He has combined with others to subject us to a jurisdiction foreign to our constitution, and unacknowledged by our laws; giving his Assent to their Acts of pretended Legislation: For quartering large bodies of armed troops among us: For protecting them, by a mock Trial, from punishment for any Murders which they should commit on the Inhabitants of these States: For cutting off our Trade with all parts of the world: For imposing Taxes on us without our Consent: For depriving us in many cases, of the benefits of Trial by Jury: For transporting us beyond Seas to be tried for pretended offences: For abolishing the free System of English Laws in a neighbouring Province, establishing therein an Arbitrary government, and enlarging its Boundaries so as to render it at once an example and fit instrument for introducing the same absolute rule into these Colonies: For taking away our Charters, abolishing our most valuable Laws, and altering fundamentally the Forms of our Governments: For suspending our own Legislatures, and declaring themselves invested with power to legislate for us in all cases whatsoever. He has abdicated Government here, by declaring us out of his Protection and waging War against us. He has plundered our seas, ravaged our Coasts, burnt our towns, and destroyed the lives of our people. He is at this time transporting large Armies of foreign Mercenaries to compleat the works of death, desolation and tyranny, already begun with circumstances of Cruelty & perfidy scarcely paralleled in the most barbarous ages, and totally unworthy the Head of a civilized nation. He has constrained our fellow Citizens taken Captive on the high Seas to bear Arms against their Country, to become the executioners of their friends and Brethren, or to fall themselves by their Hands. He has excited domestic insurrections amongst us, and has endeavoured to bring on the inhabitants of our frontiers, the merciless Indian Savages, whose known rule of warfare, is an undistinguished destruction of all ages, sexes and conditions. In every stage of these Oppressions We have Petitioned for Redress in the most humble terms: Our repeated Petitions have been answered only by repeated injury. A Prince, whose character is thus marked by every act which may define a Tyrant, is unfit to be the ruler of a free people.

Nor have we been wanting in attentions to our British brethren. We have warned them from time to time of attempts by their legislature to extend an unwarrantable jurisdiction over us. We have reminded them of the circumstances of our emigration and settlement here. We have appealed to their native justice and magnanimity, and we have conjured them by the ties of our common kindred to disavow these usurpations, which, would inevitably interrupt our connections and correspondence. They too have been deaf to the voice of justice and of consanguinity. We must, therefore, acquiesce in the necessity, which denounces our Separation, and hold them, as we hold the rest of mankind. Enemies in War, in Peace Friends.

We, therefore, the Representatives of the United States of America, in General Congress, Assembled, appealing to the Supreme Judge of the world for the rectitude of our intentions, do, in the Name, and by Authority of the good People of these Colonies, solemnly publish and declare, That these United Colonies are, and of Right ought to be Free and Independent States; that they are Absolved from all Allegiance to the British Crown, and that all political connection between them and the State of Great Britain, is and ought to be totally dissolved; and that as Free and Independent States, they have full Power to levy War, conclude Peace, contract Alliances, establish Commerce, and to do all other Acts and Things which Independent

States may of right do. And for the support of this Declaration, with a firm reliance on the protection of Divine Providence, we mutually pledge to each other our Lives, our Fortunes and our sacred Honor.

Thomas Paine, *The American Crisis*, December 23 1776

These are the times that try men's souls. The summer soldier and the sunshine patriot will, in this crisis, shrink from the service of their country; but he that stands it now, deserves the love and thanks of man and woman. Tyranny, like hell, is not easily conquered; yet we have this consolation with us, that the harder the conflict, the more glorious the triumph. What we obtain too cheap, we esteem too lightly: it is dearness only that gives every thing its value. Heaven knows how to put a proper price upon its goods; and it would be strange indeed if so celestial an article as FREEDOM should not be highly rated. Britain, with an army to enforce her tyranny, has declared that she has a right (not only to TAX) but "to BIND us in ALL CASES WHATSOEVER," and if being bound in that manner, is not slavery, then is there not such a thing as slavery upon earth. Even the expression is impious; for so unlimited a power can belong only to God.

Immanuel Kant, *Critique of Pure Reason* (1781)

Preface to the First Edition

[Our age is the age of criticism, to which everything must be subjected. The sacredness of religion, and the authority of legislation, are by many regarded as grounds of exemption from the examination of this tribunal. But, if they on they are exempted, they become the subjects of just suspicion, and cannot lay claim to sincere respect, which reason accords only to that which has stood the test of a free and public examination.] . . .

This path – the only one now remaining – has been entered upon by me; and I flatter myself that I have, in this way, discovered the cause of – and consequently the mode of removing – all the errors which have hitherto set reason at variance with itself, in the sphere of non-empirical thought. I have not returned an evasive answer to the questions of reason, by alleging the inability and limitation of the faculties of the mind; I have, on the contrary, examined them completely in the light of principles, and, after having discovered the cause of the doubts and contradictions into which reason fell, have solved them to its perfect satisfaction.

It is true, these questions have not been solved as dogmatism, in its vain fancies and desires, had expected; for it can only be satisfied by the exercise of magical arts, and of these I have no knowledge. But neither do these come within the compass of our mental powers; and it was the duty of philosophy to destroy the illusions which had their origin in misconceptions, whatever darling hopes and valued expectations may be ruined by its explanations.

My chief aim in this work has been thoroughness; and I make bold to say that there is not a single metaphysical problem that does not find its solution, or at least the key to its solution, here. Pure reason is a perfect unity; and therefore, if the principle presented by it prove to be insufficient for the solution of even a single one of those questions to which the very nature of reason gives birth, we must reject it, as we could not be perfectly certain of its sufficiency in the case of the others.

Declaration of the Rights of Man and of the Citizen (1789)

(Adopted by the National Assembly during the French Revolution on August 26 1789, and reaffirmed by the Constitution of 1958.)

Preamble

The representatives of the French people, formed into a National Assembly, considering ignorance, forgetfulness or contempt of the rights of man to be the only causes of public misfortunes and the corruption of Governments, have resolved to set forth, in a solemn Declaration, the natural, unalienable and sacred rights of man, to the end that this Declaration, constantly present to all members of the body politic, may remind them unceasingly of their rights and their duties; to the end that the acts of the legislative power and those of the executive power, since they may be continually compared with the aim of every political institution, may thereby be the more respected; to the end that the demands of the citizens, founded henceforth on simple and uncontestable principles, may always be directed toward the maintenance of the Constitution and the happiness of all.

In consequence whereof, the National Assembly recognizes and declares, in the presence and under the auspices of the Supreme Being, the following Rights of Man and of the Citizen.

Article first – Men are born and remain free and equal in rights. Social distinctions may be based only on considerations of the common good.

Article 2 – The aim of every political association is the preservation of the natural and imprescriptible rights of man. These rights are Liberty, Property, Safety and Resistance to Oppression.

Article 3 – The source of all sovereignty lies essentially in the Nation. No corporate body, no individual may exercise any authority that does not expressly emanate from it.

Article 4 – Liberty consists in being able to do anything that does not harm others: thus, the exercise of the natural rights of every man has no bounds other than those that ensure to the other members of society the enjoyment of these same rights. These bounds may be determined only by Law.

Article 5 – The Law has the right to forbid only those actions that are injurious to society. Nothing that is not forbidden by Law may be hindered, and no one may be compelled to do what the Law does not ordain.

Article 6 – The Law is the expression of the general will. All citizens have the right to take part, personally or through their representatives, in its making. It must be the same for all, whether it protects or punishes. All citizens, being equal in its eyes, shall be equally eligible to all high offices, public positions and employments, according to their ability, and without other distinction than that of their virtues and talents.

Article 7 – No man may be accused, arrested or detained except in the cases determined by the Law, and following the procedure that it has prescribed. Those who solicit, expedite, carry out, or cause to be carried out arbitrary orders must be punished; but any citizen summoned or apprehended by virtue of the Law, must give instant obedience; resistance makes him guilty.

Article 8 – The Law must prescribe only the punishments that are strictly and evidently necessary; and no one may be punished except by virtue of a Law drawn up and promulgated before the offence is committed, and legally applied.

Article 9 – As every man is presumed innocent until he has been declared guilty, if it should be considered necessary to arrest him, any undue harshness that is not required to secure his person must be severely curbed by Law.

Article 10 – No one may be disturbed on account of his opinions, even religious ones, as long as the manifestation of such opinions does not interfere with the established Law and Order.

Article 11 – The free communication of ideas and of opinions is one of the most precious rights of man. Any citizen may therefore speak, write and publish freely, except what is tantamount to the abuse of this liberty in the cases determined by Law.

Article 12 – To guarantee the Rights of Man and of the Citizen a public force is necessary; this force is therefore established for the benefit of all, and not for the particular use of those to whom it is entrusted.

Article 13 – For the maintenance of the public force, and for administrative expenses, a general tax is indispensable; it must be equally distributed among all citizens, in proportion to their ability to pay.

Article 14 – All citizens have the right to ascertain, by themselves, or through their representatives, the need for a public tax, to consent to it freely, to watch over its use, and to determine its proportion, basis, collection and duration.

Article 15 – Society has the right to ask a public official for an accounting of his administration.

Article 16 – Any society in which no provision is made for guaranteeing rights or for the separation of powers, has no Constitution.

Article 17 – Since the right to Property is inviolable and sacred, no one may be deprived thereof, unless public necessity, legally ascertained, obviously requires it, and just and prior indemnity has been paid.

Edmund Burke, *Reflections on the French Revolution* (1790)

You had all these advantages in your ancient states; but you chose to act as if you had never been moulded into civil society, and had everything to begin anew. You began ill, because you began by despising everything that belonged to you. You set up your trade without a capital. If the last generations of your country appeared without much lustre in your eyes, you might have passed them by, and derived your claims from a more early race of ancestors.

Under a pious predilection for those ancestors your imaginations would have realized in them a standard of virtue and wisdom, beyond the vulgar practice of the hour: and you would have risen with the example to whose imitation you aspired. Respecting your forefathers, you would have been taught to respect yourselves. You would not have chosen to consider the French as a people of yesterday, as a nation of lowborn servile wretches until the emancipating year of 1789. In order to furnish, at the expense of your honour, an excuse to your apologists here for several enormities of yours, you would not have been content to be represented as a gang of Maroon slaves, suddenly broke loose from the house of bondage, and therefore to be pardoned for your abuse of the liberty to which you were not accustomed, and ill fitted. Would it not, my worthy friend, have been wiser to have you thought, what I, for one, always thought you, a generous and gallant nation, long misled to your disadvantage by your high and romantic sentiments of fidelity, honour, and loyalty; that events had been unfavourable to you, but that you were not enslaved through any illiberal or servile disposition; in your most devoted submission, you were actuated by a principle of public spirit, and that it was your Country you worshipped, in the person of your king?

Had you made it to be understood, that in the delusion of this amiable error you had gone further than your wise ancestors; that you were resolved to resume your ancient privileges, whilst you preserved the spirit of your ancient and your recent loyalty and honour; or if, diffident of yourselves, and not clearly discerning the almost obliterated constitution of your ancestors, you had looked to your neighbours in this land, who had kept alive the ancient principles and models of the old common law of Europe meliorated and adapted to its present state – by following wise examples you would have given new examples of wisdom to the world.

You would have rendered the cause of liberty venerable in the eyes of every worthy mind in every nation. You would have shamed despotism from the earth, by showing that freedom was not only reconcilable, but, as when well disciplined it is, auxiliary to law. You would have an unoppressive but a productive revenue. You would have had a flourishing commerce to feed it. You would have had a free constitution; a potent monarchy; a disciplined army; a reformed and venerated clergy; a mitigated but spirited nobility, to lead your virtue, not to overlay it; you would have had a liberal order of commons, to emulate and to recruit that nobility; you would have had a protected, satisfied, laborious, and obedient people, taught to seek and to recognize the happiness that is to be found by virtue in all conditions; in which consists the true moral equality of mankind, and not in that monstrous fiction, which, by inspiring false ideas and vain expectations into men destined to travel in the obscure walk of laborious life, serves only to aggravate and embitter that real inequality, which it never can remove; and which the order of civil life establishes as much for the benefit of those whom it must leave in an humble state, as those whom it is able to exalt to a condition more splendid, but not more happy. You had a smooth and easy career of felicity and glory laid open to you beyond anything recorded in the history of the world; but you have shown that difficulty is good for men.

Compute your gains: see what is got by those extravagant and presumptuous speculations which have taught your leaders to despise all their predecessors, and all their contemporaries, and even to despise themselves, until the moment in which they became truly despicable. By following those false lights, France has bought undisguised calamities at a higher price than any nation has purchased the most unequivocal blessings! France has bought poverty by crime! France has not sacrificed her virtue to her interest, but she has abandoned her interest, that she might prostitute her virtue. All other nations have begun the fabric of a new government, or the reformation of an old, by establishing originally, or by enforcing with greater exactness some rites or other of religion.

All other people have laid the foundations of civil freedom in severer manners, and a system of a more austere and masculine morality. France, when she let loose the reins of regal authority, doubled the license of a ferocious dissoluteness in manners, and of an insolent irreligion in opinions and practices; and has extended through all ranks of life, as if she were communicating some privilege, or laying open some secluded benefit, all the unhappy corruptions that usually were the disease of wealth and power. This is one of the new principles of equality in France.

France, by the perfidy of her leaders has utterly disgraced the tone of lenient council in the cabinets of princes, and disarmed it of its most potent topics. She has sanctified the dark, suspicious maxims of tyrannous distrust; and taught kings to tremble at (what will hereafter be called) the delusive plausibilities of moral politicians. Sovereigns will consider those, who advise them to place an unlimited confidence in their people, as subverters of their throne; as traitors who aim at their destruction, by leading their easy good nature, under specious pretences, to admit combinations of bold and faithless men into a participation of their power. This alone (if there were nothing else) is an irreparable calamity to you and to mankind.

Remember that your parliament of Paris told your king, that, in calling the states together, he had nothing to fear but the prodigal excess of their zeal in providing for the support of the throne. It is right that these men should hide their heads. It is right that they should bear their part in the ruin which their counsel has brought on their sovereign and their country. Such sanguine declarations tend to lull authority asleep; to encourage it rashly to engage in perilous adventures of untried policy; to neglect those provisions, preparations, and precautions, which distinguish benevolence from imbecility; and without which no man can answer for the salutary effect of any abstract plan of government or of freedom. For want of these, they have seen the medicine of the state corrupted into its poison. They have seen the French rebel against a mild and lawful monarch, with more fury, outrage, and insult, than ever any people has been known to rise against the most illegal usurper, or the most sanguinary tyrant. Their resistance was made to concession; their revolt was from protection; their blow was aimed at a hand holding out graces, favours, and immunities.

Mary Wollstonecraft *A Vindication of the Rights of Woman, with Strictures on Political and Moral Subjects* (1792)

An extract from Chapter 5, "Animadversions on Some of the Writers Who Have Rendered Women Objects of Pity, Bordering on Contempt"

I now appeal from the reveries of fancy and refined licentiousness to the good sense of mankind, whether, if the object of education be to prepare women to become chaste wives and sensible mothers, the method so plausibly recommended in the foregoing sketch, be the one best calculated to produce those ends? Will it be allowed that the surest way to make a wife chaste, is to teach her to practise the wanton arts of a mistress, termed virtuous coquetry by the sensualist who can no longer relish the artless charms of sincerity, or taste the pleasure arising from a tender intimacy, when confidence is unchecked by suspicion, and rendered interesting by sense?

The man who can be contented to live with a pretty useful companion without a mind, has lost in voluptuous gratifications a taste for more refined enjoyments; he has never felt the calm satisfaction that refreshes the parched heart, like the silent dew of heaven – of being beloved by one who could understand him. In the society of his wife he is still alone, unless when the man is sunk in the brute. "The charm of life", says a grave philosophical reasoner, is "sympathy; nothing pleases us more than to observe in other men a fellow-feeling with all the emotions of our own breast."

But, according to the tenor of reasoning by which women are kept from the tree of knowledge, the important years of youth, the usefulness of age, and the rational hopes of futurity, are all to be sacrificed, to render woman an object of desire for a short time. Besides, how could Rousseau expect them to be virtuous and constant when reason is neither allowed to be the foundation of their virtue, nor truth the object of their in-quiries?

But all Rousseau's errors in reasoning arose from sensibility, and sensibility to their charms women are very ready to forgive! When he should have reasoned he became impas-sioned, and reflection inflamed his imagination, instead of enlightening his understanding. Even his virtues also led him farther astray; for, born with a warm constitution and lively fancy, nature carried him toward the other sex with such eager fondness, that he soon became lascivious. Had he given way to these desires, the fire would have extinguished itself in a natural manner, but virtue, and a romantic kind of delicacy, made him practise self-denial; yet, when fear, delicacy, or virtue restrained him, he debauched his imagination; and reflecting on the sensations to which fancy gave force, he traced them in the most glowing colours, and sunk them deep into his soul.

He then sought for solitude, not to sleep with the man of nature; or calmly investigate the causes of things under the shade where Sir Isaac Newton indulged contemplation, but merely to indulge his feelings. And so warmly has he painted what he forcibly felt, that, interesting the heart and inflaming the imagination of his readers; in proportion to the strength of their fancy, they imagine that their understanding is convinced, when they only sympathize with a poetic writer, who skilfully exhibits the objects of sense, most voluptuously shadowed, or gracefully veiled; and thus making us feel, whilst dreaming that we reason, erroneous conclusions are left in the mind.

Why was Rousseau's life divided between ecstasy and misery? Can any other answer be given than this, that the effervescence of his imagination produced both; but, had his fancy been allowed to cool, it is possible that he might have acquired more strength of mind. Still, if the purpose of life be to educate the intellectual part of man, all with respect to him was right; yet, had not death led to a nobler scene of action, it is probable that he would have enjoyed more equal happiness on earth, and have felt the calm sensations of the man of nature, instead of being prepared for another stage of existence by nourishing the passions which agitate the civilized man.

But peace to his manes! I war not with his ashes, but his opinions. I war only with the sensibility that led him to degrade woman by making her the slave of love.

> . . . "Curs'd vassalage,
> First idoliz'd till love's hot fire be o'er,
> Then slaves to those who courted us before."
>
> Dryden.

The pernicious tendency of those books, in which the writers insidiously degrade the sex, whilst they are prostrate before their personal charms, cannot be too often or too severely exposed.

Let us, my dear contemporaries, arise above such narrow prejudices! If wisdom is desirable on its own account, if virtue, to deserve the name, must be founded on knowledge; let us endeavour to strengthen our minds by reflection, till our heads become a balance for our hearts; let us not confine all our thoughts to the petty occurrences of the day, nor our knowledge to an acquaintance with our lovers' or husbands' hearts; but let the practice of every duty be subordinate to the grand one of improving our minds, and preparing our affections for a more exalted state!

Beware then, my friends, of suffering the heart to be moved by every trivial incident: the reed is shaken by a breeze, and annually dies, but the oak stands firm, and for ages braves the storm.

Were we, indeed, only created to flutter our hour out and die – why let us then indulge sensibility, and laugh at the severity of reason. Yet, alas! even then we should want strength of body and mind, and life would be lost in feverish pleasures or wearisome languor.

But the system of education, which I earnestly wish to see exploded, seems to presuppose, what ought never to be taken for granted, that virtue shields us from the casualties of life; and that fortune, slipping off her bandage, will smile on a well-educated female, and bring in her hand an Emilius or a Telemachus. Whilst, on the contrary, the reward which virtue promises to her votaries is confined, it is clear, to their own bosoms; and often must they contend with the most vexatious worldly cares, and bear with the vices and humours of relations for whom they can never feel a friendship.

There have been many women in the world who, instead of being supported by the reason and virtue of their fathers and brothers, have strengthened their own minds by struggling with their vices and follies; yet have never met with a hero, in the shape of a husband; who, paying the debt that mankind owed them, might chance to bring back their reason to its natural dependent state, and restore the usurped prerogative, of rising above opinion, to man.

FURTHER READING

Isaiah Berlin, *The Age of Enlightenment: The 18th Century Philosophers Selected, with Introduction and Interpretive Commentary*, New American Library, New York, 1956.

Alexander Broadie, *The Cambridge Companion to the Scottish Enlightenment*, Cambridge University Press, Cambridge, 2003.

Peter Gay, *The Enlightenment Vol 1: The Rise of Modern Paganism*, W.W. Norton & Co, New York, 1995.

Peter Gay, *The Enlightenment Vol 2: Science of Freedom*, W.W. Norton & Co, New York, 1995.

A.C. Grayling, *Toward the Light of Liberty: The Struggles for Freedom and Rights That Made the Modern Western World*, Walker & Co, New York, 2007.

A.C. Grayling, *Descartes: The Life and Times of a Genius*, Walker & Co, New York, 2006.

Arthur Herman, *The Scottish Enlightenment: The Scots' Invention of the Modern World*, Fourth Estate, London, 2003.

Jonathan Hill, *Faith in the Age of Reason: The Enlightenment from Galileo to Kant*, Intervarsity Press, Illinois 2004.

Paul Hyland, Olga Gomez and Francesca Greensides (eds), *The Enlightenment: A Sourcebook and Reader*, Routledge, London, 2003.

Jonathan I. Israel, *Radical Enlightenment: Philosophy and the Making of Modernity, 1650–1750*, Oxford University Press, Oxford, 2002.

Isaac Kramnick (ed.), *The Portable Enlightenment Reader*, Viking Portable Library, Penguin, New York, 1996.

Roy Porter, *Enlightenment: Britain and the Creation of the Modern World*, Penguin, London, 2001.

John W. Yolton, Roy Porter, Pat Rogers and Barbara Maria Stafford (eds), *The Blackwell Companion to the Enlightenment*, Blackwell, Oxford, 1991.

INDEX

Notes: Where more than one page number is listed against a heading, page numbers in bold refer to significant treatment of a subject

Britannica®

Since its birth in the Scottish Enlightenment Britannica's commitment to educated, reasoned, current, humane, and popular scholarship has never wavered. In 2008, Britannica celebrated its 240th anniversary.

Throughout its history, owners and users of *Encyclopædia Britannica* have drawn upon it for knowledge, understanding, answers, and inspiration. In the Internet age, Britannica, the first online encyclopædia, continues to deliver that fundamental requirement of reference, information, and educational publishing – confidence in the material we read in it.

Readers of Britannica Guides are invited to take a FREE trial of Britannica's huge online database. Visit

<u>https://ideas.britannicaguides.com</u>

to find out more about this title and others in the series.